ARTHURIAN STUDIES XXX

T. H. WHITE'S
THE ONCE AND FUTURE KING

ARTHURIAN STUDIES

ISSN 0261–9814

Previously published volumes in the series
are listed at the back of this book

T. H. WHITE'S

THE ONCE AND FUTURE KING

Elisabeth Brewer

D. S. BREWER

First published 1993 by D. S. Brewer, Cambridge

D. S. Brewer is an imprint of Boydell & Brewer Ltd
PO Box 9, Woodbridge, Suffolk IP12 3DF, UK
and of Boydell & Brewer Inc.
PO Box 41026, Rochester, NY 14604, USA

ISBN 0 85991 393 7

British Library Cataloguing-in-Publication Data
Brewer, Elisabeth
 T.H.White's 'Once and Future King'. –
(Arthurian Studies, ISSN 0261–9814)
I. Title II. Series
823.912
ISBN 0–85991–393–7

Library of Congress Cataloging-in-Publication Data
Brewer, Elisabeth.
 T.H. White's The once and future king / Elisabeth Brewer.
  p. cm. – (Arthurian studies, ISSN 0261–9814 ; 30)
Includes bibliographical references and index.
ISBN 0–85991–393–7 (alk. paper)
 1. White, T. H. (Terence Hanbury), 1906–1964. Once and future
king. 2. Arthurian romances – Adaptations – History and criticism.
I. Title. II. Series.
PR6045.H20534 1993
823'.912–dc20   93–11658

The paper used in this publication meets the minimum requirements
of American National Standard for Information Sciences –
Permanence of Paper for Printed Library Materials, ANSI Z39.48–1984

Printed in Great Britain by
St Edmundsbury Press Ltd, Bury St Edmunds, Suffolk

Contents

Acknowledgements

My thanks are due, first, to Richard Barber who originally suggested that I should attempt this book. I now know why so few have written on *The Once and Future King*: its protean nature constantly eludes all efforts to define, categorise or evaluate. I have, however, been inspired by Professor Kurth Sprague's superb but unfortunately unpublished doctoral thesis: *From a Troubled Heart: T.H. White and Women in 'The Once and Future King'*. I have to thank for their kind help both Professor Sprague and Professor François Gallix, who has generously allowed me to quote from his *Letters to a Friend*. Richard Garnett brought me closer to T.H. White himself, through his memories of visiting him in Ireland, and by most helpfully letting me see some as yet unpublished letters. I am also deeply indebted to the Harry Ransom Humanities Research Centre at the University of Texas at Austin, for allowing me to make use of their archive material. There, access to White's journals and other unpublished material enabled me to come to know him better and there, the kind helpfulness and patience of the staff made a lasting impression on me.

I am also indebted to David Higham Associates, the literary executors of the Estate of T.H. White, for permission to quote from *The Once and Future King* and other of White's writings, published and unpublished, and to the University of Texas Press for permission to quote from *The Book of Merlyn*.

I owe a special debt of gratitude to Elsie Duncan-Jones, once my tutor, ever since my friend, whose recollections of 'Timothy' when they were close friends in their third year at Cambridge brought him back to life for me in the splendour of his happy youth. I am also grateful to my husband and my family for their encouragement and for the inspiration I derived from their distinguished examples.

I ask readers to forgive, if possible, such errors and ineptitude as may be found in this work, in the hope that it may nevertheless enhance their appreciation of White. Like his master, Sir Thomas Malory, he too was a 'knyght prisoner', confined not by stone walls but by the fetters of intellectual isolation and emotional deprivation, yet following Malory, he gave the twentieth century, in *The Once and Future King*, its greatest retelling of the Arthurian story.

Abbreviations

I have used the following abbreviations in the text:

BM	*The Book of Merlyn*
CW	*The Candle in the Wind*
EHMB	*England Have My Bones*
FF	David Garnett: *The Familiar Faces*
IMK	*The Ill-Made Knight*
LF	François Gallix: *Letters to a Friend*
OFK	*The Once and Future King*
QAD	*The Queen of Air and Darkness*
SS	*The Sword in the Stone*
STW	Sylvia Townsend Warner: *T.H. White: A Biography*
Vin	Vinaver, Eugène: *The Works of Sir Thomas Malory*
W/GL	David Garnett: *The White/Garnett Letters*
WW	*The Witch in the Wood*

1

T. H. White

The Once and Future King is the book by which T.H. White will be remembered. It reflects his own protean nature: it is the work of a sad man who also saw the funny side of things. It is by turns comic and tragic, farcical and romantic, serious in its presentation of historical material and highly anachronistic. Our encounter with White's flamboyant personality and his total commitment to his story makes for a uniquely engaging Arthurian experience. Into it he put so much of himself – his personality, his experience, his learning – that some knowledge of his life and a sense of the times in which he lived is needed for the full understanding and appreciation of his great work. No author could be more fortunate in his biographer than was White, and it is to Sylvia Townsend Warner's fine *T.H. White*[1] that the interested reader should go for a fuller account of his life. What follows here is a brief sketch of the general context of White's Arthuriad.

Though T.H. White's childhood seems to have been, superficially at least, a happy one, the circumstances into which he was born were not propitious. It is not difficult to see in them the origins of the psychological problems which blighted his adult life, though they also, on the more positive side, contributed significantly to some of his most successful fictions. He was born in Bombay on 29 May 1906, the only child of a District Superintendent of Police and of the daughter of an Indian Judge (who was of course, at that time, English). Like other children in such situations, he was looked after much of the time by native servants, who – as in the case of Rudyard Kipling – indulged and spoilt him. This had the unfortunate effect of making his mother jealous of the affection which he naturally felt for his Indian nurse. The relationship between his parents appears to have been troubled from the beginning and there seems never to have been any love lost between them. His father took to drink, and there were desperate quarrels between the parents, apparently even over the baby's cot, as a poem in White's journal for 1 December 1938 suggests:

---

[1] *T.H. White: A Biography*, London, Cape with Chatto & Windus, 1967. (Referred to hereafter as STW)

Of hapless father hapless son
My birth was brutally begun
And all my childhood o'er the pram
The father and the maniac dam
Struggled and leaned to pierce the knife
Into each other's bitter life.
Thus bred without security
Whom dared I love, whom did not flee?

Well blest! Now, in ten million sighs,
One can stand on without surprise.[2]

Constance White seems to have been an extremely difficult woman: her son adored her when he was a child, but disillusionment set in later. She could refer to him when he was an undergraduate, embarrassingly in the presence of his friends, as 'my baby'. His reaction against her was to contribute significantly to *The Once and Future King*. In spite of this he still felt responsible for her and was generous towards her to the end of her life.

Like Rudyard Kipling, White was sent 'home' at an early age, but he was very much more fortunate than the young Kipling in the home that received him. In 1911, his mother brought him back to England, to live with her parents, who were also looking after his three cousins, and here he seems to have enjoyed a comparatively carefree existence in a tolerant and loving environment.

His happy childhood came to an end when in September 1920 he was sent away to Cheltenham College, a school with a strong Anglo-Indian connexion, and so a natural choice for his secondary education. He was placed on the military side which prepared boys for careers in the army. As with many of his contemporaries who attended public schools at this time, his experiences at Cheltenham were very unhappy. Corporal punishment was taken for granted as a feature of daily life, his housemaster was, he claimed, sadistic, and prefects as well as masters were allowed to cane younger boys. 'The prefects used to beat us after evening prayers. . . . I knew in a dumb way it was a sexual outrage, though I could not have phrased that charge', he later recorded (STW 30–1), adding that it had the effect of turning him into a flagellant. But there were also some more positive results from the years at Cheltenham. He was introduced to Malory's *Le Morte Darthur* by C.F. Scott, one of the masters, and he was eventually to do well in his examinations.

By this time his parents were on the verge of a judicial separation, and their matrimonial problems achieved notoriety by being reported in some detail in the *Evening Standard* newspaper for all to see, including of course White's contemporaries at Cheltenham. He was now high up in the school

---

2 'Poem for the Outbreak of Hostilities', in Sprague, Kurth ed.: *A Joy Proposed: Poems by T.H. White*, London, Bertram Rota, 1980.

hierarchy, and so immune from the savage punishment of his early years there, but he was clearly not sorry to leave the institution that he later satirised as the castle of the giant Galapas in the first edition of *The Sword in the Stone*.

Every stage of White's life seems to have contributed something to his later writing. He was by nature a gifted teacher; in need of money, he took a temporary teaching post before going up to Cambridge to read English in 1925. There, at Queens' College, he was fortunate in having as his tutor L.J. Potts, a man who though he achieved no great reputation as a scholar or a writer, was a splendid life-long friend to White – indeed probably the best friend he ever had. In a letter to his former tutor when he was engrossed in the writing of *The Sword in the Stone*, fearing that he must be boring him, he wrote 'forgive my reverting to it – I have nobody to tell things to'[3] – a state of affairs which was to become almost permanent. He was fortunate, too, in being up at a time when such well-known literary figures as I.A. Richards, E.M.W. Tillyard and T.R. Henn were active. White must have been attracted to Tom Henn with his flamboyant personality and Irish background; he also shared Henn's sporting interests and benefitted from his expertise. Tillyard and Richards, each famous in his particular field, remained benefi-cent powers for White after he left the university, supplying vital references and judiciously reading his manuscripts occasionally when he was in need of advice before submitting them for publication. Later Sir Sydney Cockerell, retired Director of the Fitzwilliam Museum, was added to the few whose life-long friendship, mainly carried on by the exchange of let-ters, meant so much to him.

At the end of his first year White won a College Exhibition, which pro-vided very much needed help with his finances. But after a happy and promising start, his university course was interrupted when in his second year he was diagnosed as having tuberculosis, at that time a disease that was still often lethal. He was told (probably by his mother who liked to dramatize and to play on people's feelings) that he had only six months to live. He nevertheless insisted on taking his examinations, but was in hospi-tal from June to October. Meanwhile L.J. Potts and a number of others in Cambridge were generously contributing out of their own pockets to a fund to allow White to spend a year in Italy in the hope that he would recover away from the English winter and in the warmer climate of the south. He was in consequence able to travel a little – to visit Naples, Capri, Amalfi, Paestum and Vesuvius. He learnt Italian. He had time not only to recover his health completely, but to think and to write, and one result was his first novel, *They Winter Abroad*, and a volume of poems, *Loved Helen*.

In his final year, as part of his final examination for the English Tripos he

---

3 See Gallix, François ed.: *T.H. White: Letters to a Friend, The Correspondence between T.H. White and L.J. Potts*, Gloucester, Alan Sutton, 1984, p. 87. (Hereafter *LF*)

submitted an 'Original Contribution' (a short piece of work, which might take the form of an essay or of the first chapter of a novel, or a poem, voluntarily offered in addition to the formal written papers). This was a dissertation on Malory, an author not at that time very highly regarded by the Cambridge English Faculty: when, years later, L.J. Potts re-read *Le Morte Darthur*, stimulated by White's new treatment of the story of Arthur, he wrote, 'how could I read it and not see *anything* in it – I mean anything that *is* in it' (LF 115–16). His comment suggests both how difficult it was, even at a time when the classics of English literature were very much more widely studied than they are now, to read such a book with real under-standing, and how perceptive and innovative White's reading and re-telling of Malory actually was. But this dissertation (which unfortunately has not survived) seems to have had a mixed reception. It is reported that one of the examiners was not favourably impressed by it, apparently be-cause like *The Once and Future King* it did not treat its subject entirely seriously. Tom Henn, however, reported that he had found it wildly funny at times.

When White returned to Cambridge for his final year it was with an offer of publication for *Loved Helen*, subsequently the Book Society's choice for April. That same year he was literary editor of the *Granta*, a long-established undergraduate journal in the style of *Punch*. He contributed a poem to the first number of the Empson-Bronowski *Experiment* and had more poems in *Cambridge Poetry 1929*[4] than anyone except Empson. A column of his on Cambridge doings appeared from time to time in a London weekly.

Perhaps his closest friend in the Cambridge English School at the time was Elsie Phare, a Newnham student in her third year. She had been recommended to him as a reviewer for the *Granta* by L.J. Potts, one of the examiners who had given her a star (i.e. an indication of exceptional merit in the examination, very rarely awarded) in the English Tripos Part I, 1928. At 85, and now Mrs Duncan-Jones, she vividly remembers 'Timothy' (he was never called Terence) as he appeared when she first went to Queens' to collect the weekly copies for review. Tall, fresh-complexioned, challenging and wearing a remarkable plus-four suit of blue velvet, he looked every inch a poet: she found his conversation lived up to his looks. They went to lectures together, to plays and films, and talked of books they studied as well as those they reviewed. Her interests at that time centred on Hopkins, his still on Malory. Virginia Woolf's *Orlando* came out in October 1928 and her recollection is that Timothy spoke of it with some severity then, though in *The Once and Future King* he seems to have felt its influence.[5] In Part II of

---

4 In *Hogarth Living Poets, No. 8*, London, Hogarth Press 1929.
5 Personal communication.

the Tripos both had stars. In the spring of 1930 he wrote to her that he was hoping to have a holiday in France and tentatively raised the possibility that she might join him: 'I should ask you but don't know if you would think it proper. I am still harmless.' She didn't go and has no more of his letters.

Probably because he had already been so successful as an author, there seems to have been no question of White's going on to a research degree: Potts advised him to embark at once upon a career as a writer. Afterwards White seems sometimes to have regretted the missed opportunity of an academic career. After going down from Cambridge, he spent the autumn in the British Museum, working on a book to be called *Three Lives*, biographies of Joanna Southcott, Admiral Byng and Sir Jeffrey Hudson. It was never published.

The next year, 1930, in need of more money, he became an assistant master in a preparatory school in Reigate, a job for which he was much over-qualified, but which allowed him to do some writing in his spare time. Little seems to be known about his experiences here, although in an undated letter to Elsie Phare, he wrote:

> Yes, I'm a quite happy, efficient, moral and almost high-class school-master in Sussex. Much golf and physical existance (sic), teaching boxing, indeed, and drill. Nor need you laugh. I don't think I do it at all badly (I should say rather that I do it fairly well.) And I rise at seven twenty. It is my vocation.[6]

White's natural gift for teaching and his enjoyment of the society of children and young people no doubt made his work quite congenial, but at the same time he knew that he was wasting his talents. 'I feel that it's rather preposterous to teach Latin in a prep school after getting a First in English', he wrote to Potts (LF 28). He now proposed to write a book on Gerard Manley Hopkins in his own name, while continuing to write novels under the pseudonym that he had used for *They Winter Abroad*, James Aston. He had also collaborated with another master to produce a murder story, *Dead Mr Nixon* (1931). But unfortunately, and perhaps not surprisingly, his individuality and unconventionality did not recommend him to his headmaster, who disapproved of some of his activities such as his reading John Masefield's delightful and entirely innocuous *The Midnight Folk* to his form of twelve-year-olds. Worse still, he seems to have failed to muster the stern disapproval required of him, of close friendships between young boys. Sylvia Townsend Warner tells the story of how two little boys had been found in the same bed, and so were expelled. 'White was charged to

---

6 Personal communication.

accompany them to London. During the journey, he asked what they had been doing. They admitted that they had been talking. Asked what they had been talking about, they replied, "Buses and trains" (STW 55). Towards the end of 1931 the headmaster, referred to in a letter to Potts as 'Dr Prisonface', indicated to White that his services were no longer appreciated: 'To all intents and purposes I have been fired from this school owing to my Socratic intransigence. There was nothing wrong, or anything of that sort . . .' he wrote to Potts (LF 28). By the end of February, however, he was writing to him again with the good news that he was to be head of the English Department at Stowe School from September. In this year he published two novels in addition to *They Winter Abroad*: *First Lesson*, as well as *Darkness at Pemberley*, which he claimed to have written in three weeks.

He was extremely successful at Stowe. The school had been established for less than ten years when he joined its staff, but under the headmastership of the enlightened J.F. Roxburgh it already had a high reputation. It was even described as the 'new Eton'. It was modern and in many ways progressive without being cranky, aiming to be in the best public school tradition, but without the time-honoured corporal punishment and bullying usual in the older public schools. Although White was initially rather prickly, he later came to appreciate his new headmaster (sometimes referred to as his 'circus-master') and to regard him as a friend. He was soon in trouble: correspondence from the publisher about *First Lesson*, written under the name of James Aston, was accidentally delivered to one of the boys, James Ashton, which eventually led to White's identification as the author. A parent on discovering this objected to the book on moral grounds, and indicated his view that the author was no fit person to have the education of his child. Roxburgh stood by his head of English, but made him write a letter condemning his novel as 'an undergraduate scrape', after which the whole trouble blew over.

One of his colleagues described White at this time as 'this daemonic and brilliant man'. His energy must indeed have been demonic in view of the bulk of his publications, but his books were not produced at the expense of his conventional duties. He was considered a responsible tutor, and an inspired and inspiring teacher, though one of his pupils later recorded that he was also a very severe one, who would pour scorn on those who tried to impress by their cleverness rather than by the sincerity of their writing. Influenced himself by the innovative teaching of I.A. Richards and other Cambridge dons, he must have been able to bring a new and lively approach to the study of language and literature; and must have found teaching English literature to intelligent adolescents much more satisfying than teaching little boys Latin grammar. White was a charismatic, if somewhat bohemian figure, who not only still found time to write, but also engaged in a great range of other activities. In 1931, while still at Reigate, he had written to Potts that he had decided to take up 'gentility' (LF 15). So in due course at Stowe he fostered his country-gentleman image by driving about in a black Bentley and participating in various sports. He bought a horse, and kept a Hunting Diary, a Fishing Diary, a Shooting Diary and a Flying Diary. The passion for learning things and for acquiring skills that was never to leave him was not only indulged during the years at Stowe, but was also shared with some of his pupils. He was a man who collected techniques, his biographer says of him, but his flying-instructor later commented that 'when he'd got what he wanted, he never went on with it' (STW 74).

The hunting, shooting and fishing in which White engaged while at Stowe provided material for his next two books, *Earth Stopped* (1934) and *Gone to Ground* (1935), both in the manner of Surtees, and promptly followed by the very successful *England Have My Bones* (1936). Despite his action-packed life, he was unhappy, craving more time in which to write, but unable to see how to finance full-time authorship, since his novels had failed to bring in enough money to live on. A deeper unhappiness lay beneath the surface of his life: the demonic activity which filled every moment at Stowe stemmed from the need to stifle his misery. In an attempt to come to terms with his problems he underwent psychoanalysis, which seemed to do some good. 'I am partially in love with a quite perfect barmaid', he was soon writing to Potts – a love-affair appears to have been recommended as part of the treatment. Unfortunately (or otherwise) it came to nothing. The immediate effect of the analysis was to make him much happier, if only temporarily so: for a time he certainly believed that he was cured (LF 62). He had been recommended to the analyst by a man who had been a sadistic homosexual, but who had later been able to marry and become a father. White was not so fortunate himself: the whole of his life was darkened by his sadistic and homosexual tendencies, which he believed had had their origins in his family relationships and his experiences at Cheltenham College. In his final year at Cambridge, in the spring of 1929, he had told Elsie Phare that he was a homosexual, a fact which remained for some time a closely guarded secret because he was very conscious of the disadvantages, e.g. the illegality, of homosexuality. One cannot but admire the iron will with which he kept this side of his nature under total subjection, apparently throughout his life. The long-term consequence of it all was a life-time of loneliness and at least partial frustration. Though someone who knew him described him as a self-tormented person, and he could be self-pitying, he was also a man whose generous and loving impulses could find few outlets. 'I have always wanted to be someone's best friend, but never succeeded', he wrote to Potts; 'I have no friends, only acquaintances.' (STW 97)

With the publication of *England Have My Bones* which was chosen both by the *Daily Mail* and the Book Guild as the book of the month, White was becoming increasingly successful as an author. He was asked to give papers in both Oxford and in Cambridge; and the same year (1936) also saw the beginning of the friendship with David Garnett which was to help to sustain White – though mainly through the exchange of letters – for the rest of his life. Now, aged thirty, he began to think of resigning from Stowe to devote himself to writing: 'Actually I would rather have no money at all than be a schoolmaster', he wrote to Garnett.[7] Eventually he decided to burn his boats, sending in his resignation in the Easter holidays, but by this time he had to admit that the psychoanalysis had only got him 'about one quarter of the way' that he needed to go. What he hoped to do was to live in a cottage, preferably near a trout stream, with neighbours who would allow him to shoot half a dozen times a year, and to write. What finally became available was a gamekeeper's cottage on the Stowe estate. It was isolated and primitive: water had to be drawn from a well, and there was no indoor sanitation, but it made it possible for him to do what he was longing to do, to 'revert to a feral state', a phrase which he had encountered in a book on the training of falcons. It also gave him the opportunity of trying to train a falcon himself, beginning with Gos, sent over from Germany. This was more than just a passing fancy on White's part: he persevered with the enormously demanding and often extremely frustrating process partly because he expected that his livelihood in the near future would depend on the book which it was his intention to write on falcons. In its place, when his plans were ruined by the loss of Gos, he wrote *Burke's Steerage, or the Amateur Gentleman's Introduction to Noble Sports and Pastimes* (1938), in which he enjoyed making fun of all sorts of vulgar pretentiousness and snobbery. He did not give up the idea of training falcons: he tried again with Cully, acquired two sparrowhawks, and then very briefly an owl called Archimedes, later immortalised as Merlyn's companion. The book that he had intended to write out of his experience with falcons, *The Goshawk*, was not published until 1951.

It was in the gamekeeper's cottage with his dog Brownie and the falcons and other livestock for company that White wrote *The Sword in the Stone*. He was in urgent need of money when the book was accepted, but its publication was put off so that it could be considered by the American Book of the Month Club. Eventually the good news came that it had been chosen, on condition that White revised three chapters, which he immediately did, enabling it to be published in New York in 1939. Earlier in the year he had extended his experience in a way that, later on, also fed into *The Sword in the Stone*, by his visit to Wells-next-the-Sea in Norfolk to shoot wild geese. Sir Sydney Cockerell invited him to Kew and showed him a facsimile of the twelfth-century bestiary which many years later he was to translate and publish as *The Book of Beasts* (1954).

White was deeply disturbed by the preparations for war and by the

---

7   See Garnett, David ed.: *The White/Garnett Letters*, London, Cape 1968. (Hereafter *W/G L*)

Munich crisis of August 1938. There was no getting away from the sense of impending doom. In the uneasy months that followed, he made a move that significantly affected the rest of his life. When he was invited by Garnett to join him on a fishing holiday on the river Boyne in Ireland, White was wanting to find a quiet retreat in which he could finish *The Witch in the Wood*, the second volume of his Arthurian tetralogy, later to become *The Queen of Air and Darkness*, which was now well under way. Ray, David Garnett's wife, went to a nearby farm, Doolistown House, near Trim (about forty miles from Dublin), and asked if they would take a lodger. In the end, White's stay at Doolistown, originally intended to last only a few weeks, lengthened into six years, and was to be crucial for his career as a writer in several ways.

The Witch in the Wood was finished in May 1939, leaving him uncertain as to what he ought to do, as it became increasingly apparent that World War II was imminent. He was acutely depressed by the threat of war, and also exasperated by his publisher's insistence that he should drastically modify *The Witch in the Wood*. He had hoped to gather a party of friends together in Ireland for grouse-shooting and good company, but these plans were also thwarted, to his intense disappointment. He had rented a shooting lodge in the west of Ireland, at Sheskin (now a nature reserve) but the owners changed their minds about the dates, so that White was not able to have the use of it in the month of August as he had expected. When he got there it was too late: with the onset of war, his hoped-for gathering of friends could not take place. Poland had been invaded by Hitler, and on 3 September Great Britain declared war on Germany. Ireland (apart from Ulster, Northern Ireland) remained neutral. It was generally expected that a full scale attack would immediately be unleashed on England, and young men were at once called up for military service. White was exempt both on the grounds of age and of physical fitness, and also because he was resident in Ireland, though subsequently he was to make many abortive attempts to contribute to the war-effort. Eventually, he came to feel that the most important business in which he could engage was the finishing of his work on Malory. In his journal for 21 September 1939 he wrote:

> I can do much better than fight for civilisation: I can make it. So, at any rate until Arthur is safely through the press, I have ceased to bother about the war.

At the same time, he recorded that he had 'vaguely volunteered' for the Ministry of Information.

Despite the difficult political situation, David Garnett came to Sheskin at the beginning of September 1939 with members of his family, but he had to return to England almost immediately, leaving his children and his wife Ray who was desperately ill with cancer. Perhaps the best thing to come out of the disastrous venture was the consolidating of White's friendship with Ray, who gave him some invaluable advice about how to improve his understanding of women so as to characterise them more effectively in his novels, before she too had to leave. Probably as a result of her interest, by October he was formulating the idea that a 'Much more important question than what sort of person was Lancelot is what sort of person was Guenever?' (Journal, 10 October 1939), since Ray had suggested that White did not 'attend to his women'. In a letter to David Garnett after her death White indicated his sense of his indebtedness to her by saying that if *The Ill-Made Knight* turned out to be a good book, it would be due to Ray.

As a compulsive learner as well as teacher, White had interested himself from the beginning of his stay in Ireland in the language, history and customs of the country. He took lessons in Erse, he joined in with the family devotions at Doolistown and came close to becoming a Roman Catholic. He also tried to investigate the folklore of Inniskea in the west of Ireland. The tradition of the Godstone, a mysterious object closely associated with Inniskea, the identity of which seems never to have been established, provided the starting point for *The Godstone and the Blackymor* (1959). The Godstone was supposed to improve the crop of potatoes, as well as to calm raging seas, and White held the view that it had originated in a fertility cult. His stay in the west of Ireland, though it was productive in so far as his book was concerned, was made miserable by the fact that his activities aroused suspicion and feelings of hostility in the local people. He was thought to be spying for the English; and it was even rumoured that he concealed illicit maps under the waterproof coat that his dog Brownie wore in bad weather. Since even his landlady at Doolistown, not too far from Dublin in the east, claimed to have heard the banshee, and was able to indicate the size of fairies as being two or three feet high, the credulity of the inhabitants of Belmullet in the far north-west (where White had been staying) is hardly to be wondered at.

By the summer of 1940 *The Ill-Made Knight*, the third volume of his Arthuriad, was finished and White, back at Doolistown, turned to what was to become the last volume of the tetralogy, *The Candle in the Wind*. It already existed in the form of a play written some time before, but turned down by Noel Coward as being insufficiently dramatic to be viable. White was able to use it as the basis for his fourth volume, from which he immediately went on to write *The Book of Merlyn* (which would have been a fifth volume, or epilogue), in which Arthur returns to his animals. Problems and frustration very soon arose with respect to the publication of the now completed Arthurian work. When *The Candle in the Wind* and *The Book of Merlyn* were completed, White wanted the publisher, William Collins, to bring out a new edition which would comprise his five 'Arthur' books, the earlier ones in newly revised and final form, together with the last two. Collins replied that they had not, in war-time, the resources to undertake so large a project. Considerable annoyance seems to have been experienced on both sides, and the result of it all was that the publication of the four volumes together of *The Once and Future King* was held up until 1958, when it first appeared as a one-volume work (published first by Collins and then by the Reprint Society). Even then it was without the fifth and final *Book of Merlyn*, only published after White's death by the University of Texas Press in 1977, on the advice of Sylvia Townsend Warner.

When his Arthurian book was finished at last, White began to think seriously of returning to England to make a contribution to the war-effort. He made elaborate plans for the well-being and weaning away from him of his dog Brownie, but the thought of leaving her was misery: he wrote in his journal for 24 October 1941:

> By going, I am sacrificing everything I have. I never had much. I had no wife, children or home. . . . I did have one thing for seven years, a red setter bitch who went with me everywhere I went . . . I have, like Abraham slaying his son, to leave her here and go away.

If the tone could be regarded as self-pitying, nevertheless it was undeniable that he felt he 'never had much', and that Brownie was everything to him for that reason. Since he was not eligible for conscription, he applied to join the Royal Air Force Volunteer Reserve on the strength of having qualified as a pilot while at Stowe, but was turned down. He asked David Garnett to look for a suitable job for him but nothing came of that, either. Although he accepted that, in his own words, 'Hitler is the kind of chap one has to stop', and declared himself ready to help in the process, there was no suitable role for him, not even writing propaganda, which he had assumed he could usefully do.

His next move was to apply to the Irish government for an Exit Permit so that he could return to England to look for some other way in which he could help. This attempt was also frustrated: evidence of employment was required before a visa could be granted. At least his conscience was now clear that he had done his best to make his contribution, and that it was not wanted.

Unable to leave Ireland, White suffered a period of ill-health and severe depression, partly as a result of the social and intellectual isolation of his life at Doolistown, particularly when he was without a major creative project to engage his attention. Without:

> the encouragement of equal minds, the stimulation from other intellects, isolated from a surrounding war, with letters spied on, journalism censored, wireless stuffed with lies, and ignorance all round one, the writer's life is that of the slaves set to make bricks without straw,

he had written early in the war (STW 182), and by 1942 he was more acutely lonely than ever before, lacking even the heart to keep up his correspondence.

Eventually, perhaps when he was finally convinced that he could not do anything in the war, he seems to have accepted his situation. On 6 July 1943 he wrote to Garnett:

> Six months ago I realised the fact (with pleasure) that I was not a normal human being. The great thing about not being normal is that you don't have to do the usual things – go to war, etc. Here had I been forcing myself to be normal for thirty years quite unnecessarily and vainly. It was a great relief.   (W/G L 126)

He took up gardening, built a greenhouse, grew exotic vegetables, and began work on *The Elephant and the Kangaroo*.[8] He sent some drafts of this to Garnett, who was both impressed and encouraging. He also started to translate the bestiary in October, deriving great satisfaction from an intellectually challenging task which enabled him to see himself in a new role. 'I was always intended to be a scholar', he later wrote to Potts (LF 148). *Mistress Masham's Repose*[9] was soon under way, and *The Age of Scandal* begun. But just when everything seemed to be going better, the parting which he had found almost unbearable to contemplate in 1941 took place with the death of Brownie in November 1944, of whom he wrote 'she was the central fact of my life'. 'With her death', says Sylvia Townsend Warner, 'he lost the only being he dared to love' (STW 211). Her trust 'had become the thing he depended on'. On David Garnett's advice he at once looked for and acquired a setter puppy, in the hope that it would take her place in his affections, but her loss was irremediable and he was overwhelmed with grief.

At last, however, the war was almost at an end, offering White the opportunity of returning to England, seeing the old friends with whom he had almost lost touch, and so ending his isolation. It seemed likely that Doolistown would be sold, and the prospect of remaining there as the tenant of strangers was not attractive. David Garnett was able to offer White a cottage, Duke Mary's, in Swaledale in Yorkshire, where his only neighbours were grouse, and the nearest shop had to be reached by taking a precipitous walk of four miles. His books, he wrote to Sir Sydney Cockerell, he would have to drag up the crag with a horse and sledge.

At first he seems to have been very happy: he was very short of money, but both of his most recent books had been offered to an American publisher, and eventually the news came that they had been accepted, and again he was a Book of the Month choice. The financial reward was considerable, but he had to pay heavy taxes in both the United States and in Britain. He had no other assets or financial resources and was considering emigrating

---

8 London, Cape 1948; New York, G.P. Putnam's Sons, 1947.
9 London, Cape 1947; New York, G.P. Putnam's Sons, 1946.

to America to lessen the drain on his income, when David Garnett again came up with a solution to his problems, which was to move to the tax-haven of the Channel Islands. White first tried Guernsey, but it proved to be inhospitable; then Sark, but that island had to be rejected because no bit-ches were allowed there. In the end, he settled on Alderney.

The story is told of how, infuriated by the attitude of the people in the hotel in Guernsey, debarred from Sark and unable to fly to Alderney be-cause dogs were not allowed on the plane, White found a miserable little boat which was just leaving and embarked on it. It was an extremely rough crossing, and there was some doubt as to whether the boat would be able to make harbour. It did, however, and first off was his dog Killie, followed by the bearded figure of White, drenched and streaming with water. A voice from the spectators on the quay was heard to exclaim: 'The boat must have gone deep. They've fetched up Father Neptune' (STW 238). But a warm welcome was awaiting him on Alderney, first from the owners of the Gros-nez Hotel, who took him in, dog and all, and then from other inhabitants. Alderney suited him, and at last he had found somewhere he could settle and perhaps put down roots. The remaining sixteen years of his life were mostly spent there, and by July 1947 he had bought a three-storeyed house in which he was later able to have friends to stay.

In the spring of 1949, while on a visit to White, his publisher had ac-cidentally discovered a manuscript lying about the house which turned out to be *The Goshawk*, and was eager to publish it, despite White's reluct-ance. It had been written in 1936, and White had come to think of it as amateurish as far as the training of hawks was concerned. David Garnett was consulted and insisted that it ought to be published forthwith, assert-ing that 'It will be an intensely popular book among all thirty British and American austringers and falconers' (STW 244). It was to become a classic, still in print today.

As when he was in Ireland, White had a problem with alcohol – it had by this time in effect become chronic – but now he was writing again. He was still at work on *The Age of Scandal* and its sequel, *The Scandalmonger*, as well as on the bestiary. He was also doing some more rewriting of *The Sword in the Stone*, removing *The Book of Merlyn* from the intended final version of *The Once and Future King*, and incorporating from it into his first volume the visits to the ants and geese. This last revision was finished on 17 April 1957.

In many ways the move to Alderney gave White a new lease of life. *The Book of Beasts* was at last finished after many years of intermittent labour: it was by this book that he believed that his name would survive, for it had demanded much scholarly enquiry and effort in the translating. To a cer-tain extent he was right; the copy in the University Library of Cambridge bears witness to considerable use, but the recognition that he had so keenly hoped for at the time of its publication was not forthcoming, because the title raised misleading expectations. In consequence, he did not get the serious scholarly reviews that it was not unreasonable to expect for such a work. His next book was very different: *The Master, an Adventure Story* (1957), described by White as 'My Treasure Island Story' and intended for children. At the same time, he was doing a certain amount of book-reviewing, for the *Times Literary Supplement* in particular, for despite the remoteness of Alderney, he was able to keep in closer contact with the literary world than was possible while he was in exile in war-time Ireland.

More practical interests also offered themselves. White was able to take up snorkelling and diving, which included, in 1956, the experience of going down in a deep-sea diving-suit, of which mention was made in Chapter 2 of *The Ill-Made Knight* in the final revision, completed in the following year. He acquired a sailing-dinghy, the Popsie, and so added sailing to the tally of his skills. He learned the deaf-and-dumb alphabet, following it with Braille, because of his sympathy with the plight of the deaf-blind, and for several summers he offered hospitality in his home to these sufferers, beginning with Puck, a middle-aged deaf-blind lady, whom he taught to swim, greatly to her delight. It was typical of his sympathy and generosity, as of his patience and predilection both for learning and for teaching. He also managed to interest some of the local children in these summer visitors, teaching them the deaf-and-dumb alphabet, so that they too could communicate with his guests.

When in 1957 he at last got *The Once and Future King* off his hands in its final form, the year was also made noteworthy by the presence of some young boys, on holiday from London, who stayed in his house, among them Zed. White fell in love with Zed. 'It has been my hideous fate to be born with an infinite capacity for love and joy with no hope of using them', he wrote to Garnett (STW 277–8); and to Mary Potts (whose husband had quite recently died) he later wrote of the boy as 'the heir on whom I had pinned all my love and trust' (LF 255). He claimed that he never told the boy what he felt for him, and the friendship – if that is what it should be called – lasted for four years, until Zed grew away from him. It undoubtedly brought White much more unhappiness and frustration than joy. Sylvia Townsend Warner, in a letter written when she was working on his biography, records that 'it was like feeling at home in hell when last summer I read through those diaries ... with White's raving, despairing soliloquy whispering on and on in my ear.'[10] In March 1959 he had written in his journal:

> If I had no insight into my condition, really I would say I was insane. I am in a sort of whirlpool which goes round and round, thinking all day and half the night about a small boy – whom I don't need sexually, whose personality I disapprove of intellectually, but to whom I am

10 Maxwell, William ed.: *Letters: Sylvia Townsend Warner*, London, Chatto and Windus, 1982, p. 227.

committed emotionally, against my will. The whole of my brain tells
me the situation is impossible, while the whole of my heart nags on. . . .
What do I want of Zed? – Not his body, merely the whole of him all the
time. It's equivalent to a confession of murder.

White took up new projects, filming puffins and trying unsuccessfully to
sell the film to the BBC. *The Once and Future King* had got on to the Ten
Bestsellers list in the United States for three successive weeks, and interest
was being shown there by Lerner and Loewe in making it into the musical
Camelot. In November 1959 White met Julie Andrews who was to star in
Camelot, and she and her husband became kind and valued friends during
the last years of his life. The following November (1960) he flew to Boston
for the opening night of the musical which got off to rather a slow start with
a good many teething-troubles, but promised to make White a rich man all
the same. His return from America was followed by what he described as 'a
sort of minor nervous breakdown' (LF 252) resulting in excessive drinking,
but the next year his loneliness was cheered by a first meeting with a cousin
and her husband and two children. Together they had a very successful
holiday in France, and they spent Christmas together in 1961. He was able
to lavish on them, particularly on the children, the love for which it was
otherwise so difficult for him to find an appropriate outlet.

White's career as a writer was by this time virtually finished. In the
winter of 1962 he went to Italy again, staying in Rome and in Florence, but
alienating many acquaintances by drinking and talking too much. He was
looked after and made welcome by the Verney family, whose generosity
and loving tolerance enabled them to put up with his eccentricities. In May
he was in Naples, adopted and looked after this time by a family of Italian
costermongers. 'His wealth spouted from him like wine from a fountain on
a royal birthday', says Sylvia Townsend Warner of this period (STW 327),
and much of it was lavished on the costermongers who later exploited
him.

White was back in Alderney again in June. He had been invited to visit
the United States for a lecture tour in the autumn of 1963. He insisted on
going by sea, in the Queen Elizabeth, accompanied by Carol Walton, the
sister-in-law of Julie Andrews, who had gallantly offered to undertake the
very demanding task of organising all the travel arrangements and generally taking care of him. He gave a large number of lectures, many of which
were very successful, though as sometimes happens with such enterprises,
there were occasions when things went rather wrong. For a long time his
health had been breaking down and he had been feeling his age, indeed
more than feeling his age, but under Carol Walton's excellent care, he
enormously enjoyed the tour. At the end, Carol had to fly home for
Christmas, leaving White to make his way back to Europe on a semi-cargo
vessel, with the intention of going on to Egypt, the Lebanon and Greece. He
expected to be back in Alderney by about February. At Naples, he picked

up a member of the costermonger family, Vito Moriconi, whom he had got
to know the previous spring. It was Moriconi who, on the morning of 17
January 1964, found White lying on the floor of his cabin, dead. Three days
later he was buried in the Protestant Cemetery in Athens. The inscription
on his tombstone, devised by Sylvia Townsend Warner, reads:

T. H. WHITE
1906 – 1964
AUTHOR
WHO
FROM A TROUBLED HEART
DELIGHTED OTHERS
LOVING AND PRAISING
THIS LIFE

2

The Genesis of
The Sword in the Stone

i. *Literary Influences*

When White eventually gave up his post at Stowe and went to live in the gamekeeper's cottage at Stowe Ridings, he was at last able to revert to 'a feral state' as he had longed to do. With no modern facilities, he was living in primitive conditions and in such isolation as was often still possible in England in the 1930s; in conditions, moreover, which in many ways had remained unchanged since the Middle Ages. With his hawks and his hound for sole company, like the knight in the ballad, he must often have felt himself to be existing in a time-warp. In his journal for 28 April 1939, he wrote:

> When I have finally finished my quadruplets about Arthur, I think I may fairly write a little Introduction to them. Perhaps, after a quarter of a million words, one earns the right to an introduction. . . . Since there are perhaps a quarter of a million words in this edition, I think there is the right to tell one anecdote. I began writing the history without conscious premeditation. When I was a young boy at Cambridge I had done a thesis upon Mallory, and now, when I was thirty years of age, I was living alone in a tiny cottage which contained almost nothing except a representative library and several live hawks or owls. One evening, exhausted of everything to read, I took down the Morte d'Arthur once more in the lamplight and began to read it for recreation as if it were as simple as Edgar Wallace. There was nothing else to read. To my astonishment, which many will understand to be usual in the writer of a thesis upon the Morte d'Arthur, I found that the book was just as simple. . . . I read it with passion, knowing how Launcelot would behave in any circumstances, how Arthur, how Gawaine. They were real people. I finished it in two days, with my heart in the reading eyes, and came upon the final words of that most chivalrous and learned tragedian. "I pray you all" he wrote, "gentlemen and gentlewomen that read this book . . . pray for me while I am on live that God send me good deliverance, and, when I am dead, I pray you all pray for my soul." I did pray for his soul, and wrote this book for it

from this moment onwards, and now I ask any readers, who may come
to it after 1939, that my own soul may be joined in the same petition.

This was how the brilliantly original idea of White's 'preface to Mallory'
dealing with Arthur's boyhood, and soon to grow into the very large
project which White later saw as his epic, came into being.

The achievement of his first months at Stowe Ridings was proclaimed to
Potts when on 14 January 1938 White wrote to say that he had a new book
in the press:

> I think it is one of my better books, so probably no-one else will. It is a
> preface to Mallory. Do you remember I once wrote a thesis on the
> Morte d'Arthur? Naturally I did not read Mallory when writing the
> thesis on him, but one time last autumn I got desperate among my
> books and picked him up in lack of anything else. Then I was thrilled
> and astonished to find that (a) The thing was a perfect tragedy, with a
> beginning, a middle and an end implicit in the beginning and (b) the
> characters were real people with recognisable reactions which could be
> forecast. . . . Anyway, I somehow started writing a book. It is not a
> satire. Indeed, I am afraid it is rather warm-hearted – mainly about
> birds and beasts. It seems impossible to determine whether it is for
> grown-ups or children. I will send a copy for my godson's birthday, if
> out in time, and you must try it on him when he is about twelve. It is
> more or less a wish-fulfillment of the kind of things I should have liked
> to have happened to me when I was a boy. . . . I should have liked it to
> be like Masefield's *Midnight Folk*, a book which I love this side of
> idolatry. It is called *The Sword in the Stone*. I did a lot of research into the
> 14th-15th centuries, in a mild way.   (LF 86)

The Sword in the Stone gave White great scope for indulging the interest in
history that he had not been able to satisfy at Cambridge, since it allowed
him to take freely from medieval history the materials he wanted to create a
secondary world as background for the life of his young hero. His very
diverse antiquarian interests and enormously wide reading were dedicated
to the task of interpreting *Le Morte Darthur* for the modern reader, particularly for the young and inexperienced reader who needed to be drawn in to
what is still for many people at the present day an inaccessible work. By
representing the events of Malory's story in modern terms, he makes it
comprehensible and enlists our sympathies. Beginning with Arthur's childhood in what is primarily a children's book, he moves on into the adult
world as the story advances towards its tragic denouement.

In creating a medieval background White was performing a complex feat
by presenting the story's setting as he imagined Malory might have
visualised it – if he had been the sort of writer given to such imaginative
activity – and by bringing this vanished world vividly to life in very visual
terms, often even drawing his images from medieval manuscript illustrations. *The Once and Future King* is probably the last major retelling of the

story based on Malory, set in the Middle Ages and in the chivalric tradition. Most subsequent writers have gone further back in time to a more primitive age and chosen a Romano-British setting. None has so lovingly and minutely evoked the medieval scene, or so painstakingly endeavoured to interpret *Le Morte Darthur* for his contemporaries, showing us not only how Arthur's tragedy unfolded, but also endeavouring to bridge the gap between medieval ways of thinking and our own.

In *The Once and Future King* White was not simply devising a modernised version of the traditional story, but by his interpretation bringing out its mythic power. Perhaps the impact of World War II increased a general interest in myths developed by various scholars and writers, not least in Cambridge, and also in psychoanalysis. White was following a literary interest of the day in being consciously or unconsciously attracted to the mythic.

His fascination with the past was both romantic and scholarly. He had the added advantage of not being limited by a fixed historical period, as also of not setting out to write an historical novel. In the end-paper of his copy of Lord Lytton's *The Last of the Barons*, there is a note in White's hand which says:

> Point out that neither my nor Mallory's book is strictly an historical novel.

History inspired and furnished his fantasy world, yet did not constrain him. Malory gave him the basic plot and the characters – more even than he needed – while leaving him free to devise the setting. Although Malory in so far as he created a background for his story at all, set it in his own age, with occasional references to earlier times when things were better, he provided virtually no colourful detail to enable the reader to imagine the scene, thus giving White his opportunity. Like many late nineteenth- and twentieth-century writers, he enjoyed looking back to an imaginary golden age in the past. In *The Sword in the Stone*, he devised his own utopia, 'a sort of fanciful fairyland', as he describes it in the note quoted above, consisting partly of the world as seen by a happy child, and partly of his vision of what pre-industrial England might have been like. His chosen setting allowed him to give way to his school-masterly tendency to instruct, the counterpart of his own life-long desire to learn. His real interest in the Middle Ages was above all in how things were done, so that by explaining how Sir Ector's castle was constructed, how the hay-harvest was got in, how the mews were organised, how boar-hunts were conducted and so on, with an enormous amount of relevant detail, he was able to create an image of the medieval world that has its counterpart in the art of the Middle Ages. With disarming zest he updated anything that might cause problems to the uninstructed modern reader. Sir Grummore, after passing the port, suggests that the Wart and Kay should be sent to Eton, though:

It was not really Eton that he mentioned, for the College of Blessed
Mary was not founded until 1440, but it was a place of the same sort.
Also they were drinking Metheglyn, not Port, but by mentioning the
modern wine it is easier to give you the feel.[1]

White manages to have it both ways: to give some idea of the realities of
medieval life (usually through rose-tinted spectacles) and to exploit to the
full the opportunities for humour and comedy offered by comparing and
contrasting them with modern circumstances. Thus he avoided, by paradoxically invoking them, charges of anachronism and inconsistency. Even
while creating a picture of the quaint 'medievals' of popular imagination,
he also manages to inject a good deal of factual information for the better
instruction of the reader. Sir Ector and Sir Grummore Grummursum are
presented as caricatures of Old Etonians, but we hear that in their boyhood
they were 'doin' all this Latin and stuff at five o'clock every morning', in
accordance with some actual medieval educational practice. White's school
history lesson continues with a close-up of Sir Ector's castle – something
which Malory never dreams of giving the reader in *Le Morte Darthur*. The
scene is idealised and romanticised: it is July, 'and real July weather, such as
they had in old England'. Like Kipling in *Puck of Pook's Hill* (1906), a book
which White knew well, he contrives an interaction both between past and
present, to enhance the young reader's awareness and understanding of
the past, and at the same time an interplay between the adult's and the
child's worlds. As author he appears in the guise both of mentor and of
omniscient narrator. He tells his tale somewhat in the manner of the medieval oral story-teller, but he goes far beyond medieval convention in the
extent to which he allows his personality, his experience and his views to
impinge upon the reader.

Writing notes for a review of Martyn Skinner's *Return of Arthur* in 1955,
White comments somewhat scornfully: ' "a novel in verse" (the work's
subtitle) is exactly what it is.' He goes on to express the view that the
versification is adequate and the poetry nil, 'the cerebration is interesting
and, in the Dylan Thomas sense of imagery, humour and compassion, there
is not a trace of poetry anywhere.' His intention when he was writing *The
Sword in the Stone* was that it should be 'poetic' in 'the Dylan Thomas
sense', and in this he succeeded, above all in his depiction of an idyllically
happy childhood, but also by conjuring up a vision, worthy of William
Morris's *News from Nowhere* (1891), of an idealised Old England in which
everyone was happy.

No medieval writers had written of the childhood or 'enfances' of
Arthur. The story of Arthur in Malory, as in many modern versions, begins
with an account of his birth: Uther's desire for Igraine, the subsequent

---

1 *The Once and Future King*, London, Collins, 1958, the first one-volume edition, p. 4. All
subsequent page references are to this edition.

killing of Gorlois her husband, and the begetting of Arthur, brought about through Merlin's agency, followed by Arthur's upbringing in secrecy and seclusion, also arranged by Merlin. In traditional story, the birth of the hero is often clothed in a mystery which gives it special importance: the origins of the man born to be king are not just like those of ordinary people. The circumstances of his birth are singled out for attention in preference to the details of his upbringing. Clearly defined conventions govern his coming into the world: usually he is born into obscurity, often in unusual circumstances, brought up not by his natural parents in princely splendour, but by humbler folk as is Siegfried, or even by animals, as in the case of Romulus and Remus. He has no material or social advantages, and his exceptional qualities are at first unrecognised. He must prove himself, convince his society of his pre-eminence, his intrinsic worth, his claim and unique right to be the leader of his people. His experiences between birth and recognition are usually of minimal importance: the details of his upbringing and education and of his everyday life in childhood are often omitted altogether in such stories. The strange circumstances of the hero's conception, as with Perseus in Greek myth, begotten upon Danae by Zeus in a shower of golden rain, or of Arthur himself, set him apart from ordinary men. The young hero's claim to recognition, by freeing Andromeda from the sea-monster in the story of Perseus, or drawing the sword from the stone in the case of Arthur, is the true centre of narrative interest.

White had his own reasons for not wishing to follow Malory and his medieval predecessors by adopting the traditional pattern, which drew attention to Arthur's mysterious origin and passed over in silence the years between his birth and his drawing the sword from the stone. In the first instance, the 'facts' of Arthur's begetting and birth, invented for him in accordance with the conventions of traditional storytelling, were such that they would have been awkward to explain to White's intended readership in the 1930s, a period when the 'facts of life' themselves were still surrounded by an aura of mystery for many young people, an aura often only to be dispelled by judicious revelations to small groups in headmasters' studies as White himself had been instructed, as he comments in one of his journals. White did not intend to change, conceal or bowdlerise the story of Arthur's origins: he simply chose to direct his readers' attention to other matters, to his own nostalgic recreation of a vanished world, a never-never land which should also be a kind of ideal. Although we are given to understand that the Wart, as he facetiously but significantly nicknames Arthur, did indeed come into this world in the way related by Malory, the manner of his birth is of minimal importance in *The Sword in the Stone*. Instead of looking back to the dim and distant legendary past for Arthur's origins, White focuses on the intensity of the child's current experience, appropriately since children are seldom much aware of past or future time. So, in going back in imagination not only to the Middle Ages when Malory had begun his story, but to childhood too, he addressed himself primarily if not wholly intentionally to such young readers as those with whom he had shared some of the books he loved at Reigate and at Stowe. It was a complete departure from his earlier fictions, *They Winter Abroad* and *Darkness at Pemberley*.

The strongly contrasting educational systems that White had himself directly experienced, both as pupil and as teacher, at Cheltenham, at Reigate and at Stowe, naturally led him to think about what might constitute an ideal education. The tutoring system and the enlightened and liberal attitudes which had allowed the masters at Stowe to treat boys as individuals and to take a personal interest in them provided the basis for Merlyn's programme. (It is now familiar under the title of child-centred education.) So instead of beginning the story of Arthur in the conventional way, White decided to fantasise about what might constitute the ideal boyhood, what educational programme might best prepare a young prince for his regal responsibilities; or which might, as Edmund Spenser says in his letter to Sir Walter Raleigh, expounding his intention in writing *The Faerie Queene*, 'fashion a gentleman or noble person in vertuous and gentle discipline'. (White had *The Faerie Queene* in mind shortly before he wrote *The Sword in the Stone*, since a quotation from it forms an epigraph to one of the sections of *England Have My Bones*). His genuine and sympathetic interest in young boys, and his life-long passion for both learning and teaching led him readily to cast himself as tutor in the shape of Merlyn. Writing at the end of two decades which had seen a considerable amount of innovation in education, he embarked enthusiastically upon the construction of a scheme which allowed freedom within limits, while its first aim was to make the pupil think for himself by extending his experience and challenging his assumptions. White's interest in the content of the school syllabus is recorded, from the very beginning of his career as a schoolmaster, in his letters to Potts, so that it is hardly surprising that he should have chosen to make Arthur's upbringing the most important feature of his first volume. The tragedy inherent in his story – that the best education in the world could not devise a way of avoiding, might even contribute to, the ultimate disaster – was one which White did not have to confront until much later.

In describing the kind of boyhood he would have liked to have had himself, White necessarily to some extent identified with the Wart, even though he also projected himself as Merlyn. Arthur – the Wart – is the product of parents who, it might be said, were patently unsatisfactory, although he appears not to suffer in consequence of being the child of Uther the ruthless military man and of Igraine the absentee mother. White seems to have felt that his own situation as a young boy had been rather similar, brought up as he was in the first instance by Indian servants, and then by his grandparents. He was as parentless to all intents and purposes as Arthur, except in so far as he had in the background an active mother who was not like the gentle Igraine, but whom he later came to hate and to characterise as a witch. His experience of psychoanalysis, begun not long

before he moved to Stowe Ridings, made him acutely aware of the importance of early upbringing and of parent/child relationships, and he believed
that his own adult unhappiness and neurosis had their origins in his childhood.

By choosing a topic entirely neglected in the Arthurian stories of the
Middle Ages, White was deliberately choosing to write in a genre which
was very popular in the last years of the nineteenth century and the earlier
decades of the twentieth, but which is now largely forgotten. As a literary
topic, or even a general concept, childhood was virtually 'discovered' in the
nineteenth century, and there followed a number of books – often written
ostensibly for children but in a mode which had a greater appeal for adult
readers – of which the subject is the myth of the idyllic childhood. The form
is pastoral, usually characterised by a pervasive nostalgia for the vanished
'dream days', combined with sophisticated jokes quite lost on young
readers. When the present-day reader wonders whether *The Sword in the
Stone* was really written for children or for adults – as its author did, too –
the answer is that it is a hybrid among other hybrids. This form of pastoral,
as Kathryn Hume points out, encourages the reader to draw on personal
recollections. She comments: 'For readers who do have suitable memories
. . . such pastoral offers a Proustian experience.'[2] The carefree life of the
Wart and Kay in Sir Ector's castle, though the element of fantasy is dominant because it is set in the remote past, removes us temporarily from 'the
real world' and brings back memories of childhood adventure and the
intensity of childhood experience. Thus *The Sword in the Stone* takes its
place beside such classics as *The Wind in the Willows* (1908) and *Winnie the
Pooh* (1926) as an example of a form of fantasy pastoral, characterised by a
sense of freedom from responsibility. The 'songs and the abundant food
from no visible economical source'[3] are features of this form: features which
thanks to Merlyn are also to be found in *The Sword in the Stone*. In creating
his images of happy childhood, White drew on his own experience of life
with his grandparents between leaving India and going away to school. In
his journal for 17 April 1942 he comments, 'For six years [5–11] I grew
straight and rampaged and was protected.' His grandparents, he says,
'made a paradise for one little boy', and he continues, '. . . now that you are
dead I know what you gave me and what has gone out from the beauty of
the world.' A few days later he reverts again to his childhood happiness,
remembering 'West Hill House, paragon of all houses and seat of the best of
grandparents', and going on to list, in a passage reminiscent of his description of Sir Ector's castle, all the rooms and special features of the house.

One of White's most influential predecessors in this genre (though without White's pervasive humour) was Richard Jefferies whose books he knew

2   Hume, Kathryn: *Fantasy and Mimesis*, New York and London, Methuen, 1984, p. 62.
3   *Ibid.*

and admired. Jefferies' *Wood Magic* had come out in 1881 and his *Bevis* in 1882 (both to be more fully discussed later). Kenneth Grahame in two books which were popular well into the 1930s, *The Golden Age* (1895) and *Dream Days* (1898) somewhat similarly celebrates the world of childhood adventure in which imagination and fantasy play an important part, and in which the sphere of the children's activities is sharply demarcated from that of the grown-ups, the Olympians (to use Grahame's term).

Although in *The Sword in the Stone* the adventures involve only the Wart and Kay, rather than a larger group of children as in the stories of Kenneth Grahame, E.Nesbit and Arthur Ransome, White like other writers in the genre is able to convey a sense of the separate world of the boys' real and imaginative experience. Their activities still take place under the authority and within the control of the 'Olympians', Merlyn and Sir Ector and the old nurse. The effectiveness of the tale of childhood experience, remembered or imagined in adulthood, is augmented in *The Sword in the Stone* by the image of the parentless child. The Wart, well looked after though he is, is like the children in Grahame's *Golden Age*, without 'a proper equipment of parents', as are also such children as Kay Harker in John Masefield's *The Midnight Folk* (1927) and Mowgli in Kipling's *Jungle Book* (1894), as well as *Kim* (1901) himself. The child without such 'equipment' is more intensely on his own, however well cared for. As we see with the Wart, his very identity may be to all intents and purposes uncertain. Like the traditional hero, he has in the end to fight for himself and for recognition.

Under the benevolent rule of Sir Ector at the Castle of the Forest Sauvage, the peasants live happy and healthy lives in the fulfilling exercise of their craftsmanship. Famine and oppression are both unknown to them, while they like their master live in close contact with a natural world as idealised as the social order. Though they live in one-roomed huts with their animals the villeins are 'healthy, free of an air with no factory smoke in it, and, which was most of all to them, their heart's interest was bound up with their skill in labour'. This vision of a well-fed and contented patriarchal society is implicitly contrasted with the miseries of the unemployed farm-labourer in the 1930s, to which White had drawn attention in *England Have My Bones*. Modern farmers, he claimed there, were faced with ruin by unfair legislation:

> And then, naturally, the labourers are on the street, pushing prams which contain all their worldly possessions, bound for unknown and distant poor houses when they have never been out of their own villages.   (EHMB 324)

At Stowe Ridings, White, like Richard Jefferies and others at the end of the nineteenth century and in the first decades of the twentieth, was able to indulge more intensely that nostalgic passion for nature which showed itself in a variety of practical ways on the one hand, and in religious awe on the other. While at Stowe, White had been a 'toff' (British slang for a rich, well-dressed or upper-class person, especially a man), huntin', shootin' and fishin' in the traditional manner, but abandoning these semi-social activities (at least in their social forms) when he retired to his cottage, he was able to establish a different kind of contact with nature such as was once also possible for many English children. 'To nature, as usual, I drifted by instinct' remarks Kenneth Grahame in *The Golden Age*, finding in it a source of consolation and enjoyment in the childhood equivalent of White's 'feral state'. So White, by presenting the 'enfances' of Arthur in terms of the myth of the idyllic childhood, exchanged the traditional opening of the story for his own romanticised recreation of a medieval boyhood in close touch with nature.

The desire for closer contact with nature that had drawn White to his isolated cottage was already well established by the time that he was writing. Beginning in nostalgia for the good old days, for an England unpolluted by the effluents of the industrial revolution, smoke, fumes and noise from trains and the internal combustion engine, uncarved up by railway lines and trunk roads, this desire took many forms and had many proponents. Enthusiasm for the craftsmanship which John Ruskin had lauded and William Morris had tried to revive professionally found popular expression at the amateur level through the development of all sorts of traditional crafts and skills, of which White's efforts to train hawks was one rather exotic example. There was also a desire to participate in the work of cultivating the soil and growing things, deriving largely from the influence of figures such as Edward Carpenter (1844–1929), whose aim in setting up a smallholding and type of commune in 1882 was 'just to try and keep at least one little spot of earth clean'. The establishment of agrarian communes and the building of garden cities was another manifestation of the same movement, while some of the new progressive schools incorporated in their regimes programmes intended to give pupils an experience of the time-honoured tasks and rituals of the farming year. At Abbotsholme school, for example, study was abandoned altogether in order to get in the hay-harvest in the summer, as seems to be the custom at the Castle of the Forest Sauvage in the case of the Wart and Kay.

The 'Back to the Land'[4] movement had its counterpart on a more ethereal plane in the form of nature-mysticism, which also took many different forms. Instead of going to church, people might go 'blue-doming' (in the facetious nineteenth-century phrase), worshipping 'under the blue dome of heaven'; or, in fiction at any rate, sense or even see the great god Pan, as in E.M. Forster's 'Story of a Panic', as also in many other contemporary fantasies by such writers as Evelyn Underhill, Arthur Machen, and Algernon Blackwood. In *The Wind in the Willows*, the Piper at the Gates of Dawn inspires awe in the Rat and Mole. This more spiritual aspect of the cult of

4 See Marsh, Jan: *Back to the Land*, London, Quartet Books, 1982, pp. 17–22, and elsewhere.

the return to the world of nature had been vigorously promoted by Richard Jefferies. In *Wood Magic*,[5] which seems intended for adults, though its subject is the experiences of Bevis, a very small boy, Jefferies draws on his own childhood and writes of an idyllically unspoilt rural world, in which Bevis can freely come and go as he pleases. Animals and insects talk to him without constraint; indeed even the Wind talks to him. Bevis lies down on the grass and hears the Wind whispering in the tufts and bunches, 'and the Earth under him answered', and what the Wind says is:

> "Bevis, my love, if you want to know all about the sun, and the stars, and everything, make haste and come to me, and I will tell you."
>
> (257)

So we see that when the Wart is lost together with Cully, before he discovers Merlyn, he sleeps well, out of doors in the woodland nest where he had laid himself down, and just like Bevis, he is aware of stars and the rustling trees before he nuzzles 'into the scented turf, into the warm ground, into the unending waters under the earth' (OFK 21).

It is a passage reminiscent of much in D.H. Lawrence, whom White admired and who, although he never wrote for children, in his own wilder way shares and exemplifies all these impulses; he also expresses similar views on education in *The Rainbow*.

Nature proves more hospitable to the Wart than to Jane Eyre, fleeing from Mr Rochester, who finds little comfort and nothing to sustain her when she has to spend a night in the open. The Wart is in fact very near to Merlyn's cottage: his night under the stars in direct contact with mother earth is in practical terms quite unnecessary. But the passage establishes at the outset of the story that closeness to and identification with nature which is soon to provide a substantial part of his education. David Garnett, in reviewing *The Sword in the Stone* on its first appearance, actually described the book as 'wood magic' in itself, drawing attention to his recognition of its affinity with the writing of Jefferies. The intense beauty of the natural world, so keenly if not necessarily consciously felt by the child, is present again to Arthur at the end of his story in *The Book of Merlyn*, when he is made young again by magic: 'He wanted . . . to lie upon the earth, and smell it; to look up into the sky . . . and lose himself in clouds.'[6] His yearning for this contact, this absorption, takes the place of the traditional, symbolic motif of Arthur's concern for the return of Excalibur to the Lake.

White certainly found Jefferies congenial for a variety of different

---

5 *Wood Magic*, 2 vols, London and New York, Cassell, Petter, Galpin & Co., 1881. See Vol. II, p. 257.
6 *The Book of Merlyn*: Unpublished Conclusion to The Once and Future King. Prologue by Sylvia Townsend Warner. Illustrations by Trevor Stubley. Austin and London, University of Texas Press, 1977. (Hereafter *BM*)

reasons: he shared his views of British education as in general a cramping system which cut children off from their natural heritage. These are matters still highly relevant and the subject of bitter controversy in the 1990s. In *The Open Air* (1885), Jefferies had written:

> We can hear the hum, hum, all day of the children . . . in the school. The butterflies flutter over us, the sun shines . . . but the children go on hum, hum, inside this house, and learn, learn.[7]

Jefferies, too, had felt that earlier ages had managed things better: 'My heart looks back and sympathises with all the joy and life of ancient time'.[8] *Bevis* may also have suggested to White another aspect of the education of nature. Little Bevis's experience of close contact with sun, wind, earth and stars is not simply pleasurable. It also confronts him with moral problems, inherent in the natural order itself. Should he release the Weasel from a trap, when the Mouse begs him not to free his dangerous enemy? When he yields to the Weasel's demand, he is taken to task by an angry Hare who also fears him. The Wart is not faced with a comparable dilemma, but he meets in the old pike and in the hawks creatures as dangerous and fierce who also provide him with food for thought.

In Jefferies as in the folklore tradition we see an interchange, a constant dialogue taking place between the human and the animal world, as distinct from the convention of talking animals on which *The Wind in the Willows* is based. This dialogue implies that man is in harmony with nature, but the exchanges are of course always one-way: human beings learn from animals, not vice versa.

Despite its pastoral nature, there is nothing escapist about White's fantasy, for even while it makes use of magic and invokes nostalgia in the adult reader it poses serious questions and offers ways of evaluating theories about upbringing and social conditioning, just as much as it also questions the need for human beings to fight each other. White very deliberately, from the very beginning, constructs a social and political order which we are invited to compare with our own present-day systems. His concern is with modern man, even when he is indulging in a quasi-medieval fantasy. It is our own world that he wants us to consider as well as the good and bad old days of a vanished age. We are confronted, particularly in the final form of the book in the 1958 edition, not only with Arthur's mistakes and failures, but with our own ungovernable folly and disposition to evil: *The Once and Future King* presents in another form Malory's own despair of his countrymen: 'Lo ye all Englysshemen, see ye nat what a

---

7 Quoted by Coveney, Peter: *The Image of Childhood*, Revised edition. Penguin, Harmondsworth, 1967, p. 238.

8 *Ibid.*, p. 235.

myschyff here was?' (Vin 708)[9] The incorrigible irrationality and wicked-ness of human beings remains unchanged.

In addition to these general influences and models, John Masefield's *The Midnight Folk*[10] was of prime importance in helping to shape White's inten-tions. As early as September 1931, while considering suitable texts for teaching English literature in school, he had written to Potts:

> Note the Masefield book. You will probably loathe it because I say it is good. . . . But in my opinion it is his *only* claim to the consideration of posterity, and a *chef d'oeuvre* of the imagination. A POET.   (LF 25)

His reference to Masefield as a poet on the strength of this particular book also suggests a close link with *The Sword in the Stone*, conceived as 'poetry' as distinct from the genres of comedy, romance and tragedy assigned to the books that followed it.

White's admiration for Masefield never wavered. In his journal for 18 October 1938, he records having just read Rudyard Kipling's *Kim* again 'straight through, at a draught', and comments:

> In all this welter of shameful misery which men have made of the world, there are wells. The bright, clear remorseless water of love springs up to shame us and shew us what could be. How they all in that book behave to one another with brimming hearts. Kipling and Masefield are the two writers I think of, off-hand, who have this impec-cable instinct for human charity, the pity which is akin to love. In this age of barbarism and neurosis, the intellectuals dare not grant the homage due to such people. But they will survive, they will be there, to bathe the soul in, for those few, too few, who will be left to remember human decency . . . there will be the old books, Kim, Midnight Folk, Pook's Hill, the Bird of Dawning, to shew how the graph once went up. From the peak it is down now, in the history of human hearts.

White undoubtedly succeeded in creating a 'well . . . to bathe the soul in' himself, a monument to human decency, in *The Once and Future King*.

Kay Harker, the young hero of *The Midnight Folk*, is in many ways a forerunner of the Wart in *The Sword in the Stone*. Although Kay is at the mercy of a disagreeable governess (who turns out to be a witch), he seems able to run wild and to converse with animals and birds as the Wart was later to do. His education, like the Wart's, is an individual one, and he learns much more from his midnight adventures than from the tedious tasks set him by the governess. The plot of *The Midnight Folk* is based on the quest for long-lost treasure, but Kay's search for it is unusual in that it is not to get hold of it for its own sake, but to bring about its restitution to the

---

[9] Vinaver, Eugéne: *The Works of Sir Thomas Malory*, 2nd edition, London, Oxford Univer-sity Press, 1971, p. 708. (Hereafter Vin)

[10] *The Midnight Folk: A Novel*, London, Heineman, 1927.

place from which it had been stolen long ago, and to bring peace to the soul of his dead grandfather who had felt responsible for its loss. The quest on which Kay is engaged, therefore, is not only a lonely but also in a sense an abstract one, in that respect resembling the Wart's quest for understanding, prompted by Merlyn and by his animal educators.

Kay's adventures, like the Wart's, involve journeys into the unknown, an indispensable feature of growing up, and several visits to the underworld. One of these takes him into a cave, another into the depths of the sea, as he tries again and again to unravel the mysteries, learning his lessons both about good and evil, and about human nature in doing so. At the same time he also learns about animal nature from Nibbins the cat, Rollicum Bitem the fox, Blinky the owl and other creatures as well. As in traditional tales generally, nature is on the side of the human being, and in particular, on the side of the child adventurer.

Masefield constantly obscures the boundaries between dream and waking experience, a technique which White was also later to adopt. Just as Kay is often not sure whether his adventures were actual, or just vivid dreams, so the reader is often uncertain, in *The Sword in the Stone*, whether the Wart has simply been dreaming, or whether what has happened has been the work of magic. The effect of the uncertainty as to the actuality of the happenings enhances the dimension of fantasy and intensifies the impact of both books. In each, moreover, otherworld adventures alternate with this-world ones. Both boys are able to fly and to swim, sharing in animal-nature to do so.

Masefield had a gift for creating character through the use of dialogue and dialect. His chip-on-shoulder, underdoggy but friendly Mr Rat, who gnaws a living from dustbins, is the forerunner of the pathetic little hedgehog whom the Wart first encounters when he has been metamorphosed into a badger. The earlier writer may well have prompted White to experiment with the hedgehog as character, judging by a few lines written in the end-papers of his copy of Masefield's *Box of Delights*:[11]

> "Ar" said my hedgehog afterwards to a somewhat higher class I went who was inclined to put on airs, "he wur a proper genl'mun, he wur. Caught hold on me one day in the arternoon, un teuk us um in a box. Lived in a real draring-rum, I did, a parlour like, and fed on all the best. Fresh en's heggs un breaden-milk un water out of er saucer. It ent many edgepigs, arter all, as av supped tap-water from Crown Derby."

The passage probably also has its origins in White's habit of catching and bringing back animals and reptiles while he was still at Stowe.

By blending the human and the animal Masefield had introduced some delightful comedy into his fantasy. On one of Kay's midnight excursions he

[11] First published in 1935.

visits the Otter and there meets the cat and the fox, the friends who are helping him in his search for the treasure, in some distress.

> "You'd both be better for a bit of fish," the Otter said. "Would you like it fresh or some that's been hung a bit?"
> "I like it well hung," Bitem said. "But Nibbins here would like it fresh, I'm sure."
> "Well, I'll bring you a bit of both," the Otter said.
> While Otter was fetching the fish, which took a minute or two, Nibbins said, "I'm not at all sure, Kay, that you oughtn't to have a look at what is beyond there. There's a queer smell . . . it's a very rich smell . . . You ought to smell it anyway."   (279)

The Otter's home looks forward to the Badger's quarters in *The Sword in the Stone*, but whereas Masefield's characters regard the Badger as 'rather a joke', because of the way in which he naturally digs, White's Badger is comic because of his human coyness about reading his learned but hopelessly disorganised treatise to the Wart. Just as the Wart has a most perfect breakfast in Merlyn's cottage, Kay had had for breakfast all the things that he was fondest of, in the cabin of *The Plunderer*:

> very hot, little, round loaves of new white bread . . . a very fat sausage . . . a bowl of strawberries and cream   (171–2)

and so on and so forth. Both feasts are equally lavish and lovingly described.

White also found a precedent for the songs in *The Sword in the Stone* in *The Midnight Folk*, but it must be admitted that Masefield's are usually better, both for their parodic elements and for their scansion. The witches' song with its sinister chorus, Rollicum Bitem's songs, and the even more rollicking songs of the octogenarian Miss Susan Pricker are worthy of Gilbert and Sullivan and achieve a polish that White never quite achieved, though it is clear that Masefield was his model in this respect.

White's sense of the past was much stronger than Masefield's, and he was more interested in the way in which people lived and the way in which things were done in former times, but both authors' sense of humour regarding the past was very similar. Masefield's children's books are some of the finest ever written: his stories are brilliantly devised and superbly told, and remarkable for the qualities on which White commented in his journal. Yet for all that they lack the passionate commitment characteristic of White in *The Sword in the Stone* – children's book though it really is – to the past, to the world of Malory and *Le Morte Darthur*, and to enabling the modern reader to discover that world for himself.

Less obviously, there are many points of similarity between Kipling's *Puck of Pook's Hill* (from which White quotes a paragraph in Chapter I of *The Book of Merlyn*) and *Rewards and Fairies*. In *Puck*, the children have a magical guide who is able to transcend time; and in *Rewards and Fairies* it is

Merlyn himself whose magic and illusion take them out of the everyday world to enlarge their experience by familiarising them with an earlier period of time. Kipling's interest in the development of the English nation and its civilisation in *Puck* and in the medieval period in *Rewards* found its counterpart in *The Once and Future King*, just as Kipling's love of the English countryside, apparent in both books and elsewhere, did too.

ii. *The English and American Editions* from 1938 to 1958

Despite White's belief soon after completing it in 1937, that *The Sword in the Stone* was one of his better books, it went through several revisions, during which he extensively rewrote it, over two decades. In consequence, it appeared in three quite distinct forms, beginning with the first English edition of 1938. This was considerably modified for publication in the United States, and the American edition was ultimately rewritten when, at the end of World War II, Collins refused to accept *The Book of Merlyn* as the last volume and White transferred the visits to the ants and geese from it into his first book. The reader familiar only with the standard 1958 edition of *The Once and Future King* may be surprised to discover a very different book in White's first version of the Wart's adventures.

To begin with, the first English edition was enriched with 42 very delightful little line drawings done by White himself, as chapter headings and sometimes in the text. These have been omitted from later editions. They often give an indication of what is to come, or add a pictorial dimension to the comedy: Sir Ector and Sir Grummore Grummursum are shown tippling together at the beginning of Chapter 1, for example, while at the end of Chapter 3, King Pellinore is seen lifting his visor and peering out of his helmet through a pair of pince-nez. The Questing Beast is depicted being carried back after the boar-hunt, slung over a pole, so that the reader can see just how White visualised that strange creature, while another graphic little picture shows King Pellinore tangled up in his hound's leash. Most of the other comic illustrations show Merlyn, with an owl perched on the very top of his wizard's hat, or sitting by the fire with his feet up on the fender. The badger similarly sits by the fire, wearing carpet slippers. The hats that Merlin accidentally calls up are neatly fitted into the text, beginning with a topper, then a Kate Greenaway school cap, a deerstalker and a child's sailor-hat. The other thirty or so illustrations are meant to be informative or simply decorative: there is a sketch of the Castle of the Forest Sauvage, of a medieval peasant, of hawks, of a pike. Some bear an obvious similarity to medieval grotesques: White includes several Anthropophagi, as well as the noseless Wat. Others effectively evoke appropriate feeling, as when the Wart is saddened by Merlyn's departure at the end of his tutorship, and is shown going off disconsolately to come to terms with the news.

One day in 1949, White wrote in his journal that he had been reflecting on the remarks of David Garnett, to the effect that he did not love human nature, ruefully agreeing that his friend was right.

> This is why all my novels are rotten. Unfortunately I lack that rather feminine interest in character. Do not find anything absorbing in the humanity which surrounds me. Am only absorbed by (a) all the arts . . . (b) philosophy and ethics (c) animals of all sorts, except cats and aphides. But a novel has to be about character. My novels are blood from a stone.[12]

A fantasy does not have to be about individual character; and *The Sword in the Stone* shows White's depth of understanding of children and especially of young boys. The Wart's distress at not being 'a proper son' to Sir Ector, whereas Kay is, and at not having 'a proper father and mother' (reflecting White's parallel situation), as well as because 'Kay had taught him that being different is wrong' is beautifully suggested à propos the foray with the goshawk in the first chapter. White's ear for small boys' talk is ever apparent, in the well-trained politeness of the Wart on meeting Merlyn and in his excited account of his 'Quest' on his return to the castle, to give only two examples. The haymaking, still in the 1930s a familiar rural activity, allows past and present to merge into a shimmering, hazy timelessness as the fabulous impinges more and more on the realistic, leading into the child's mysterious fantasy world of unaccountable happenings. So the Wart, lost in the forest in the moonlight, comes upon 'the most beautiful thing that he had ever seen in his short life' (OFK 15), the knight in full armour, who reassuringly turns out to be, not a ghost but only poor old Pellinore. The child's imaginative life, nurtured by the reading of adventure stories, is amusingly suggested when the hungry little boy, we are told:

> had heard about people who lived on berries, but this did not seem practical at the moment because it was July, and there were none. He found two wild strawberries and ate them greedily. . . . Then he wished . . . that he had not lost his goshawk Cully, so that the bird could catch him a rabbit which he would cook by rubbing two sticks together like the base Indian.   (OFK 21)

(The last two words are a typically literary allusion lost on children, though it introduces a slightly odd tone arising as it does from *Othello*.) The early chapters capture the boredom as well as the happiness of childhood. Even though, like White's grandparents' house, the castle is 'a paradise for a boy', on the cold wet evening when the Wart is turned into a hawk, he wanders about miserably with nothing to do while every grown-up sends him on his way, until at last Merlyn takes pity on him.

---

[12] Journal, 20 May 1939.

From the beginning of his story, White differentiates the boys effectively, making the Wart modest, thoughtful and considerate, anxious about Kay who is denied the experience of being changed into different animals, though the Wart is capable of boyish impertinence as well. Kay by contrast is rather conceited, short-tempered and envious.

The first five chapters of both English and American first editions are closely similar, but thereafter they diverge. When White's American publishers insisted on some modifications, the episode in which the Wart falls into the hands of a witch, Madame Mim, was the first to go. In it the influence of Masefield is once again apparent; it has of course no equivalent in Malory. Madame Mim is more threatening than Masefield's Mrs Pouncer and her coven of witches because, like the witch in Hansel and Gretel, her intention is to eat the boys. The story begins with the Wart and Kay doing their archery practice. The Wart loses his best arrow and in looking for it in Chapter Six they soon come upon a cottage just like Merlyn's, with a brass plate screwed on the garden gate which says:

> MADAME MIM, B.A. (Dom-Daniel)
> PIANOFORTE
> NEEDLEWORK
> NECROMANCY
>
> No Hawkers, circulars
> or Income Tax
> Beware of the Dragon.

(The warning notice is a parody of one often seen in the nineteen-thirties. Hawkers are beggars, circulars 'junk mail', and the Dragon replaces the dog.) In White's sketch, she is peering out from behind lace curtains, and appears to be quite a personable lady and not at all witchlike. The Wart and Kay are very soon in her power, and she is seen going about the business of sharpening knives and cleavers and boiling water, while skipping for joy, licking her greedy lips, and so on. White is much more explicit than the brothers Grimm about the intended fate of the witch's victims. Although she is presented with a certain amount of humour – she sings a number of songs in the manner of those in *The Midnight Folk* while making her culinary preparations – her treatment of the Wart is frighteningly sadistic and long drawn out. She takes his clothes off with 'a practised hand', pinches him all over to see if he is fat, and shuts him in a small cage with verminous straw, as she prepares for the 'cruel old custom' of plucking a chicken before it is dead. 'Of course a little boy doesn't feel any pain. Their clothes come off nicer if you take them off alive', she says.[13] The horror is intensified for the modern reader by a probably unintentional sexual innuendo

---

[13] *The Sword in the Stone*, London, Collins 1938, the first English edition, p. 90. (Hereafter *SS*).

when eventually the 'dreadful witch . . . lifted the Wart into the air and prepared to have her will of him' (SS 91).

The cancellation of such passages removes an element of mother-hatred which is intrinsic to White's imagination, but it is a pity that if it had to go, the lively ensuing battle between Merlyn and the witch had to go too. Just as Masefield's Kay is helped to escape from Mrs Pouncer's clutches by Nibbins, the Wart is saved in the nick of time by Merlyn, summoned by the kind and selfless goat, as a result in part of the Wart's superior resourcefulness. He is already showing his mettle, while his foster-brother Kay is merely crying in a corner of his cage. What follows is a brilliantly ingenious and amusing battle of wills and magical power between Merlyn and the witch, with Archimedes and the witch's gore crow as seconds, and Hecate on top of a step-ladder in the middle to umpire. White explains that in those far-off days, quarrels between black and white wizards were settled ceremonially, by means of duels: when the signal was given they were at liberty to turn themselves into things. This is a traditional fairy-tale motif, as for example in the story of Puss in Boots. When Madame Mim turns herself into a dragon, Merlyn causes great confusion by becoming a field mouse, which is quite invisible in the grass, and then when she becomes a cat, he becomes another cat, and stands opposite her and makes faces. When she turns herself into a dog, he becomes a dog too, so that she gets furiously angry and feels herself 'out of her depth against these unusual stone-walling tactics and experienced an internal struggle not to lose her temper.' She is finally vanquished after many more absurd transformations, when at last Merlyn wins by turning himself successively 'into the microbes, not yet discovered, of hiccoughs, scarlet fever, mumps, whooping cough, measles and heat spots', so that 'from a complication of all these complaints the infamous Madame Mim had immediately expired.' The ending of the contest is particularly ingenious, because it makes use of Merlyn's gift of 'backsight and insight' which allow him some access to modern science. All this was simply cut from the first American edition, where the chapter ends with the mysterious loss of the arrow, but when Madame Mim was moved out of *The Sword in the Stone*, she soon turned up again in a slightly modified form as the Witch in the Wood, until she was eventually driven out altogether and replaced by the Queen of Air and Darkness, a transformation that retains the essential element of all these evil and hostile mother-figures.

The cancelled passages, it must also be said, whether felt to be objectionable in terms of content or not, showed clear signs of careless or hasty writing in this episode. The not very polished verses attributed to the witch are one example, while such details as the dimensions of the Wart's cage, too low for him to stand up in at first, but in which he later runs about, show White's control slipping.

The next major differences between the first English and the first American edition occur in each case in the chapters (X–XII) in which the boys meet Robin Hood (or Wood). In the original version, the Wart and Kay encounter the Anthropophagi after their escape from Madame Mim, while in the American edition Robin leads them in an attack on Castle Chariot, the Castle of Lard inhabited by Morgan le Fay, which in one sense takes the place of Madame Mim's cottage in the wood. The battle with the Anthropophagi fits perfectly into the medieval ambience of *The Sword in the Stone*: White has already alluded to such ancient authorities as the classical author Flavius Arrianus and the late medieval *Master of Game* on the care of hounds, and given some detailed information about the techniques of jousting and archery, so that with the Anthropophagi we remain in what feels like the Middle Ages, even though there is in fact no mention of these creatures in English until 1552. He seems to have associated the Anthropophagi with Mandeville, the late fourteenth-century writer (who does not mention them) but whose mysterious identity greatly interested him: it is considered at length in some ms. notes in which White puts himself in the place of Sir John Mandeville, and argues for and against the proposition that he was in reality a certain Jean à la Barbe. The speculation indicates his capacity for identifying with historical and fictional characters. White's attention may perhaps have been drawn to Mandeville's fictitious *Travels* in the first instance by a poem by William Empson published in 1929 in the volume of undergraduate poetry to which White also contributed a number of poems:

> Mandeville's river of dry jewels grows
> Day-cycled, deathly, and iron-fruited trees;
> From Paradise it runs to Pantarose
> And with great waves into the gravely seas.[14]

In the American and later English editions, the attack on the Castle of Lard was substituted for the battle with the Anthropophagi. Even though White drew it from an ancient Irish source, it is at variance with the realism of the Castle of the Forest Sauvage and of the visit to Robin and Marian in the greenwood. It has a Disneyish quality by contrast with the traditional fairytale features of the Madame Mim episode. But the Anthropophagi of the first edition, who live in the depths of the forest and 'creep out like wolves or adders and assassinate any person that they see' (SS 166) are a formidable foe, cannibals who have captured the Dog Boy and old Wat, and constitute a real menace with their poisoned arrows. When the boys come upon them as Robin prepares the surprise attack, they present a splendid example of medieval fantasy and grotesque invention. Some have their heads growing beneath their shoulders, some have the heads of dogs, and there are pygmies and Sciopodes, who have only one foot, so enormous that they use it as an umbrella. The Nisites have four eyes, while their

---

[14] *In Hogarth Living Poets, No. 8. Cambridge Poetry 1929.*

women have long beards but are quite bald; the Scythians are accustomed to wrap themselves up in their ears at night.

The episode becomes nightmarish as the Dog Boy, old Wat and Cavall the dog are led out and tied to stakes with faggots piled about them, in preparation for the barbaric orgy of burning them. Then the battle ensues, and when it is over, it is very properly the Wart's arrow that is found sticking through the chest of the huge Sciopod, rather than Kay's. White describes the encounter with enormous zest, with not a qualm about the wiping out of every single one of the enemy: they are of course not 'real', neither human nor animal. But in the light of his subsequent horror of war and desperate desire to find an antidote, it is a surprisingly bloodthirsty episode, though good swashbuckling adventure stuff. A hint of sadism lingers, however, even in the bland American edition in which the only actual fight is against Morgan le Fay's griffin. White comments that the Wart 'had often longed to hear the noise that these gay, true, clean and deadly missiles of the air [his arrows] would make in solid flesh. He heard it.' Richard Jefferies similarly had fantasised on the satisfactions of medieval warfare:

> Give me a bow, that I may feel the delight of feeling myself draw the string and the strong wood bending, that I may see the rush of the arrow.[15]

The fight with the Anthrophagi was probably thought to have been too recondite, too medieval, and too violent for the American reader (an interesting difference from modern convention). White had to do a good deal of rewriting, and the changes he made in this part of his story were radical. His source was still medieval: the name 'Castle Chariot' was taken from Malory, while White explains that he found the description of the Castle of Lard in the medieval Irish poem 'The Vision of Mac Conglinne'. White's copy of the *Ancient Irish Tales*[16] in which he found this poem has pasted into it his own very amusing sketch of the interior of an Irish cabin with two men sitting on stools, one with an axe, the other smoking a pipe, with a gross old woman standing behind them. Beside an overturned barrel a sow lies on its side, with a cow in the background, the whole scene suggesting Mother Morlan's home in *The Queen of Air and Darkness* rather than the Castle of Lard. Underneath White has written: 'Honour, Respect and Fair Play for Women (c.f. Honour in tricking guests into a house where they can be roasted alive, fair play in murdering your son or best friend . . . and Connor's respect for the wretched Deirdre.)' 'The Vision of Mac Conglinne' is heavily annotated throughout, mainly in the form of summary, but what-

---

15 Quoted by Coveney, *op. cit.* p. 235, who here draws attention to Jefferies's cult of erotic violence and the quest for the hero, features which must also have appealed to White, whether consciously or otherwise.

16 Cross, T.P. and Slover, C.H., *Ancient Irish Tales*, London, Harrap 1936.

ever sinister undertones the tale may have had for White, as it is presented
in *The Sword in the Stone* it is much less frightening than the encounter with
the Anthropophagi. White quotes six stanzas from the poem, then trans-
lates the Celtic vision into modern terms in the detailed description that
follows: 'The place smelt like a grocer's, a butcher's, a dairy and a fish-
monger's, rolled into one', and as the boys plod over 'the filthy drawbridge
– a butter one, with cow hairs still in it', they find Morgan le Fay stretched
upon a bed of glorious lard, and the prisoners (the Dog Boy, Cavall and old
Wat) tied to 'pillars of marvellous pork' (OFK 109). It is the very opposite of
the cottage that hungry Hansel and Gretel find, made of delicious, tempt-
ing things to eat. But although Castle Chariot is sickening, it offers no real
horror, no convincing threat. The situation of the prisoners is trivial compared with the parallel passage in the first English edition. As is traditional
with such places in Irish story the castle melts away completely, leaving the
boys and the rescued prisoners standing in the forest clearing. The fight is
still to come, but the enemy is now reduced to a single griffin, eventually
vanquished by Kay, who shoots it in the eye.

The boys' adventure in both English and American editions in the depths
of the forest where they are led to Robin Wood begins as a pastoral idyll,
under the great lime. The episode suggests the innocence of childhood,
balancing and contrasting with the 'experience' of the volume which was
soon to follow. Robin is idealised as:

> a sinewy fellow whose body did not carry an ounce of fat . . . clean
> shaven, sunburned, nervous, gnarled like the roots of the trees which
> he loved; but gnarled and mature with weather and with poetry rather
> than with age, for he was about thirty years old.   (SS 159)

The outlaws are seen in an ascending scale of blissful activity in their forest
home:

> It had been beautiful to see little leather-clad Much sitting compla-
> cently at his dinner, more beautiful to see the great limbs of Little John
> sprawling in company with his dog. But now there was something
> which was most beautiful of all, for Robin Wood lay happily with his
> head in Marian's lap.   (SS 160)

He and Maid Marian are singing 'Under the greenwood tree' together, an
anachronism perfectly in keeping with the general atmosphere. Innocent
playfulness is dominant, to be contrasted with the unicorn episode in *The
Witch in the Wood*. When, in the original version of that book, the Queen
proposes that Sir Grummore should lay his head in her lap, and when
Agravaine later responds frenziedly to the unicorn's laying its head in
Meg's lap – it is for him a symbolic act which drives him on to his frantic
attack on the creature – White shows us how the corruption of the adult
world can result in the tragic loss of childhood innocence.

Kurth Sprague in his brilliant but, sadly, unpublished doctoral dissertation, *From A Troubled Heart: T.H. White and Women in The Once and Future King*[17] has drawn attention to the problems White had in portraying women. Maid Marian, however, is one of his most successful portraits. In the boys' world of *The Sword in the Stone*, there was little need for women at all. The Wart is in effect a motherless child: his bodily needs are taken care of by the old nurse in Sir Ector's castle, who seems to originate in a pleasing blend of Juliet's nurse with a comic version of a prep-school matron. She fusses over the Wart kindly, though usually ineffectually. Maid Marian is presented as a virginal young woman, rather like the boyish girls in the novels of John Cowper Powys. She is very much 'one of the boys', whose knowledge of woodcraft is not to be despised, even though at first the Wart is displeased at being assigned to her band for training. He and Kay have both been given Maid Marian's bows because they could not have drawn anything larger: although she is 'an accomplished soldier', she is really the equivalent of a young boy. Unlike Madame Mim and the Witch in the Wood, she is presented in a favourable light as an instructor rather than as a predatory mother-figure.

In the first English and American editions of 1938 and 1939, one of the Wart's educative metamorphoses was into a grass snake, an episode cancelled in favour of the visit to the ants and to the geese in the final edition. White's enthusiasm for snakes seems to have begun while he was at Stowe, where he persuaded boys to share his interest and help him find them, and continued at Stowe Ridings. In *England Have My Bones* he talks of this fascination with them:

> I used to go out with Hughesdon to catch them, and then turn them loose in the sitting-room. At one time I had about a dozen.
>
> (EHMB 107)

They are fascinating pets, it seems, 'always inevitably themselves'. White found it exciting to catch them, frightening himself with the risk that they might be adders, then (when he had decided that they were not) wrapping them up in his handkerchief and putting them in his trouser-pocket. Snakes, however, seem to have lacked individuality for him, even though they differed from each other:

> To have called them names would have been ridiculous . . . A snake cannot have a name. If it had to be addressed I suppose it would be addressed by its generic title: snake.   (EHMB 110)

From such reflections as this comes the title, T-natrix, by which the grass-snake is introduced to the Wart, just before he is turned into one himself, as a result of which he is able to talk to the 'affectionate and tender-hearted' snake, who first instructs him in pre-history and then tells

[17] University of Texas at Austin, 1978.

him a legend of a Just-So-ish kind about a human being and a python. It is a much more attractive episode than the visit to the ants, but it makes no political points. In it, White the schoolmaster and naturalist is very much in evidence, explaining the habits of snakes and how they talk. His often keen observation of nature and the ways of living things combined with his love of devising anthropomorphic fantasy thus enabled him to share his special knowledge with his readers in an amusing way.

There is wisdom in the Wart's introduction to the world of reptiles, but wisdom is even more consciously sought in a subsequent episode, later cancelled. In this, Archimedes takes the Wart not on a visit to the geese, as in the 1958 edition, but on a long and terrible journey to Athene, the Greek goddess of wisdom, defined in terms of the experience that she represents:

> He was aware that her unthinkable beauty was neither that of age nor of youth. That her eyes were the only things you thought of looking at, and that to be her was terrible, whereas to be with her was the only joy. If you can understand this, she was in herself so unhappy that words only melt in such temperatures, but towards other people she was the spirit of invincible mercy and protection. She lived, of course, beyond sorrow and solitude, and, if you follow me, the suffering which had brought her there had left her with a kind of supernatural *good manners*.
>
> (SS 263)

Athene gives the Wart a vision of the world as she holds him 'in the hollow of her kind hand', but this turns out to be, not some profound insight into human nature, or into the nature of good and evil, but a vision of the life of trees. The serious tone with which the episode begins soon gives way to White's particular brand of humour:

> "My dear Madam," said a rather society box, in smirking, urban, scholastic, eighteenth-century accents, "a decoction of boxwood pro-motes the growth of hair, while an oil distilled from its shavings is a cure for haemorrhoids, toothache, epilepsy, and stomach worms. So, at least, we are told."   (SS 266)

White's knowledge of trees was self-confessedly both superficial and idio-syncratic. In *England Have My Bones* he confesses that as far as he was concerned, trees 'used to be oaks, elms and beeches – wrongly diagnosed' (EHMB 230). 'I could put all I know about trees into three pages, and much of this knowledge would be wrong, all unacademic', he writes, with a footnote:

> I showed the following pages to an expert on trees, who nearly had a fit. It seems that there are things called ABIES and CUPRESSUS, and that my divisions are all wrong. Never mind: they work with me.
>
> (EHMB 231)

His lack of expert knowledge did not inhibit him but, amateur as he was in this field as in many others, he could still identify with trees, love them for their individual properties, and communicate his feeling for them to the ordinary reader – feeling of a kind most strikingly expressed by his contemporary J.R.R. Tolkien in *The Lord of the Rings*.

From all these strange experiences the Wart returns to the waking world, snoring like a volcano after his final vision of the 'dream of the stones' not, as later, honking like a goose when White had replaced the often somewhat ponderously instructive passages, reminiscent of Charles Kingsley and other Victorian writers of children's books, with the less obviously didactic visit to the geese.

A further adventure in the fairytale tradition and in keeping with the Madame Mim episode followed the Wart's visit to Athene in the English edition of 1938, where accompanied by Merlyn and in his own shape, the Wart encounters the giant Galapas. Here, White transmuted a significant aspect of his own painful childhood experience into a fantasy that was evidently not felt to be particularly appropriate for the American market. The giant is in fact mentioned in *Le Morte Darthur*, where Arthur as young king deals successfully with him, as with others of his kind. Some features of the episode were probably also suggested by *The Midnight Folk*. White's unhappy early years at Cheltenham provided the basic material for the chapter, however: the references to school-life are pervasive, from the schoolboy slang of the miserable prisoners in Galapas' castle, to the giant's headmasterly ' "I hope you will never forget the lessons you have learned with us here' " (SS 290). The régime at Cheltenham is symbolically indicated in the vivid little line-drawing that heads the chapter, in which the giant is shown as a gross figure with the emblems of oppression and ruthless cruelty, a hammer and sickle and a swastika, on his clothes. Behind him crouches a small figure apparently clad only in shorts, as were the victims of the corporal punishment so freely administered by the prefects in White's own schooldays. By the time he was writing this chapter, however, his experience of the much more humane regime at Stowe School enabled him, in the comparative safety of adulthood, to allow the Wart, protected by Merlyn, to look upon the fairytale representative of the sadist of the classroom with contempt. The Wart whispers his disappointment to Merlyn, ' "But he's not big at all" ', to which Merlyn replies indignantly that he is ten feet high, *extremely* big for a giant (SS 278). All the same, the adventure is not without its excitements: like Masefield's Kay Harker, the Wart becomes invisible, but 'Being invisible is not so pleasant as it sounds. After a few minutes of it you forget where you last left your hands and legs' (SS 276).

Nevertheless, White certainly saw the possibility of making Galapas an even more sinister and evil figure than at first presented: in one of his notebooks, dating from a time when he was thinking of making some revisions in *The Sword in the Stone*, he wrote 'Hitlerise Galapas'. In the end, however, the giant had to go to make way for the Wart's visit to the geese.

Even so, the Wart's metamorphoses still conformed to a pattern unintentionally created by White, but of which he only became aware well after he had finished the book. In his journal for 6 July 1942 he wrote:

> Two years after writing the Sword in the Stone, I began to learn about the development of the human foetus, of which I had known the minimum before. I was astonished to find that the Sword in the Stone was a complete allegory of this development, even getting the various steps more or less accurate. i.e. The Wart begins as a fish and ends as a mammal etc.

Both the English and American editions of *The Sword in the Stone* end with the joyful event of the young Arthur's coronation, following the drawing of the sword from the stone, in which White follows his source in *Le Morte Darthur*. The book had not yet found its final form since to it were later to be added the Wart's visits to the ants and to the geese, originally intended for *The Book of Merlyn*. In his journal for 14 November 1940, White wrote:

> Pendragon can still be saved, and elevated into a superb success, by altering the last parts of Book 4, and taking Arthur back to his animals. The legend of his going underground at the end, into the badger's sett, where badger, hedgehog, snake, pike (stuffed in case) and all the rest of them can be waiting to talk it over with him. Now, with Merlyn, they must discuss war from a naturalist's point of view, as I have been doing in this diary lately. They must decide to talk thoroughly over, during Arthur's long retirement underground, the relation of Man to the other animals, in the hope of getting a new angle on his problem from this. Such, indeed, was Merlyn's original objective in introducing him to the animals in the first place. Now what can we learn about the abolition of war from animals?

White had come increasingly to identify with Arthur, so that the legend of his going underground, on which Masefield's *Midsummer Night* of 1928 had already been based, became more and more attractive. It gave him the opportunity of 'saving Pendragon' (i.e. Arthur), while at the same time carrying on an argument about Might versus Right, and returning to the animals who had played so lively a part in *The Sword in the Stone*, and whose continuing, seemingly untroubled existence could provide a sort of guarantee that life 'will go onward the same Though Dynasties pass.' He was soon writing to Potts to declare his intentions of ending with a fifth volume, in which Arthur would return to the badger's sett of Volume I because, he explained:

> I have suddenly discovered that (1) the central theme of Morte d'Arthur is to find an antidote for War, (2) that the best way to examine the politics of Man is to observe him, with Aristotle, as a political

animal. . . . So, to put my 'moral' across (but I shan't state it), I shall have
the marvellous opportunity of bringing the wheel full circle, and ending on an animal note like the one I began on. This will turn my
completed epic into a perfect fruit, 'rounded off and bright and done'.

(LF 117–18)

In November 1941 *The Book of Merlyn* was finished and sent off to Collins with *The Candle in the Wind* and a request that the three previous books
(all of which White had once again revised) should be reprinted and all
five published together. Collins' refusal to comply left White with an acute
problem which was not solved until years later. In the end, he abandoned
most of *The Book of Merlyn* but salvaged the ant and goose episodes. The
introduction into the first book of the visit to the ants was managed very
skilfully. White cancelled the episodes of the snakes and the visit to Athene, as also to the castle of Galapas in order to make room for what he
considered to be very much more important material. He abandoned the
instructions for making a vivarium for ants with which the episode begins
in *The Book of Merlyn*, substituting some amusing dialogue between the
Wart and Merlyn as a prelude to the magical transformation, and making
various other minor alterations. The Wart as ant is called Barbarus instead
of Sanguinea, and the ants congratulate each other on being born in 'the
'A' nest', where previously they were 'born of the Sanguinea blood', and
expressed themselves as thankful that they did not belong to 'those filthy
Formicae fuscae' (BM 56). White removed some very stilted dialogue (' "I do
think our beloved Leader is wonderful, do not you?" ', for example) and
replaced it with the sort of stylised cockney dialect that he uses elsewhere
for the 'lower orders'. Essentially, however, the passage remained the
same, and so with its overt references to Hitler's Germany (such as
'Antland, Antland Over All') introduced a more sinister and sombre tone
by comparison with the light-hearted adventures of the earlier editions.
However, it was followed by the pastoral idyll describing the preparations for winter at Sir Ector's castle where 'Everybody was happy' (OFK
130), an example of the splendid ease with which White could switch
from one level of fantasy to another and change the tone of the narrative
at will.

When he had to abandon the idea of ending his Arthurian epic with *The
Book of Merlyn*, the changes which White made to *The Sword in the Stone*
undoubtedly effected an artistic improvement on the earlier version. The
Wart's transformation into a wild goose and his subsequent experiences are
more homogeneous, more in keeping with the earlier metamorphoses. On
the other hand, as with the visit to the ants, the substitution of the political
message for the fairytale-like earlier episodes introduces a more serious
tone into the first volume. Chapter XVIII still begins with the Wart's transformation into a bird, as previously, but then transfers him to a strange
landscape, absolutely flat, of an 'enormous flatness' in which:

there lived one element – the wind. For it was an element. It was a dimension, a power of darkness. In the human world, the wind comes from somewhere, and goes somewhere, and, as it goes, it passes through somewhere – through trees or streets or hedgerows. This wind came from nowhere. It was going through the flatness of nowhere, to no place. Horizontal, soundless except for a peculiar boom, tangible, infinite, the astounding dimensional weight of it streamed across the mud.   (OFK 166)

'The Wart, facing into this wind, felt that he was uncreated.' White drew on his experience of shooting wild geese at Wells-next-the-Sea in Norfolk in 1938 for his imaginative identification with them in these chapters. From the elemental world of the great wind, he swoops down to the mudflats where the White-fronted Geese are gathering in family parties, in a 'comradeship, free discipline and *joie de vivre*' which the Wart longs to share. He naturally has difficulty in understanding the customs of his companions (as of course the goose Lyo-lyok to whom he talks has in understanding human ways), but White places the Wart's transformation in the context of folk-tale by referring to the Irish story of the Children of Lir. He simplified the original episode as it appears in *The Book of Merlyn*, so as to make it appropriate as a lesson for a young boy, rather than for an aged king with extensive experience of governing his country. Arthur as king wants to know about 'nationalism, about state-control, individual liberty, property and so forth', but for the Wart, White puts his message across in a simplified way, appropriate to the level of understanding of a boy who has only been Merlyn's pupil for one year. He therefore focuses on the quintessential difference between human beings and geese: 'There are no boundaries among geese', nor have they kings, laws, or territorial rights, except for their nests. The lessons are presented in entirely modern terms, apart from a reference to the bitter Norman laws. The town of birds in which the Wart finds himself after the migration is one of streets and even slums, inhabited by birds:

> like an innumerable crowd of fish-wives on the largest grandstand in the world, breaking out into private disputes, eating out of paper bags, chipping the referee, singing comic songs, admonishing their children and complaining of their husbands.   (OFK 178)

White, who had always objected to the snob-culture of his time, still saw class differences appearing, even in the utopia of the wild geese.

The visit to the wild geese includes four songs, one of them a sort of parody of 'John Brown's Body', another reminiscent of the Norse sagas, none of them very good. The Wart is amused by 'a silly one' in which occurs the stanza:

> Then we bend our necks with a curious kink
> Like the bend which the plumber puts under the sink.
> Honk-honk, Hank-hank, Hink-hink.   (OFK 175)

It is another example of White's enthusiasm for the anachronistic.

The Wart's next metamorphosis takes place just before Kay is knighted, and so when the Wart is all but grown-up. In the meantime (we are told this in the 1958 edition only) he had been changed into countless other animals. He and Kay have had, by this time, more and more weapons as presents, as well as full suits of armour and bows nearly six feet long, despite the visits to the various animals, which seem by no means to have turned the Wart into a pacifist. His final metamorphosis, into a badger, completes his education, for he soon finds himself in 'the enchanted sett' with its Great Hall and Combination Room full of portraits of departed badgers, 'famous in their day for scholarship or godliness', and the portrait of the Founder over the fireplace (OFK 192). The scene is clearly intended to suggest a Cambridge college. White had no need to cut or replace this episode, which is the same in both the first and in the 1958 editions and which also contains the ingenious fable, or parable as he calls it, of the embryos. In it, his gift for animal fantasy is seen at its best in its diversity, as the Wart meets and spares the ridiculous hedgehog, visits the old Badger, and hears the story of how God at the beginning of time called all the embryos before Him, all looking very much the same, and asked them to choose what they wanted to be. All thought the matter over carefully and chose what specialisations most appealed to them until 'at the very end of the sixth day, just before it was time to knock off for Sunday, they had got through all the little embryos except Man.' Then:

> 'Please God,' said the embryo, 'I think that You made me in the shape which I now have for reasons best known to Yourselves, and that it would be rude to change. If I am to have my choice I will stay as I am . . . and I will stay a defenceless embryo all of my life, doing my best to make myself a few feeble instruments out of the wood, iron and other materials which You have seen fit to put before me . . .' 'Well done,' exclaimed the Creator in delighted tones. 'Here, all you embryos, come here with your beaks and whatnots to look upon Our first Man. He is the only one who has guessed Our riddle . . . and We have great pleasure in conferring upon him the Order of Dominion over the Fowls of the Air, and the Beasts of the Earth, and the Fishes of the Sea. Now let the rest of you get along, and love and multiply . . . As for you, Man, you will be a naked tool all your life, though a user of tools. You will look like an embryo till they bury you, but all the others will be embryos before your might . . . We are partly sorry for you, Man, but partly hopeful. Run along then, and do your best. . . .'   (OFK 195)

The fantasy has something of the ingenuity of Kipling's *Just-So Stories* with the addition of White's own brand of humour.

Despite the many changes that White made in the course of the years between the first publication of *The Sword in the Stone* and the appearance of the final version, the last chapters remained virtually untouched. Malory's account of the drawing of the sword is very succinct but nevertheless charged with emotion, and White for the most part follows him closely, elaborating some of the details to bring out the undercurrents of feeling implicit in the terse dialogue of his source. White's whole book has led up to this, its concluding episode, the most important event in Arthur's life, apart from his death at the end of the story. He handles the dramatic event idiosyncratically but effectively, beginning with facetious humour as the death of Uther is announced in Sir Ector's castle, and making the whole episode thoroughly modern in tone. When Kay is knighted just before the expedition sets out from Sir Ector's castle, the young man's ritual bath 'had to be set up in the boxroom, between two towel-horses and an old box of selected games which contained a worn-out straw dart-board – it was called fléchette in those days' (OFK 204). Later, the Wart's disgusted reaction to Kay's patronising offer of a shilling, if he will fetch him his forgotten sword, is convincingly realistic, and makes a fine prelude to what is to come. Then the Wart sees the great stone with the anvil on it, in which the sword is stuck: 'some sort of war memorial', he supposes, but at this point fantasy takes over. He hears music, 'whether of pan-pipes or recorders', transporting the reader to the realm of nature-mysticism, as all the 'old friends' of his childhood reappear to help him. The creatures are both real and legendary, 'otters and nightingales and vulgar crows and dogs and dainty unicorns and newts and solitary wasps and goat-moth caterpillars and corkindrills and volcanoes and mighty trees and patient stones. As a result of their encouragement, Wart felt his power grow' (OFK 208).

White differs from Malory in placing no emphasis upon the importance of the sword itself, either when the Wart first draws it, or elsewhere. Muriel Whitaker[18] has drawn attention to the significance of Excalibur as representative, with its scabbard, of Arthur's sovereign power, and to Malory's insistence that the King is first of all a knight, so that the sword takes precedence over the crown. When Arthur is eventually acclaimed at Pentecost by the Commons, he offers the sword on the altar at which the Archbishop is standing before he is knighted, and only after that 'was the coronacyon made' (Vin 10).

White presents the episode of the sword in the stone with admirably perceptive psychological realism. When Kay shows the sword to his father, Sir Ector deals with his lapse of honesty with the delicate tact of a good parent or headmaster:

> Sir Ector did not say anything silly. He looked at Kay and he looked at the Wart. Then he stared at Kay again, long and lovingly, and said, "We will go back to the church."   (OFK 209)

[18] See Whitaker, Muriel: *Arthur's Kingdom of Adventure: the World of Malory's Morte Darthur*, Cambridge, D.S. Brewer 1984.

The essentially dramatic nature of the incident is not lost in the telling, nor is its significance. When it has become clear that the Wart is none other than the new king, White moves from modern colloquial language to quote Malory directly, for this is a solemn moment for which the high style is more appropriate, as Sir Ector continues:

> "Nay, nay, my lord . . . I was never your father nor of your blood, but I wote well ye are of an higher blood than I wend ye were."
>
> (OFK 210)

White is never able to surpass Malory at the most dramatic or significant moments of Arthur's story, because the dignity and economy of language which Malory has at his command seem impossible to achieve in the twentieth century. But the remarkable fluctuations between realism of different kinds and fantasy, as between stylised and colloquial language, dramatise and interpret the scene for the modern reader, and also help to make clear its implications. Only at this point does White reveal that Sir Ector is not the Wart's real father, and he omits Arthur's words to Sir Ector:

> "ye are the man in the world that I am most beholdyng to, and my good lady and moder your wyf, that as wel as her owne hath fostred me and kepte."   (Vin 9)

The book ends with the words THE BEGINNING. White could not quite give it the happy resolution of *The Midnight Folk*:

> You may be sure that there is no more witchcraft in the house, nothing but peace and mirth all day and at night peace, the owls crying, the crickets chirping and all sorts of fun going on among THE MIDNIGHT FOLK.

It was probably, however, as positive an ending as the story allowed.

White's library contained a volume of critical essays, *Laughing Truths* (1927) by Carl Spitteler. As with many of his books, it was heavily annotated, often with the comment 'Bosh' in the margin. However, some paragraphs in an essay on 'Naïveté' won White's approval, and he marked them 'Good'. They are interesting now because they well describe what, in *The Once and Future King*, White himself attempted and achieved:

> He produces naively who tries to solve the problems set him by his inspiration and theme, simply by following a bee-line to his goal, regardless of models, rules, and prohibitions, or of the wisdom and judgment of his contemporaries. One may be naive in creation, even if one is a man of the highest culture, possessing the most extensive knowledge and even exhibiting a subtle and sophisticated quality of mind.
> . . .
> And, lo and behold, the threshed-out sheaves produce new grains of wheat, and the by-paths blossom under his feet, as if they were the

very spot chosen by spring as its dearest haunt. Teach and prove as much as you will that so-and-so cannot be done, the naive writer proceeds to do it and shows that it was not only possible but easy.

A preliminary condition of naiveté is richness of endowment . . . naiveté is only . . . successful when the poetic pictures fill the soul of the creator so richly and with such illuminating power, that they gain undisputed sovereignty without demur.   (215)

3

From *The Witch in the Wood* to *The Queen of Air and Darkness*

In his second Arthurian book, White felt it necessary to introduce into the story the circumstances that eventually brought about the final disaster in the downfall of the Round Table and the death of Arthur at the hands of Mordred. Malory tells us that:

> 'a grete angur and unhappe' arose which 'stynted nat tylle the floure of chyvalry of alle the worlde was destroyed and slayne.
>   And all was longe uppon two unhappy knyghtis whych were named sir Aggravayne and sir Mordred, that were brethirn unto sir Gawayne. For thys sir Aggravayne and sir Mordred had ever a prevy hate unto the quene, dame Gwenyver, and to sir Launcelot.'   (Vin 673)

His emphasis falls on the hatred stirred up by the love affair of Launcelot and Guenever. Though Malory mentions that Arthur had attempted to have his bastard child Mordred killed, he makes nothing of this personal motive for hatred. Mordred, like Aggravayne, is accepted without any attempt at individual characterisation as a man with a grudge. At first their joint hatred is directed against Launcelot, and Mordred only becomes Arthur's enemy when he betrays his trust as regent in the king's absence and tries to win the kingdom. The dénouement in *Le Morte Darthur* develops out of Mordred's and Aggravayne's hostility to Launcelot, whose prowess and nobility are carefully enhanced by Malory as the story progresses. We are thus made strongly aware of the nature of the tragedy: that so noble a knight as Launcelot, the prop and stay of the most glorious society that the world has ever known, because of his undying love – in itself a noble emotion – should bring about the destruction of the Round Table and the death of the king, his lord and his best and life-long friend. The emphasis therefore falls upon the love of Launcelot and Guenever as the cause of the disaster. This must have been apparent to White, but he chose to tell the story in a different way.

Although he was very well aware of the importance of education in deciding the pattern of the child's future life, he also believed that parent-child relationships largely control our future destinies. In his narrative,

Mordred has the misfortune to be illegitimate, but at Arthur's court he later finds himself lovingly treated 'by the King-father whom his mother had taught him to hate with all his heart'. In consequence, 'confused between the loves and hatreds of his frightful home' (OFK 553) he has grown up misshapen in mind as well as body. In both *The Witch in the Wood* and the later version, *The Queen of Air and Darkness*, White implies that it is the incest between Arthur and Morgause that is the most important single cause of the downfall of the Round Table, combined with the destructive relationship between Morgause and her sons. While most recent writers of Arthurian fictions, following Malory, have taken the begetting of Mordred as an unfortunate mishap indeed, but no more than that, White had his own reasons for making very much more of the episode. For him it was impossible to deal with the topic with the unexcited sureness that other writers have been able to bring to it.

On the 28 June 1939 White wrote to Potts from Doolistown, asking him if he would read the typescript of the recently completed *Witch in the Wood*, because William Collins was in doubt as to whether it was suitable for publication. In his letter he explained:

> *The Witch in the Wood* . . . is Book II of a projected 4 books about the doom of Arthur. Book III will give the Lancelot-Guenever tangle (it will be romantic) and Book IV will bring the three tragic themes together for the final clash. The three tragic themes are 1 The Cornwall Feud, existing ever since Arthur's father killed Gawaine's grandfather, 2 The Nemesis of Incest, which I have found frightfully difficult to introduce without gloom or nastiness in the book which Collins sends you, and 3 The Guenever-Lancelot romance. You know, the real reason why Arthur came to a bad end was because he had slept with his sister. It is a perfectly Aristotelian tragedy and it was the offspring of this union who finally killed him.

Continuing on his intentions and the problems that he had encountered with this book, he said:

> I cannot think of a better way to introduce this nasty incest business, and yet keep the books fairly sweet, than the way I have used. Morgause (the sister) is really far more important in the doom than even Guenever is, both through being associated with the Cornwall feud (it is her influence on Gawaine/Agravaine which help to ruin Arthur) and through the incest theme (for her son Mordred finally brings the ruin). I had to shew her as a bad mother and the kind of person who would bear more of the incest onus than my hero (Arthur). Error or frailty. If I hadn't made her nasty, it would have been *more* than an error or frailty in Arthur and I should have spoiled the tragedy. Yet I had to make her nasty without 1 making the book stink, 2 making her so nasty that it was incomprehensible of Arthur to sleep with her. You see it has been a frightfully difficult book to write (the next volume will

be easy) and I am conscious that it doesn't quite come off. . . . Well,
there is the problem.   (LF 98–9)

There are two quite distinct versions of White's second Arthurian book,
differing markedly from each other. The first, *The Witch in the Wood*, was
published in the United States by George Putnam's Sons in October 1939,
after Potts had read the typescript and White had made some modifications
to his original draft. It also came out in an English edition somewhat
revised, and with line drawings like those in *The Sword in the Stone*, published by Collins, in April 1940, the same year in which *The Ill-Made Knight* was
published in the United States. The final version, entitled *The Queen of Air
and Darkness*, the one with which most modern readers are familiar, did not
come into existence until after White had written both the third and fourth
books (*The Ill-Made Knight* and *The Candle in the Wind*) and what he intended to be the concluding book, *The Book of Merlyn*. Both versions of the
second volume are to some extent the product of the psychoanalysis which
White underwent before he left Stowe Ridings for Doolistown, and which
seems to have helped to bring about a radical change of attitude to his
mother, whom he had idolised in childhood and adolescence.[1]

If the extended treatment of his boyhood constituted an unusual approach to the story of Arthur, White's second volume was quite as original.
He could have chosen to continue with Arthur as his central figure; or he
could have taken from Malory one of the books or passages that he in the
end completely ignored. He could have made something of the tale of
Balin, or of Sir Gareth, or indeed of the story of Tristram. The enormous
trouble that his second book gave him might have been avoided if he had
chosen to follow Malory more closely. There was in fact not the slightest
need for him to write about the home-life of Gawaine and his brothers, and
particularly of Morgause. He could have dealt with the 'incest business'
perfectly adequately by simply relating the bare facts, as indeed he eventually does on the very last page. But if he wanted to invent 'enfances' for
Sir Gawaine and his brothers, to contrast with the upbringing of Arthur,
this desire was secondary to the overwhelming compulsion that he felt to
revenge himself on his mother, caricatured in the figure of Morgause.

Masefield and other modern writers as well as Malory had helped to
shape his first Arthurian book, but the hag-ridden White had no appropriate literary model when he began his second volume. Unlike most of his
nineteenth- and twentieth-century predecessors, he seems to have felt com-
pelled to make Arthur's incest a significant feature of his narrative. Realis-
ing that the story of Arthur was a perfect tragedy of epic proportions, he
was convinced that he must show how its seeds were sown in the begetting
of Mordred, but he nevertheless decided to make the whole story into farce,

---

[1] White had dedicated his first book, *Loved Helen and Other Poems* (London: Chatto and
Windus, 1929) to his mother, in a Latin dedication expressive of deep affection.

'smuggling in the tragic theme under the cloak of it', because he could not think of a better way to introduce what was to him a painful topic. He could not, at this point, deal with it either in a tragic or even a consistently serious mode. It was therefore hardly surprising that he experienced very severe problems with this book. Another reason for this was that even in its final form, with Arthur and Merlyn playing a more significant part than he had originally intended, there was no-one within the compass of the book with whom he could identify. Merlyn had finished his work as tutor by the end of *The Sword in the Stone*, and although he subsequently makes possible the dialectic on the topic of Might v. Right, he is no longer a dynamic figure. (Indeed, White may well have begun to have doubts as to the validity of Merlyn's ideas, since from this time onwards the wizard starts to decline into an anarchist whose theories do not seem to work.)

On the other hand, White could no longer identify with Arthur in his second volume as he had done in his first. The Wart had been the author himself, experiencing a happy imaginary childhood; but with Arthur as a 'young fellow, just on the threshold of manhood', with 'a rather stupid face', a kind young man 'because he had never been beaten' White could not feel that he was recreating his own late adolescence. The impetus for his writing could only come from his bottled-up fury against his mother. He had begun to analyse his feelings towards her in his earlier book, *England Have My Bones*, and to realise or at least to convince himself of the psychological damage she had inflicted on him. In a passage ostensibly about pets, he spoke of the 'curse of possession or motherhood. Mothers ruin their children, choke them like ivy' (EHMB 120). Later, strangely, he expresses his fixed belief, which seems to have had unfortunate consequences, that of all little boys in the world, he was the worst (EHMB 349). 'I think I must have had a mistaken mother', he continues.

> When she pleaded so movingly that I should grow up a big brave and honourable man, she was conditioning me to fear the reverse. I felt myself incapable of being any of those noble things; and the result was that whenever anything appeared to be truly noble I found myself incapable of doing it *ipso facto*.   (EHMB 350)

Eventually his mother had come to seem very much more than merely mistaken. Now he felt unable to live up to the ideal that had been created for him in boyhood. The psychological approach which he had adopted for telling Arthur's story only led him into the deep waters of family relationships. Now, Madame Mim, the Witch in the Wood vanquished by Merlyn in the first English edition of *The Sword in the Stone*, came to life again in a more virulent and unpleasant form as Morgause the central figure in Volume II.

The Witch in the Wood was in many ways a strange and inappropriate title: to begin with, Morgause is not obviously a witch at all. Even the love-philtre with which she tries to ensnare Arthur at the end is procured from old Mother Morlan, not concocted by herself. She is, moreover, never seen in a wood: there are no woods in Dunlothian as far as one can tell. The title seems to be a carry-over from the first edition of *The Sword in the Stone* in which the Wart and Kay captured by the wicked witch barely escape with their lives. In that episode, nature and the powers of good magic, represented by the brave goat and Merlyn, protect the innocent. The witch in the wood in fairytale is generally a symbol of all the dangers and terrors that can threaten the unprotected child, struggling on his own through the unforeseeable perils of this world. At the end of White's second volume Arthur, though now king and just adult, is still an innocent, but unprotected by either friendly animals or Merlyn's magic, hopelessly vulnerable when confronted by quite new experience. He is still in the wood, as it were, when Morgause arrives at Carlion, easily falling prey to sexual enchantment.

The serious underlying theme of *The Witch in the Wood* is present from the first, made particularly apparent in the earlier version, which begins with a long quotation from *Le Morte Darthur*:

> Then after the departing of King Ban and of King Bors, King Arthur rode unto Carlion. And thither came to him Lot's wife of Orkney, in manner of a message, . . . and she came richly bisene, with her four sons Gawaine, Gaheris, Agravaine, and Gareth, with many other knights and ladies. For she was a passing fair lady, therefore the king cast great love unto her, and desired to lie by her; so they were agreed, and he begat upon her Mordred, and she was his sister, on his mother's side, Igraine. So there she rested for a month, and at the last departed.
>
> *Le Morte Darthur*, Book I, Chapter XIX.[*]

The passage continues with Merlin's disclosure of Arthur's parentage, warning to him that he has 'done a thing late that God is displeased with', and revelation that he has 'gotten a child that shall destroy you and all the knights of your realm' (Vin 27–31). For the reader of the first edition of *The Witch in the Wood*, the origins of the tragedy to come were outlined before White began his story, but this long epigraph was removed in the course of White's many revisions. It was not surprising that he found it hard to handle the topic of incest since the book was still to some extent intended for young readers. His attempt to solve the problem by making it a comedy was only partially successful. A few days after his letter of late June 1939 he was writing to Potts again, admitting that perhaps there was 'considerable truth in the charges of cheap anachronism and 'determined facetiousness' which had been brought against him by William Collins. But he was reluctant to change the tone of the book, although he was prepared to comply with one of Collins' suggestions by adding several 'nature bits' at the beginnings of chapters, to bring it more in line with *The Sword in the Stone*.

In Malory, Morgause is a mysterious figure. White, however, had decided to update her, making her grotesque at the same time. She is 'the loveliest of the Cornwalls' and like Morgan le Fay:

* White was quoting from Caxton (Dent: Everyman, 1935).

she had black hair and eyes which reminded one of fresh prunes, but her particular form of witchcraft lay in preserving this beauty. . . . She had contrived to turn her finger nails into bloody talons, which always shone as if fresh from a vampire's meal. . . . Sometimes her eyelids went green, as well as shiny, and sometimes they were violet. When they were violet she wore black, and kept them drooping, and looked sideways out of them, and smoked through a silver cigarette-holder studded with gems.

She becomes 'a sort of fashionable witch' with 'an uncanny book of charms which Morgan had got for her out of the future, called *Vague*' (WW 14) (a facetious pun on the fashion magazine *Vogue*). She is ruthlessly selfish, given to self-deception and constantly posing. White reverts again and again to her 'magic changes into another person' (WW 83), to her 'blue-stocking transubstantiations' – her repertoire 'was as extensive as the seed of Abraham' (WW 113) – and he makes her speak with a sickening coyness. ' "Do you . . . believe in Reincarnation?" ' (a topic which had been fashionable in the earlier decades of the twentieth century) she asks Sir Grummore, insisting that he had been a little flower in a previous incarnation. ' "I was a little Dicky Bird, and I hopped down beside this flower and gave it a peck . . . More like a kiss" ' (WW 86), she continues.

Soon after finishing *The Witch in the Wood* (at 3.30 on 3 May 1939, as he notes in his journal) White made another entry which showed how much his mother was on his mind:

My mother was (is) a woman for whom all love had to be dependant. She had to be the senior partner in love, the incubus, and the result was that she chased away from her, her husband, her lover and her only son. All these fled from her possessive selfishness, and she was left to extract her meed of affection from more slavish minds. She became, a quarter of a century ago, a lover of dogs. This meant that the dogs had to love her.

Like Constance White, Morgause is therefore fond of little dogs, grotesquely named Oodlums, Dovekins, Sweetie-Peetie, Ucky-Ducky, and Ickle-Petty-Wetty.

She treats her four sons with both physical and mental cruelty: when she wants to punish them, she strips them naked and beats them with the leg of a stool, hitting at them indiscriminately. Her constantly changing attitude leaves them confused: 'they didn't know where they stood'; 'there was a cauldron seething in each of them', and 'peculiar chemical changes' happening 'secretly in their insides' (WW 169). The Queen who insists on having four hot-water bottles in bed with her at a time treats her four sons as if they too existed purely for her comfort and gratification. She likes to keep them in a constant state of emotional upheaval, saying the rosary with her darlings at bedtime, but pretending that their father King Lot has been killed in battle because 'It tortured the children more' (WW 231). The extent to which White was writing out of his own unhappy personal experience is further suggested by the description of the domestic quarrel which follows King Lot's return from the wars, probably derived from early memories of his parents' quarrels before they eventually separated.

Morgause of *The Witch in the Wood* is above all else a bad mother, one who loves to torment her children while deceiving herself that she is sacrificing herself for them, and again and again in the later books of *The Once and Future King*, White refers to the relationship between Morgause and her sons and the harm that it has done them. As the Queen of Air and Darkness in the final version, however, she remains a heartless mother but less attention is drawn to the fact.

White represents Morgause as hungry for sex, trying in vain to seduce King Pellinore (who is besotted with his love for Piggy, daughter of the King of Flanders) and Sir Grummore, who has been married for thirty years. So, whether in the rôle of mother or of vamp, she is always putting on an act, while with the knights she tries to pose as a sex-symbol. Her silly affected language and attempts to be intense are, not surprisingly, wasted on them. White introduces a farcical episode in which she organises a tournament on the ice (WW 141ff.) which ends with her ridiculous attempt to gain attention by falling through it and her indignation when she is rescued by the wrong person. White also goes out of his way to make her physically repulsive. Her secret chamber smells strongly of 'some overpowering scent like Hyacinth, mingled with the smell of dirty stockings, sandal wood, banana oil, scented salts, greasy fur, lingerie, and the excrements of Sweetie-Peetie . . . There was also a faint smell of mice' (WW 126). The description could have been, but clearly is not, an attempt at historical realism. The subsequent passage in which Morgause is in her bath, wallowing vigorously in a 'consommé of snails' blood' (WW 272), is childish in its crudity and was cut from later editions. When she goes to Arthur's court with the intention of seducing him it is therefore rather surprising to the reader to find that it is her beauty rather than her magic that causes him to succumb.

The Morgause episodes are predominantly farcical, and originally included some scenes depicting the homelife of the Queen of Orkney and King Lot in which he tells her that she looks like a death's head, and she calls him Fat Boy. King Lot's letters home from the war, though rather amusing, were subsequently cancelled, as were such scenes from domestic life as the following, where banality is almost raised to the level of genius:

> "My dear Umbawse, do have some more of this syllabub."
> "Well, I don't mind if I do."
> "Splendid syllabub this, your majesty."
> "Do you think so, Sir Umbawse? How very kind of you."
> "So well cooked, you know."
> "Yes, it is cooked."
> "Cooked by the cook."

"Cook cooks. Of course."

"Of course."

"Cook – "

"Cook – "

"Cuckoo!"

"Why did you do that?" asked the Queen sharply.

"I don't know," said the King.

Not unnaturally both the publisher and Potts felt that revision and prun-
ing were required: White's tormented mind seems to have had to find relief
through the crude form of caricature, before he could create in the later
Queen of Air and Darkness a witch of somewhat greater subtlety and more
sinister power. But the image of his mother that he had formed for himself
remained to haunt him and was not much diminished by time or distance.
In the autumn of 1940, when he had completely rewritten his second
volume, he wrote to David Garnett asking him to call on Constance White
in Sussex, meanwhile warning him: 'She is a witch, so look out, if you go.
Probably she is a poor old witch by now.'.[2] In the following year he claimed
that every time he had to write to her it was 'like being crucified' (W/G L
85).

His problems and dissatisfaction with the second book still continued
even after the first edition had appeared. On 9 April 1940, shortly before the
English edition came out, he was writing to Potts to the effect that he 'might
have to scrap the whole thing'. In the same month, in a letter to David
Garnett he said:

> there are many parts much too vulgarly farcical. I want to appeal to
> some man of decent feelings to blue-pencil the shoddy passages for me
> ... If you will do this for me, I will cut out all the parts you object to.
>
> (W/G L 67)

In June he was still contemplating re-writing the book completely, while in
his journal for 25 October 1940 he wrote:

> I shall have to rewrite the Witch in the Wood, cutting out 75% of the
> horseplay and treating Morgause seriously, against a background of
> Celtic witchcraft. This will be the *fourth* draft of the wretched work.
> ...You could perhaps build up her character by adding all their [her
> children's] characteristics together. Gawaine bad-tempered, amoral,
> clannish, fierce, with several decent instincts. Gaheris (my interpreta-
> tion, not Malory's) stupid. Agravaine brutal, bullying, cunning,

---

[2] See *W/G L* p. 75, where White also writes: 'probably I ought 'to be ashamed of myself. I
am. But I have tried to get on with her, and every year or two I try again. . . . She must be
nearing seventy, and is alone. It is because she has chased away her husband, lover and
son, by her own efforts. But this does not alter the fact that she is 70 and alone.'

envious. Gareth beautiful, a dear. Mordred intelligent, crooked, bitter, ironic, pitiless.'

There follows a list of people that Morgause might have been like:

Clytemnestra
Cleopatra (Shakespeare's)
That matron at St David's, whatever her name was
Aunt Lilian – very slightly
My mother
The witch in Snow White
A claw-padded, secret cat. Yes, and one who goes upon the tiles.
Some Faustine or other out of Swinburne
A fanatical anti-Norman, a Countess Marcevwitz
Mrs Bywaters – or Thompson
Mme Bovary

He follows this with a further analysis:

Morgause should haunt you. She should have all the frightful power and mystery of women. Yet she should be quite shallow, cruel, selfish . . . One important thing is her Celtic blood. Let her be the worst West-of-Ireland type: the one with cunning bred in the bone. Let her be mealy-mouthed: butter would not melt in it. Yet also she must be full of blood and power. Let her shew one character to one person and one to another. . . . But I must be able to love or understand or sympathise with her: at least I must be able to write her from inside. This is why the Witch in the Wood is proving so frightfully difficult. I loathed the woman. . . . I tried to get round it by satirising or mocking her, but this did not do.

In the following December, presumably not having been informed of the rewriting that was now going on, Potts was still trying to help:

The trouble about book 2 of Arthur is really that you never published the *pirate* book ['Rather Rum'], or *You can't keep a good man down*. Between them they got rid of a good deal of waste matter projected in your mind by Morgause. . . . I can't think what you're to do with Morgause, except keep her right out of the book . . . or of course leave her as she is . . . there is too much of her – she is too much exposed in all her vulgarity – for the final scene of the book – it sickens one. . . . But you *are* quite right in saying you hate M. too much to do any good with her; and if you re-write the book I don't see what you can do but cut out almost all of her . . . Don't actually show her in her bath – but do it somehow indirectly. (LF 120ff.)

At last it seems that White's mind was to some extent purged of the 'waste matter' that Potts had mentioned. The witch was, as it were, being driven out of the wood, and her baneful power at least beginning to be exorcised. His reply to Potts's letter shows the advance that he had made:

As a matter of fact you suggested the very alterations to *The Witch in the Wood* which I had already carried out in my 3rd(?) draft. As I told you, even that turned out to be a failure, so I am re-doing the whole thing with a different woman altogether as Morgause. I have chucked overboard all idea of building her on my mother . . . Instead, she is now a pure melodramatic WITCH (rather fun) who goes about boiling black cats alive and so forth. Housman wrote a poem about her. (Her strong enchantments failing, Her towers of fear in wreck, Her limbecks dried of poison etc.) I shall make her wildly seductive.   (LF 122)

He omits to mention in his letter the lines that follow in Housman's poem, perhaps even more significant than those quoted, in that they suggest that this queen, too, is not without power over the young man:

> The Queen of air and darkness
> Begins to shrill and cry,
> 'O young man, O my slayer,
> Tomorrow you shall die'.[3]

However, with his new concept of the character of Morgause, White had the opportunity to create a powerfully symbolic figure – of the female who threatens and destroys the male. She is represented without the savage animosity, personal bitterness and particularly the physical disgust that got in the way in the earlier version: the change from the concept of the witch to the Queen of Air and Darkness marks his progress from childish vituperation to a more sophisticated mode of characterisation. Even so, he still did not manage to make Morgause either a frighteningly evil or a 'wildly seductive' figure: she remains essentially trivial. She does not seem to be adequately motivated as a character; nor does she even command great magic, because she is too vain and idle to work at it.

There are, however, some strengths in the scenes in which as Queen of Air and Darkness she appears. The boiling of the cat in the opening chapter is very vividly realised in all its horror, and made the more revolting by the

---

[3] See *Complete Poems of A.E. Housman*, New York, Henry Holt 1959. From 'Last Poems', 1895. In its entirety the poem reads:

> Her strong enchantments failing,
>   Her towers of fear in wreck,
> Her limbecks dried of poisons
>   And the knife at her neck.

> The Queen of air and darkness
>   Begins to shrill and cry,
> 'O young man, O my slayer,
>   To-morrow you shall die.'

> O Queen of air and darkness,
>   I think 'tis truth to say,
> And I shall die to-morrow;
>   But you will die today.

fact that Morgause is merely amusing herself, and trying to pass the time in her dismal castle in Lothian. White's hatred of cats and well-repressed sadistic tendencies probably found an outlet in this rather gratuitous piece of nastiness, but it is an effective substitute for the crude and almost scato-logical description of the queen in her bath in the first two editions, by which he had originally tried to make her repellent. The effect is intensified as a result of the contrast between her activities in the room below the one in which her four young boys are rehearsing their family history and de-claring their devotion to their mother. They adore her 'dumbly and uncriti-cally' (OFK 217). White made this first chapter more disturbing by ironically interweaving the most disgusting moments of the cat-boiling episode with an account of Gareth's sensitivity towards other members of his family, and the boys' declaration of devotion to their mother:

> "We must avenge our family."
> "Because our Mammy is the most beautiful woman in the high-ridged, extensive, ponderous, pleasant-turning world."
> "And because we love her."   (OFK 223)

Morgause's device for enthralling Arthur at the end of the book also makes use of magic – again a 'piseog (a dialect word for a minor magical device) rather than a great magic' – the spancel with which she ensnares him. The device, like the boiling of the cat, is also gratuitously unpleasant: other modern writers allow Morgause to achieve her ends by exploiting Arthur's vulnerability in more usual ways, generally of course by relying on her sexual attractions. White gives a graphic description of how a span-cel (a rope or fetter for hobbling cattle, horses etc., but here in the special sense of a long unbroken strip of skin taken from the body of a dead man for magical purposes) is made and used, but when at the end Arthur is seduced, we are told, 'It is impossible to explain how these things begin. Perhaps the Spancel had a strength in it'. Since its magical powers are not, it seems, indisputable, it is not even essential to Morgause's evil purpose. It shows what an unpleasant character she is, but in an unnecessarily horrible way. Nevertheless, Morgause is very much more convincing as Arthur's seductress in *The Queen of Air and Darkness*. Although in the first version of the story, she makes a dramatic entrance, 'knowing that she is looking her best', and White hints that she might have managed to slip a love-potion into Arthur's drink, he incongruously suggests (since she has consistently been presented in physically disgusting terms previously) that beauty is her main weapon. Equally strangely, in the 1958 version, she appears at Arthur's bedside, with the intention of seducing him, with her four child-ren. An entry in White's journal dated 10 October 1939 reads: 'Arthur was hardly a judge of nice people, or he would not have had a child by Morgause'. He is represented as being attracted by her maternal appear-ance rather than by her beauty: she is twice his age, old enough to be his mother, and the 'rôle of mother love' which she seems to manifest takes him 'between wind and water' when he sees her there with her children. This hint of an Oedipal situation suggests that despite all his efforts, White's neuroses still controlled his mode of telling the story. There seems also to be an inconsistency in the pattern of family relationships as he represents them: if Morgause was as bad a mother as White maintains, how was it that Gareth and Gaheris, and on the whole Gawain, grew up comparatively unscathed?

The changes that White made to the character of Morgause constitute the most significant difference between the two versions. Her presence pervades *The Witch in the Wood*, while in *The Queen of Air and Darkness* she is only in the foreground of four chapters, and then as a much more convincing figure. In the end, almost all of what was most splenetic and tasteless was removed from the final version. Exerting her influence from behind the scenes, the later Morgause is now more credible. The opening scene in which she is experimenting with the spell to make herself invisible by boiling the cat effectively communicates a sense of the cruelty of her essentially trivial nature. She still works at seducing the English knights, but White only hints at these activities, and almost entirely refrains from suggesting her fantasies. Her sons are beaten – after the unicorn incident, since the ice-tournament was cut out – but Morgause has them whipped, rather than inflicting the punishment herself. She soon discovers that she hates the English knights (Sir Grummore and King Pellinore) and declares that she is interested in nothing but her darling boys (OFK 280).

Even after Morgause had become merely 'a pure melodramatic WITCH' in *The Queen of Air and Darkness*, the theme of incest still remained intractable. Malory, addressing himself to adult readers, simply says of Morgause that 'she was a passynge fayre lady'; and continues, 'Wherefore the kynge caste grete love unto hir and desired to ly by her. And so they were agreed, and [he] begate uppon hir sir Mordred' (Vin 27). White obviously still has the twelve-year old readers of *The Sword in the Stone* in mind in his second volume. They have just been made spectators at the marriage feast of King Pellinore and his Queen and of St Toirdealbhach and Mother Morlan, with its peacock pie, jellied eels, Devonshire cream, curried porpoise, iced fruit salad, and two thousand side dishes – and White remains the schoolmaster delicately handling the topic of sex in the next passage: 'Whatever the explanation may have been, the Queen of Air and Darkness had a baby by her half-brother nine months later. It was called Mordred' (OFK 322–3). Continuing in the same vein, he says: 'And this, as Merlyn drew it later, was what the magician called its pied-de-grue', meaning the 'pedigree' or family tree of Mordred. This learned pun he probably owed to his reading of Augustin Thierry's *Norman Conquest of England*:[4] 'pied-de-grue' means

---

4   Thierry, Augustin: *History of the Conquest of England by the Normans*, translated by W. Hazlitt, 1847.

the family tree of a bastard, literally 'foot of a crane' (the bird); 'grue' is also French slang for a prostitute.

White did not reach this ingenious ending easily: in a discarded draft of *The Witch in the Wood*, he had written:

> Now comes the difficult part and the end of the story, which explains why there had to be a whole book about the Cornwall feud and about the character of the Cornwall Queen . . . Neither Arthur nor Morgause knew of their relationship when they met . . .

A pencilled note has been added by an unknown hand: 'This part, the last page, in longhand, T.W. is doubtful about, and may decide to omit.' In the end he had to grasp the nettle, and did so with complete success.

ii.

As White had originally conceived his second volume there was, rather surprisingly, very little mention of Arthur in it at all. (Arthur had, of course, nothing to do with the upbringing of the Orkney clan, or with the family in general until his encounter with King Lot in battle, and his subsequent affair with Morgause.) White's compulsive need, when he began to write *The Witch in the Wood*, to make Morgause the central figure, which also involved the topic of incest, was accompanied by his determination to make farce the dominant mode. Much space was given to scenes of low-life in Lothian, figuring the local saint as well as Sir Palomides, Sir Grummore and King Pellinore. His usual inclination towards facetiousness found outlets not only in the Gaelic scenes with the not always sober saint, but also in those in which Sir Grummore and Sir Palomides construct the pantomime-style Questing Beast to distract the grieving Pellinore from his love. Both these elements were much reduced in *The Queen of Air and Darkness*, resulting in greater unity, though not without some loss. On a more serious level, White wanted to account for the later actions of Gawaine and his brothers, to give the reader an understanding of the reasons for their fierce hatreds and their unshakeable loyalties. By showing them growing up in a milieu very different from Sir Ector's castle he was thus able to suggest the motives for their later behaviour, while at the same time drawing on his own current experience for local colour.

Presumably, had it not been for the fact that he was marooned in Doolis-town during the war years, the chapters based on 'the village' would never have come into existence at all. Particularly in the first edition, he drew on his own day-to-day experience in Ireland and turned it into fantasy. His firm intention had been that the 'hero' of *The Witch in the Wood* should be 'the village', meaning the people of Lothian, presumably to offset the evil implicit in Morgause. As in his later fantasy, *The Elephant and the Kangaroo*, his life at Doolistown where he immersed himself in the life of the area and tried to learn the language contributed substantially to the comic aspects of the book. These were augmented by the introduction of St Toirdealbhach (St Torealvac in *The Witch in the Wood*) who in *The Queen of Air and Darkness* becomes the tutor, in so far as they have one, of Gawaine and his brothers in place of Sir Palomides. The somewhat bibulous and garrulous, most unsaintly saint turns out to be none other than the author himself in another of his disguises. On 1 August 1939, when he was beginning to learn Erse, White wrote to Mary Potts actually signing the letter 'Toirdealbac', the Gaelic form of Terence.[5] In both versions he adds to the comedy in various ways. Potts in his letter to White of December 1940 commented that the 'whole of the Saint, which you added is good; and all the village is lovely' (LF 121). Since he had found so much of the first version distasteful, his enthusiasm for these episodes is not surprising. So, in the first American and English editions, there are some lively scenes in which the Saint appears, such as the night of revelry in the Lobster Inn, later cut – a scene which gives the impression of being based on many a convivial evening in which White had himself participated. It is the counterpart of the Christmas feast at Sir Ector's, but less functional. Here, St Torealvac, in his fifth heresy, has his arm round the waist of the somewhat disreputable Mother Morlan, and a good many songs, mostly of a parodic nature, are sung. In these White satirises with his usual facetiousness what he sees as rural Irish ineptitude and uncouthness. The English knights and Sir Palomides carouse with the locals and leave very much the worse for the landlord's mead, King Pellinore spending the night in a ditch. All this was eventually cut out, together with an amusing episode reminiscent of P.G. Wodehouse, in which White describes the frightful hangover experienced by the knights, whose sufferings are intensified by the butler's deliberate and persistent offers of greasy breakfast dishes next morning. The other passages involving 'those tedious knights', as White later called Pellinore, Grummore and Palomides, such as their encounters with Queen Morgause and adventures with the Questing Beast, which had provided the other main source of comedy, were also much reduced.

White cut some good comic scenes when he demoted Palomides and made him merely a minor character. In *The Witch in the Wood*, in racist jokes very typical of the late nineteen-thirties, but no longer acceptable to the present-day reader, he is presented affectionately as the 'old blackamoor', a Failed Bardic Bachelor of Arts (WW 45). He is:

a very learned man, who had been educated in one of the bardic schools of the East, with a large, round, shiny face and horn-rimmed

---

5 See *LF* 104. Although White's first name was Terence, he 'was known as Timothy or Tim to his friends at Cambridge and elsewhere, by reference to a well-known chain of chemists (now no longer in existence) called Timothy White's.

spectacles. The whites of his eyes were shot with a sort of toffee colour. He was charming, but not good at teaching boys.   (WW 30)

Palomides was also caricatured in the little sketches which White drew for the first edition. His patronising and unsympathetic attitude to his subject is surprising, in view of his happy early years in India. In the first edition, however, Palomides was also the source of some excellent literary jokes, which include his brilliantly absurd sonnet to Isoud.* His attempts, as tutor to Morgause's sons, to educate his disrespectful and recalcitrant pupils and to instruct them from a preposterous syllabus were also very amusing. With characteristically boyish insolence and misbehaviour they try to get the embarrassed Palomides, with predictable results, to explain the facts of life while he is trying to give them an elementary Latin lesson. White's extensive knowledge of the mentality of schoolboys enabled him convincingly to represent the devilish ingenuity with which children will exploit a weak teacher.

Palomides, in the early versions of the second book, also has the formidable task of trying to help King Pellinore to write love-poems to Piggy: naturally great problems arise with various aspects of form, for Pellinore is quite unable to find rhymes or to understand the rhyme-scheme of the sonnet. Palomides is thus almost a major character in *The Witch in the Wood*, but in *The Queen of Air and Darkness* he is much less important. His dissociation from the unicorn hunt allowed that episode to become more serious and significant, since it focused the reader's attention on the reactions of Gawaine and his brothers. When all these reductions in Palomides' role had been made, however, the construction of the pantomime Questing Beast was virtually all that was left for the Saracen knight. The episodes concerning the Beast had originally sprawled over much of the second half of *The Witch in the Wood*, but in the end they were reduced so as to take up little more than two chapters. In the place of these cancelled passages, White put in the rather less entertaining chapters involving Arthur and Merlyn, leading up to the battle of Bedegraine.

In the course of rewriting, he completely abandoned the original opening of his second book, which had begun with an attractive picture of the land of Lothian and Orkney, rather in the mode of *The Sword in the Stone*:

> It is a country of bog and mountain, where the wind whistles all day and at night the turf fires glow with small flames in a kind of rusty saffron . . . It is all heather and loveliness, and the town people say: "Aow, aint it 'orrible. I can't bear them lonely places with nothink in them. It's sort of melancholy, annit?"
>
> Five hundred years ago the land of Lothian looked much as it does today. The castle which stands at the top of the tremendous Atlantic cliffs was in better repair, of course, and there were several Irish saints who lived in beehives along the edges of the same cliffs, who are not there now. Also there were unicorns on the mountains, and elks in the

---

* See Sprague, Kurth: *A Joy Proposed: Poems by T.H. White*, London, Bertram Rota, 1980, p. 53.

bogs – their antlers are still dug up sometimes by peat cutters . . . So we may as well visit it now, in the hope of seeing a few sorcerers and an Irish saint or two . . .   (WW 9–10)

He vividly evoked a picture of 'that lovely old Gaelic bustle which people find so difficult to picture nowadays, if they are just looking at the bare stones':

> The place was a town in itself, a busy node of the lonely and ancient and savage north. There were old wives spinning and milkmaids churning and bards composing and turf-boys keeping the fire boxes full of sods and pump-boys looking after the water supply and house-maids carding wool and butchers salting down meat for the winter and carpenters, ploughmen, tinkers, cowboys, drovers, thatchers. The lanterns swung to and fro across the courtyards before the darkling downs and under the wild northern lights. Nothing can ever be entirely wrong in the land of the Gael, and, as the poet Aodhagan O Rathaille has put it, there were
> Companies coming to the ancient mansion without sorrow,
> Companies falling down with feverish pulse,
> Companies inebriate without offence to their neighbours,
> Companies of pride discoursing uproariously.   (WW 17)

His enthusiasm for the land of the Gael was unfortunately not destined to last until the end of his stay there. Eventually, because he considered that this and some other descriptive passages relating to the 'village' made the book seem too 'Gaelic', White put in their place the very much more vivid and dramatic opening focused on the tower in which Morgause is dabbling in magic while her sons go over their family history together. However, he retained the boys' first visit to Mother Morlan and Saint Toirdealbhach which in itself gave plenty of local colour, at the same time suggesting a primitive society which takes for granted the natural savagery of children allowed to run wild, as the boys ill-treat the donkeys in the village street. He ironically refers to this as an 'Eden-like scene', since the boys are innocent in so far as they are simply being thoughtlessly cruel in a cruel world. (The same effect had been achieved less economically in the first version by a conversation in broad dialect between the Saint and the land-lord of the Lobster Inn, who reports having seen the Queen, 'yon wum-man', pulling a butterfly to pieces, an action later repeated by Agravaine.)

iii.

In the final version of *The Queen of Air and Darkness* (1958) White at last managed to solve the problems of proportion and focus that had plagued him earlier. As the book gained greater symbolic power through the substitution of the Queen for the Witch in the Wood, so the different way in which the unicorn-episode was presented in the final version much enhanced its effect, making it the central feature of the book. The idea for the hunt must have arisen at one level out of the medieval bestiary on the translation of which White worked for many years, and which was to become *The Book of Beasts*. Although he made little change in the actual form of the hunt, by cutting down the comic scenes in which it had been embedded he enhanced its depth and seriousness.

Originally, in *The Witch in the Wood*, the unicorn hunt was introduced as part of a farcical sequence involving King Pellinore. As he appears to be going mad after an encounter with Morgause on the cliffs, Palomides suggests distracting him by encouraging him to go hunting. The Questing Beast has disappeared, so some other quarry must be found. The bestiary is got out, and it is decided to interest Pellinore in Unicorns. The idea is mentioned to Morgause, and she immediately insists on being the requisite virgin: ' "I am just a Virgin at Heart" ', she explains to the puzzled Grummore (WW 85). The Queen then has a temporary tower constructed on the mountainside by six sweating villagers, and when no unicorn appears, tries to get Sir Grummore to take its place: ' "You are a Unicorn, Sir Grummore," ' cries the Queen in desperation, as she unsuccessfully tries to persuade him to lay his head in her lap: ' "You are a Unicorn and I am a maiden" ' (WW 90). Then, sometime later, in order to get her attention because they have not seen their mother for a week, the boys decide to have a unicorn hunt. White rightly saw no reason to change the form of the children's hunt in *The Queen of Air and Darkness*, despite the fact that some early readers had criticised the episode. It is a brilliant piece of invention, even though one's attention may distracted from its deeper significances by the farcical touches.

In the final version, the preliminary unicorn hunt in which Morgause had participated is merely discussed some time afterwards by her four sons. Agravaine who, it has been hinted, has an abnormal relationship with his mother (substantiated in *The Ill-Made Knight* by the reference to his murder of Lamorak out of jealousy (OFK 453)), is half-aware of her activities with the two Sassenach knights, and so, it seems, is Gaheris. They give an account of it to their brothers, thus allowing White to suggest the nuances of feeling which the story arouses in the boys:

> "What was our mother at doing," asked Gawaine, as they made their way toward St Toirdealbhach's cell one morning, "with the knights on the mountain?"
> Gaheris answered with some difficulty, after a long pause:
> "They were at hunting a unicorn."
> "How do you do that?"
> "There must be a virgin to attract it."
> "Our mother," said Agravaine, who also knew the details, "went on a unicorn hunt, and she was the virgin for them."
> His voice sounded strange as he made this announcement.
>
> (OFK 257)

The innocent little Gareth says that he didn't know his mother wanted a unicorn. ' "She has never said so" ', he finishes, to which the twelve-year old Agravaine knowingly replies, ' "Half a word is sufficient to the wise man" ', as they plod on their way, 'reluctant to disclose their thoughts'. At the point in the narrative shortly before the boys decide to have their own hunt, White in his final version suggests by means of a subtle combination of dialogue and authorial comment the growing sexual awareness of the brothers, who are nevertheless not quite able to understand what is going on. Ironically, they hope to buy their mother's love and attention by taking her 'what she needs' (OFK 269), a phrase which suggests their recognition that her principal role is that of a witch, constantly requiring bizarre ingredients for her magic. On their arrival at the saint's cell, he gets out his bestiary to look up unicorns for them, so that instead of Palomides explaining to the English knights the habits of such creatures from his bestiary, the information is now more appropriately communicated directly to Gawaine and his brothers. When the hunt begins, it gradually takes on a meaning of its own as the boys, in identifying Meg the kitchenmaid with their mother and themselves with Sir Grummore and King Pellinore, seem to be about to engage unwittingly and innocently in sexual games.

As they set about organising their hunt, the introduction of the unicorn itself into the very realistic scene of the boys' squabbling and contriving gives the episode a surrealistic quality which effectively raises questions as to its meaning. White dwells on the noble beauty and trustfulness of the mythical beast which at first holds the children spellbound, its wonderful eyes killing 'all other emotion except love' (OFK 265). It is Agravaine, of course, who rushes out to stab and kill it, bawling ' "This girl is my mother. He put his head in her lap. He had to die." ' (OFK 266). He alone attacks it, while his brothers try to restrain him. The scene looks back to the idyllic and innocent scene in the greenwood in *The Sword in the Stone*, between Robin and Marian, and forward to Agravaine's murder, much later on in the story, of his mother 'in a storm of jealousy, on discovering her in bed at the age of seventy with a young man called Lamorak' (OFK 553). Again, long afterwards, when Mordred and Agravaine are conspiring against Lancelot and Guenever, Gareth recognises a pattern which has its focal point in the killing of the unicorn, in Agravaine's behaviour as he threatens his brothers with his sword as he remembers: 'Their murdered mother, and the unicorn, and the man now drawing, and a child in a storeroom flashing a dirk' (OFK 557).

The unicorn is a symbol of trust, innocence and beauty, the qualities of happy childhood; in coming to Meg the kitchenmaid, it gives itself up in complete trustfulness to her protection. But Meg is seen by Agravaine as his 'mother' (because she is doing what his mother was thought to be doing on the previous day, while supposedly trying to catch a unicorn) and as such, she does nothing to defend the symbol of uncorrupted childhood, just as the boys' mother betrays their trust and destroys their childhood innocence and happiness. The unicorn's death leaves them in an even greater state of psychic upheaval and confusion than before. There seems to be no way in which they can gain their mother's love and the attention that they crave, though to do so they had been prepared to sacrifice the embodiment of all beauty and goodness.

White makes much of the 'gralloch', the cutting up of the unicorn preparatory to trying to get it back to the castle:

> At the gralloch, the three remaining huntsmen were in trouble. They had begun to slit at the skin of the belly, but they did not know how to do it properly and so they had perforated the intestines. Everything had begun to be horrible, and the once beautiful animal was spoiled and repulsive. All three of them loved the unicorn in their various ways, Agravaine in the most twisted one, and, in proportion as they became responsible for spoiling its beauty, so they began to hate it for their guilt. Gawaine particularly began to hate the body. He hated it for being dead, for having been beautiful, for making him feel a beast. He had loved it and helped to trap it, so now there was nothing to be done except to vent his shame and hatred of himself upon the corpse.
>
> (OFK 268)

When eventually the boys get the unicorn's head back to the castle, and set it up to impress their mother, she does not even see it. But:

> When she found out about the unicorn later in the evening she had them whipped for it, for she had spent an unsuccessful day with the English knights.   (OFK 270)

The incident displays the differences between the brothers, to be carefully developed later as the story unfolds. At the beginning of the book, they are represented very much as if they were a litter of puppies, little differentiated, but individual traits are distinguished in each, so that towards the end of *The Candle in the Wind* they have very distinct personalities.

The murder of the unicorn is in itself a tragedy, and it becomes symbolic of the subsequent annihilation of goodness and trust in the destruction of the Round Table and the death of Arthur, through the enmity of Agravaine and Mordred.

iv.

When Gawaine and his brothers are repeating their family history at the very beginning of the book, they stop short of the story of the actual begetting of Arthur. Their grandmother 'was forced into marrying the King of England – the man who had slain her husband' (OFK 220), and there the story ends, as the boys 'considered the enormous English wickedness in silence, overwhelmed by its dénouement.' White comes back to Arthur's ancestry in the last chapter, reminding us – as Merlyn remembers too late what he should have told his pupil – of the subject of the Orkney children's conversation at the very beginning of the book. The pattern of destiny must work itself out, the 'tragedy, the Aristotelian and comprehensive tragedy, of sin coming home to roost' (OFK 323) cannot be avoided. But Arthur's ignorance, which can be equated with innocence, leaves him defenceless against Morgause.

White's problems in dealing with the begetting of Mordred arose not simply out of his difficulty in imagining the episode in the first place and in identifying with either of the participants in the action, but also out of the difficulty of deciding how to deal with it within the style of narrative that he had chosen, and for his particular readership. Yet this intractable episode was of crucial importance to the structure of the story, for apart from what he felt to be the morally unacceptable aspect of this part of the story, there was the problem of Morgause's motivation which could not be entirely avoided. He tried presenting her as the injured and resentful wife:

> Very well, she was thinking: now I have had enough. I have borne [Lot's] insults, his cruelty, his drunkenness, his physical assaults. Beaten, pinched, insulted in front of my guests, sneered at, deprived of every consideration, humiliated before the servants: still I have borne it all, for the sake of my Beloved Children. . . . Meek, womanly, mis-understood, maltreated but too loyal to admit it, I shall make my way to King Arthur's court with my darling orphans. Lot says that Arthur is only twenty years of age, and Grummore was telling me that he was one of the finest looking men he had ever seen. And think of all the glories of Court at Carlion . . . Humble, self-sacrificing, motherly, shy, nay, mouselike, I shall throw myself upon Arthur's mercy, with my babes about me. Then we shall see.   (WW 272–3)

Ultimately White greatly enhanced the subtlety and the sinister effect of the incest-episode by cutting rather than by amplification. Morgause has been told about the 'strength, charm, innocence and generosity' of the victorious Arthur, and after lying sleepless beside King Lot on the night before her departure for Carlion, she goes to her coffer and gets out her magic device, the spancel. This, if thrown over the head of the man you love and tied in a bow while he is asleep, may have two different effects, White tells us:

> If he woke while you were doing this he would be dead within the year. If he did not wake until the operation was over, he would be bound to fall in love with you.   (OFK 317)

Morgause's motives are not explored: the implication is that she is prompted by an inherently evil nature. At the same time the question of whether she knows of her true relationship with Arthur is avoided, and she is seen as a mother-figure rather than as a sister. Her action seems gratuitous: although she has never met Arthur she is determined to seduce him, presumably to avenge the wrong inflicted on the Cornwall family, even though he is guiltless of it. White struggles to explain how the disaster could have happened:

> Perhaps it was because Arthur was always a simple fellow, who took people at their own valuation easily. Perhaps it was because he had never known a mother of his own, so that the role of mother love, as she stood with her children behind her, took him between wind and water.   (OFK 322)

Individual responsibility cannot ultimately be avoided, however, and Arthur is to feel an increasingly heavy burden of guilt to the end of his days. He did not fully understand what he was doing, 'but it seems, in tragedy, that innocence is not enough' (OFK 323).

v.

In *The Queen of Air and Darkness*, the alternation of chapters concerning Morgause and her family with those involving Arthur and Merlyn give a sense of two totally disparate worlds, each existing in almost complete ignorance of the other, but which are destined to impinge violently upon each other in the fulness of time. There is very much less realistic historical detail in this book than in *The Sword in the Stone*. In the first chapter, as the four boys relate what they know of their family history, thus explaining the situation which has led to the feud between Gael and Gall, vivid details suggest what it would have been like to live under the primitive conditions existing in the ancient castle in far-away Lothian. But as the second book is only half the length of the first and White had already created an historical context for his story, it is perhaps not surprising that he largely refrains from interpolating the descriptive passages so lovingly woven into the story of the Wart. There are, however, some typical set pieces, such as the plain of Bedegraine with its forest of pavilions and attendant crowds:

> All round and about the tents there were cooks quarrelling with dogs who had eaten the mutton, and small pages writing insults on each other's backs when they were not looking, and elegant minstrels with lutes singing tunes similar to "Greensleeves", with soulful expressions, and squires with a world of innocence in their eyes, trying to sell each

other spavined horses, and hurdy-gurdy men trying to earn a groat by
playing the vielle, and gipsies telling your fortune for the battle. . . .

                                                                    (OFK 271)

Time passes in as remarkable a way as in *The Sword in the Stone*: the battle of
Bedegraine was 'in some ways the twelfth century equivalent of what later
came to be called a Total War' (OFK 306), while the fifteenth century
(though White does not say so) has clearly been reached by the time of the
arrival of the wedding party at Carlion, since pretty ladies are 'mincing
along in high dunces' caps with veils floating from the top of them' (OFK
319): he never much bothered about historical precision. He for the most
part fills out the background of his narrative with the farcical Questing
Beast episodes, rather than with scenes from medieval life.

In the place of the cancelled passages relating to the 'village' and
Palomides in *The Witch in the Wood*, White by putting in the much more
serious chapters involving Arthur and Merlyn, leading up to the battle
of Bedegraine, at last managed to solve the problems of proportion, focus
and tone that had troubled him earlier. By inserting the discussions between Arthur and Merlyn on the subject of Might versus Right, he keeps
Arthur before the reader, and prepares effectively for the establishment
of the Round Table in *The Ill-Made Knight*. Similarly, by sharpening up
the alternating scenes in which Gawaine and his brothers appear, he was
able to suggest their future importance as actors in the unfolding drama,
and so to motivate the rest of the action in *The Once and Future King* as
a whole.

White's original plan for his second Arthurian book to be purely comedy
proved in the end to be unworkable. However in its final form the book
forms a bridge between Arthur's untroubled childhood and the problems
and achievements of his reign, as well as showing how the seeds of the
ultimate disaster were sown. The final version as it appears in *The Once and
Future King* of 1958 achieves a much more unified tone: comedy remains,
but the element of farce is markedly reduced. In *The Witch in the Wood*, there
were only four chapters in a total of thirty-four in which the scene changed
from Orkney to Arthur and Merlyn and the crucial battle. After White's last
revision, in the book as we now have it, no less than seven out of fourteen
chapters take the reader back to Arthur and his problems. Chapters II to IV
are all concerned with Arthur, and thereafter every alternate chapter relates
to the King. In Chapter XII, moreover, White as 'historian' gives a serious
account of the great battle, replacing the original humorous report given by
King Lot in his letter home. The final version thus takes up a very different
attitude to war.

White keeps before the reader the progress from barbarism to civilisation
associated with Merlyn's continuing tutelage of Arthur by means of the
alternation between Lothian, far away in the North, and Arthur's camp.
The seven chapters which deal with Arthur's affairs show him abandoning

the view that battles are great fun, and eventually forming the intention of
trying to harness Might in the service of Right. He still has many lessons to
learn when we first see him as king in *The Queen of Air and Darkness*. He is
young and thoughtless, with a young man's natural energy, and he regards
fighting as fun, but now it is time for him to begin to think seriously about
the state of the country. Merlyn is still active as his mentor, accusing him of
being stupid, while Arthur obtusely fails to see what he is doing wrong. At
first he is quite unable to think of his kerns (humble foot-soldiers or serfs)
as human beings. Merlyn points out to him that battles are all very well for
knights in armour, but a very different matter for the kerns. ' "When you
said about the battle being a lovely one, you were thinking like your
father" ' (OFK 228), he says. In other words, he is behaving like a conquering Norman when he should be helping on the progress of civilisation.
Merlyn explains to him the difference between the glamour of chivalry –
defined as merely being rich enough to have a castle and a suit of armour –
which guarantees safety to the well-armed knight, and the inevitable suffering which war, even when it is masquerading as chivalry, brings to
ordinary people:

> Look at the barns burnt, and dead men's legs sticking out of ponds,
> and horses with swelled bellies by the roadside, and mills falling
> down, and money buried, and nobody daring to walk abroad with
> gold or ornaments on their clothes. That is chivalry nowadays. That is
> the Uther Pendragon touch. And then you talk about a battle being fun!
> (OFK 229)

Merlyn, as he explains 'the immortal feud of Gael and Gall', the hostility
between the Celts and Picts, or Old Ones, and the Normans, once again
tries to make Arthur think for himself, as he had done when he was a boy.
But Merlyn cannot deny that the reasons why wars break out are usually
complex, as ancient enmities interact with the force of personalities; and as
he denounces nationalist movements, his instruction seems only to add to
Arthur's confusion. All the same, at this point, Arthur as a young king is
still happy, like 'the man in Eden before the fall' (OFK 230), enjoying his
innocence and good fortune – a state of affairs not destined to last for long.

Merlyn's instruction continues by means of a reference to the pacifism,
which he now condemns as wrong-headed, that had been fashionable in
his youth, presumably, since he lives 'backwards' in time, in the 1930s.
However, he is still ready to insist that wars are so wicked that they must
not be allowed, 'though you might have a sort of duty to stop them'. (OFK
237)

> There is no excuse for war, none whatever, and whatever the wrong
> which your nation might be doing to mine – short of war – my nation
> would be in the wrong if it started a war so as to redress it. . . . Wrongs
> have to be redressed by reason, not by force.   (OFK 238)

The problem of the aggressor who is not able to reason is not considered. The discussion allows White to incorporate his current personal views on war into the narrative, while at the same time indicating how the enmity of Morgause and the Gaels constitutes a threat for the future. White's attitude to war was a source of anxiety to himself: the onset and progress of World War II was becoming an ever greater torment to him, intensified by his own uncertainty as to what part he ought to play in it, and what course of action he should take. Since he was too old to be conscripted there was no obvious obligation. The liberal-pacifist views of the 1930s were still powerful and in their way civilised influences. At the same time the nature of the Nazi evil was becoming ever more obvious and more dangerous. In 1938 he had written to several friends for their advice: Sir Sydney Cockerell had advised him not to join up, but to wait until a suitable occupation should appear. J.F. Roxburgh had written from Stowe to say that he should not go out as cannon-fodder but should do something in Intelligence. The advice which most appealed to him, however – and which he deliberately took – was Ray Garnett's. In his journal for 9 October 1938 he wrote that Ray:

> said almost anybody could be taught to stick bayonets into people, but it took much longer to teach the rules of grammar. So we decided that we would try to help with our pens, while there was time, because we had to do something, however little it was.

Earlier in the year similar ideas had occurred to him: on 31 March 1938 he wrote:

> it is the duty of the intelligent, imaginative and loving men to preserve themselves alive. It is this duty to be repositories of culture in the medieval darkness which looms ahead. If they do not survive, to tell somebody of love and beauty, all will be Hitler, all be Mussolini, all Chamberlain and Stalin, all fortified, bestial, boarish (sic) and mad, all subservient to robber-barons in the tortured gloom of mindless misery.

So the growing Arthurian epic became more and more concerned with the problem of finding an antidote to war, while White's internal conflict was at last resolved by the discovery that for some extraordinary bureaucratic reason he, an Englishman, was not allowed to leave Ireland.

In accord with these developments, Merlyn's position gradually changes and he abandons completely the pacifism that he had fervently upheld in the Boer War. He now admits that when 'the aggressor is as plain as a pikestaff' it might be the duty of decent men to fight the criminal. Arthur has succeeded to a kingdom torn with racial hatreds, in which the nobility fight each other for fun, and the poor suffer. He cannot rely on pure reason to control the still primitive nobility. He must teach them reason and morality by force – the old, ancient and dangerous dilemma for the good man.

The moral as well as the practical necessity for the battle of Bedegraine was perhaps suggested by White's reading of Victor Duruy's *Short History of France*,[6] in the end-paper of which he wrote:

> The course of power in all countries seems to have been from antagonistic petty kings to a single king (he has to make a revolution against them) and then from the single king to the people (they have to make a revolution against him).

In the same book he marked a passage which reads:

> The king's peace was imposed upon the turbulent vassals of the crown; the king's justice and the king's money were established and the crown legislated for all.

White based his account of the battle on Malory's in Book I of *Le Morte Darthur*, in which Arthur with the help of Merlion overcomes the eleven kings who are opposed to him with their vast armies. The strategy of the surprise attack at night, followed by the ambush, are both suggested by Merlion, who after 45,000 have been slain in the battle by Arthur's forces, comes to him on a great black horse and asks him if he has not had enough, before he leaves him victorious to go to his 'master Bleise in North Humberland', as White has it. Arthur's great battle is justifiable in order that the realm may enjoy peace and stability, but while he is struggling to find some way to deal with the problems of aggression, Gawaine and his brothers in the next chapter, in their conversation with St Toirdealbhach, make plain the nature of the difficulties he will have to encounter in trying to change the attitudes of his own knights. With the exception of Gareth, they are incorrigibly aggressive, for they have not surprisingly inherited the old-fashioned knightly view of armed combat and regard war as a form of sport. Arthur will have to deal not only with the old guard but also with the younger generation if he is to try to phase out aggression. In the cell of St Toirdealbhach, the boys delight in stories about war. They hear how the King of Ireland laments his inability to fight: ' "It's a hard fortune evidently, when a man can't be fighting a little bit unless he comes to the end of his days" ' (OFK 244). The saint, who enjoys more than anything else the chance to use his shillelagh in a good hand-to-hand encounter, regards war as 'the grand thing', though not it seems if very large numbers are involved, for then 'how would you know what you are fighting about at all?' (OFK 245) The boys, knowing nothing about the subject apart from what they have heard in these tales, are naturally very much in favour of wars. Only Gareth takes a more civilised view: 'what is the good of killing poor kerns who do not know anything?' (OFK 246).

When next we see Arthur he seems to have learned Merlyn's lesson: he

---

6 Duruy, Victor: *Histoire de France*, 1874. Translated as *A Short History of France*, London, Dent Everyman, 1928. For a fuller discussion of White's use of this book, see Chapter 9.

summons a council to talk about chivalry, reverting to the problem of Might versus Right. He feels his way towards the idea that it is necessary to establish domination first, and then to find some way of channelling the knights' aggressive instincts. He sees it as his task to bring a new order of things into being when the leaders of the old order – 'Lot and Uriens and Anguish and those' – have been subdued. It is tacitly admitted that chivalry cannot simply be abolished, but Might may still be harnessed 'so that it works for Right'. It is at this point that what is later to become the Round Table is conceived: the order of chivalry of which Arthur dreams will be an institution to which all knights will aspire to belong. At the same time the idea of what in Malory is called the Pentecostal Oath[7] (though White does not call it that) to which all the knights must subscribe, and which they must renew each year, also comes into being.

While the plans for the battle of Bedegraine are being drawn up, and Arthur's army awaits the beginning of hostilities, much discussion goes on about the new order. But while Arthur is a willing though apparently not very apt student of Merlyn still, Kay (like the Orkney clan) holds staunchly to the traditional notions of his class, despite Merlyn's continuing efforts to educate him too. He horrifies Merlyn by stating succinctly that a good reason for starting a war is simply to have a good reason. A king, he says, who discovered a new way of life for human beings might have to force it on them by the sword, if they would not otherwise accept it. Merlyn is convulsed with rage at the very suggestion. His reply alludes to Hitler as a man who had actually done this. He maintains that what is wanted is for ideas to be made available, but not imposed on people. Kay is unwilling to be put down, however: he points to the difficulty of deciding the rights and wrongs in political and military matters, and claims that: ' "Arthur is fighting the present war . . . to impose his ideas on King Lot" ' (OFK 274).

The Arthur and Merlyn chapters not only keep Arthur before the reader and allow White to incorporate his own views on the ethics of war, but also prepare for the final scene in which Morgause arrives at court with her designs on Arthur. Merlyn repeatedly but vainly tries to remember what it was he had to tell Arthur. His own future entanglement with Nimue is discussed, together with warnings about Guenever and Lancelot, and about the care that Arthur must take when using Excalibur, but still he cannot remember whether the warning has to do with the future or the past. Of course, it concerns both, but his exemplum about the man who rode to Aleppo to escape Death suggests that in any case the warning would be useless.

> There is a thing about Time and Space which the philosopher Einstein is going to find out. Some people call it Destiny.   (OFK 295)

---

7 See Vin 75.

As Merlyn's past foretells Arthur's future, the magician quotes Arthur's epitaph, while the young king unhappily wonders what the people of the future will be like, and whether they will even remember the Round Table: past, present and future flow into each other to suggest the timelessness of the legend.

The 'Arthur' chapters culminate appropriately in the actual battle, to which White devotes considerable space:

> It was a decisive battle, because it was in some ways the twelfth-century equivalent of what later came to be called a total war.
>
> (OFK 306)

King Lot's idea of war is now shown to be old-fashioned beside Arthur's: Lot's is 'the image of foxhunting without its guilt, and only twenty-five per cent of its danger' (OFK 306). As Merlyn had pointed out, the knights have little wish to kill each other, but no hesitation whatsoever in killing the serfs, any more than if they were vermin. Between the two enormous opposing armies of Old Ones and Sassenachs, there is serious racial enmity, but Arthur is at last learning the lesson that Merlyn has for so long been trying to teach him, and has 'begun to set a value on heads, shoulders and arms . . . even if the owner was a serf' (OFK 307). He now abandons the old idea of war as being for sport and acquisition; no ransoms are to be demanded, and his knights are to fight only their equals.

Arthur begins the battle with what in his opponents' eyes is 'an atrocity', with a surprise attack by night, and he follows it up with another; he ignores the infantry, made up of humble kerns, and goes straight for the knights. By giving a direct account of the battle himself instead of reporting it, White is able to set in opposition the old and the new modes of waging war, and to treat the whole episode with greater seriousness. The young Arthur's aim is to put an end to war by waging real war, until its 'real lords' are 'ready to refrain from warfare, being confronted with its reality' (OFK 307–8). In a moment of insight, he realises that it is to be his destiny throughout life 'to deal with every way of twisting decency by threats of Power'. White stresses the importance of duty, of 'doing a hateful and dangerous action for the sake of decency', without reward. His emphasis falls on these traditional but now unfashionable British virtues which, however he may sometimes seem to mock them, were in fact fundamental to his attitude to life, and very firmly held.

Much as he has deplored war, he nevertheless in a highly rhetorical passage gives a very zestful account of the battle – perhaps because it can be seen as 'fair', since knight fights knight, and since Arthur's cause is good. The reader is invited to imagine a cavalry charge:

> . . . you may have seen a cavalry charge. If so, you know that "seen" is not the word. It is heard – the thunder, earth-shake, drum-fire, of the bright and battering sandals! Yes, and even then it is only a cavalry

charge you are thinking of, not a chivalry one. Imagine it now, with the horses twice as heavy as the soft-mouthed hunters of our own midnight pageants, with the men themselves twice heavier on account of arms and shield. Add the cymbal-music of the clashing armour to the jingle of the harness. Turn the uniforms into armour to the jingle of the harness. Turn the uniforms into mirrors, blazing with the sun, the lances into spears of steel. Now the spears dip, and now they are coming. The earth quakes under feet. Behind, among the flying clods, there are hoof-prints stricken in the ground. It is not the men that are to be feared, not their swords nor even their spears, but the hoofs of the horses. It is the impetus of that shattering phalanx of iron – spread across the battle-front, inescapable, pulverising, louder than drums, beating the earth.   (OFK 310)

Among the infantry, there are three Gaels to every Gall but Arthur, though wishing the kerns and gallowglasses[8] no harm, realises that 'they would have to be allowed their fight'. The sentence draws attention to what seems a paradox of men's attitude to war: the poor kerns are to be pitied when they are killed in Arthur's first battle, yet at Bedegraine, they themselves will be disappointed if they are prevented from having a good fight. There may be no excuse for war, but one of the reasons why it does occur is that there are always men like St Toirdealbhach who really do want to fight, and plenty of others ready to join them.

The significance of the battle is suggested by an undated entry in one of White's notebooks, at a point when he was revising his second Arthurian book once again:

He put down, at Bedegraine and against the Dictator of Italy, the feudal idea of Might in sporting ransom-hunting warfare with little danger to the Ms.F.H.[9] He substituted a sort of Total War, to stop the sporting one.

It is Arthur's only great military success in *The Once and Future King*: he is not otherwise presented as a mighty conqueror. The celebration which ends the book is not a 'triumph', and does not include jousts and tourneys as often in medieval Arthurian stories: it is of course the absurd episode of the double wedding of King Pellinore with Piggy and St Toirdealbhach with Mother Morlan, which brings Morgause to Arthur's court with disastrous consequences.

---

8 'Gallowglass' or 'galloglass' is a now obsolete term dating from the early sixteenth century, denoting 'One of a particular class of soldiers or retainers formerly maintained by Irish chiefs' (O.E.D.).

9 Masters of Foxhounds.

4

The Ill-Made Knight

The Ill-Made Knight, the Book of Sir Lancelot, is a brilliant amalgam of fantasy and realism. It includes Arthur's consolidation of the Round Table and his position as king, the long loves of Lancelot and Guenever, and the Grail Quest. But if the two earlier books are difficult to categorise, *The Ill-Made Knight* is even more so. White had intended that its genre should be romance, but it has many of the features of the realistic novel. As such, it effects a transition between the 'poetic' *Sword in the Stone* and the often farcical *Queen of Air and Darkness*, and the developing tragedy in the final book.

White, referring to his third Arthurian volume as 'The Idea in the Mind' when he was in the early stages of writing it, had repeatedly emphasised in his letters to Potts and others that its genre was to be 'Romance'. That what he ultimately achieved was rather different is suggested by his own declaration in a letter to David Garnett when, in August 1941, he gives an indication of what he had tried to do in the now completed book:

> Mallory states the actions and some few of the conversations, but he does not pursue the motives and characters behind them, which is what I tried to do. In any case I never pretended to be more than a footnote to Mallory: it is a kind of literary criticism of him.
>
> (W/G L 91).

The following month, in a letter to Garnett's son Richard, who had offered some criticism of the book to the effect that it was too compressed, he said:

> I have been through the Ill-Made Knight on your advice, putting in little bits of scenic effect – stained glass windows, September corn fields and all that sort of thing. It was quite true that the book lacked visualisation. I dont think that I have put in enough even now, but I am afraid of distracting from the main object of that particular section, which was to deal with Lancelot & Guenever as characters.
>
> (W/G L 96)

Although he evidently accepted that there was a need for some revision, the book had been much easier to write than *The Witch in the Wood*, with the rewriting of which he was still struggling that summer. In his third book he identified with Lancelot, as a result of which it flowed into a unity that he had not been able to achieve before. This identification must have been in some ways more congenial than his earlier self-projection as Merlyn, and it gave his writing an impetus which the troubled and angry obsession with the evil mother-figure of Morgause in the second book could not. The third book is both deeply felt, and a triumph of imagination.

i. Love and Romance

Umberto Eco in *Postscript to the Name of the Rose* says that 'Romance is the story of an elsewhere'.[1] His definition, which embraces Tolkien and the Gothic novel, is probably broad enough to include *The Once and Future King* in its entirety, even though for White the work as a whole was an epic. In romance, says Eco, we have 'the past as scenery, pretext, fairy-tale construction, to allow the imagination to rove freely'. In *The Ill-Made Knight* it can rove freely, the more since the work includes the quest for the Holy Grail and the problems with which Arthur finds himself threatened by the Orkney faction, but this book can hardly be called a romance, properly speaking, since the main characters are individuals rather than types, and the pattern of the quest for love, concluding in the happy union of the lovers, does not really apply here. Nor – though the love-story of Lancelot and Guenever has always been felt to be 'romantic' – is White's version romantic in tone. The torment and complexity of Lancelot's internal conflict and the jealousy of Guenever militate against romantic feeling, and what start out as tender scenes between the lovers often end in the disharmony of misunderstanding. Because White amplifies where Malory merely hints, the tension and frustration which both lovers feel are made more explicit:

> They had hysterical scenes together, about his weakness and shamness, alternating with other scenes of a more affectionate kind. . . . But two lines came between her eyebrows, and she had a frightening eye sometimes, which glittered like a diamond. Lancelot began to have a dogged look. They were drifting.   (OFK 521)

The psychological realism of the modern novel rather than the idealism of medieval romance dominates *The Ill-Made Knight*. But we have to take White's word for it (as indeed we do with Malory, too) that ungovernable passion bound the lovers together throughout their adult lives, for their love is observed from a distance.

---

[1] Eco, Umberto: *Postscript to The Name of the Rose*, translated by William Weaver. San Diego, New York and London, Helen and Kurt Wolff, 1983.

White was not interested in so-called courtly love, as manifested in medieval literature, in many Arthurian stories, such as one of Malory's ultimate indirect sources, Chrétien's *Le Chevalier de la Charrette*,[2] the archetypal medieval romance of love. Medieval convention gives place to modern naturalism in the relationship between the lovers, though Guenever is scarcely less demanding than in Chrétien. White followed Malory closely, except in conflating Elayne the mother of Galahad with Elayne of Ascolat, thus removing from his book what is probably Malory's most romantic tragic love-story. In *Le Morte Darthur*, the young and beautiful Elayne falls passionately in love with Lancelot, nurses him back to health when he is dangerously wounded, and eventually dies when he rejects her. Malory's Elayne of Ascolat has a charm denied to White's composite Elaine, who is made to seem physically unattractive, unappealing as a personality and inclined to be over-possessive; and since the account of her death is very briefly narrated, the pathos is greatly reduced. The force of her attachment to Lancelot is felt (as of course is Guenever's), but her plainness and persistence de-romanticise it. Like Morgause and Guenever, she too is a man-eater.

Although the love between Lancelot and Guenever is the mainspring of the action in *The Ill-Made Knight*, Guenever's love only finds expression in jealousy, while Lancelot is much of the time shown as a reluctant lover who would prefer to follow a religious vocation. White's success in convincing the reader of the intensity of their emotions and the indissolubility of their relationship derives in the first instance from the intrinsic power of the traditional narrative, and secondly from his sympathetic insight into the reactions of Arthur, aware of but not consciously recognising or acknowledging what is going on. The love-affair is embedded in the on-going life of the realm, taking its place amongst the problems arising from other matters, and it begins with an unromantic falling in love. The process is simply indicated: Guenever takes it upon herself to help Lancelot when he is hawking, and does it badly. He is impatient and rude, and then realises that he has hurt 'a real person', someone who is able to think and feel. Uncle Dap notices what is happening and remonstrates, while Arthur's reaction is complicated, but he decides that the best thing to do will be to take Lancelot with him to the Roman war. It is not love at first sight, as in the medieval romance tradition, nor is there much indication of the subsequent development of the relationship, nor are there really any passionate exchanges between the lovers, as in some Victorian re-tellings of the story. Instead, the affair is represented in a down-to-earth way, in terms of twentieth-century conventions. It proceeds quite gradually, and eventually becomes apparent to other people as Lancelot's behaviour gives the game away. White takes it for granted that we all know how deeply attached to

2   See Chrétien de Troyes, *Arthurian Romances*, translated by D.D.R. Owen. London, Dent Everyman 1987.

each other the lovers were, so there is little need to put in any tender scenes, much less show them in bed together. In this respect he remains close to Malory, and his avoidance of anything sexually explicit marks the difference between his version of the story and most modern versions. Although *The Ill-Made Knight* seems to be aimed at adult rather than juvenile readers, there is nothing that even in the 1940s would have made it unsuitable for the young and innocent. Just occasionally White hints at the strength of the lovers' feeling for each other, as when Lancelot returns from his adventures with all his captives, and he and the Queen look at each other 'with the click of two magnets coming together' (OFK 379). A little later, concealment is becoming difficult:

> Arthur, whose head was still in his hands, raised his eyes. He saw that his friend and his wife were looking at each other with the wide pupils of madness, so he quickly attended to his plate.   (OFK 381)

Since White was never to experience happy and fulfilled love himself, it is hardly surprising that he did not amplify Malory's terse narrative in this respect. The nearest that he is able to get to describing the lovers' happiness is by a rather bizarre comparison with salmon. After his seduction by Elaine, Lancelot returning to Camelot and the Queen, 'came like an arrow to the heart of love', and he and Guenever had a year of joy:

> twelve months of the strange heaven which the salmon know on beds of river shingle, under the gin-clear water.   (OFK 398)

This must be one of the oddest images of happy sexual love ever to have been created, but despite the gin, it has a certain purity and genuineness of effect, and it evokes a self-contained, fulfilled placidity in an enclosed and beautiful world where movement is graceful and unaffected.

White expands his source-material by making the reader aware of the problems inherent in the eternal triangle, and by emphasising the lovers' dilemma rather than their delight in each other. Even in the scene intended to illustrate their happiness in the first year, their real incompatibility is apparent. Guenever can neither comprehend nor sympathise with the spiritual side of Lancelot's nature. ' "Well, I can't say I understand" ', she says as he talks about his aspirations and his miracles: ' "The whole thing seems fanciful to me . . . I don't understand it" ' (OFK 400).

Guenever's ungovernable jealousy soon dominates the relationship, as it does in *Le Morte Darthur*. Malory shows us the queen 'nyghe oute of her wytte' when she discovers that Launcelot has been in bed with Elayne. She reproaches him with vehemence:

> "A, thou false traytoure knyght! Loke thou never abyde in my courte, and lyghtly that thou voyde my chambir! And nat so hardy, thou false traytoure knyght, that evermore thou com in my syght!"   (Vin 487)

White makes a great effort to understand how Guenever must have felt – in relationship to Arthur, to Lancelot, and to Elaine and her baby. Although he resorts at times to speculation rather than to dramatisation, his attempts are both sympathetic and successful. On the other hand, he also allows her to make scenes reminiscent of Morgause in *The Witch in the Wood*. When, for example, she sees Lancelot after being confronted with the *fait accompli* of Elaine and her baby, 'her sweetness and reason are gone' and she speaks as if addressing a meeting, but this is as nothing to what follows, when Lancelot has again been tricked into spending the night with Elaine:

> Guenever was stiff, as if she were in a rigor, and her face was drained white – except that there was a red spot on either side of her nostrils. She looked as if she had been seasick. (OFK 413)

She is continually railing at Lancelot: ' "I suppose you will go to be near your trull?" ' . . . ' "Am I to watch you flirting with that turnip?" ' (OFK 514–15). She grows old ungracefully, and cries and makes scenes like a fishwife, giving Mordred the opportunity of remarking that he can understand a fishwife, but not a fishmistress. For all his reading of the Russian novelists recommended by Ray Garnett, there were still times when White seems unconsciously to have taken his mother as his model once again.

He makes it clear that, like Malory, he is telling a 'story of love in the old days, when adults loved faithfully – not a story of the present, in which adolescents pursue the ignoble spasms of the cinematograph' (OFK 539). So we see Lancelot in castle Bliant with Elaine, nursed back to health after his madness, 'looking towards Camelot with desperate eyes' (OFK 433). He and Guenever struggle for a quarter of a century to reach their understanding: meanwhile, the long time-span of their love and of Arthur's noble endurance is set against the background of the nation's gradual progress towards civilisation under his rule. Experience proceeds at different speeds, concentrated and condensed as it was in the Wart's educative visits to the various creatures, or seeming long drawn out as is the growth of the trees in the first edition of *The Sword in the Stone*.

While the lovers are approaching their Indian Summer, Arthur's land of Gramarye, as White calls England at its best, is at peace, Fort Mayne replaced by an embryonic system of justice, so that (in *The Candle in the Wind*), they can look at the sundown of chivalry as they sing together in harmony (OFK 570). White later emphasises – in a way that Malory never does – their age. Just before Mordred's attack, Lancelot is brushing the grey hair of his 'sweet old Jenny'. The embarrassing homeliness of the scene between this elderly pair drastically reduces its dignity. White never achieved the austere splendour of Malory's way of indicating the lovers' relationship at this crucial point:

> Than he toke the quene in hys armys and kyssed her and seyde, 'Most nobelest Crysten quene, I besech you, as ye have ben ever my speciall good lady, and I at all tymes your poure knyght and trew unto my power . . . that ye woll pray for my soule if that I be slayne' (Vin 676).

But, as White remarks elsewhere, 'That way of telling the story can only be done once' (OFK 459). The differences are significant. Malory surrounds Guenever with an aura of nobility and dignity, while at the same time suggesting the passionate nature of the lovers' relationship and its intimacy. But the physical contact is set within the context of Launcelot's lifelong devotion and service and Guenever's acceptance of it, from her superior position: 'as ye have ben ever my speciall good lady' . . . 'your poure knyght and trew'. The passage suggests an underlying attitude approaching worship on the part of Launcelot, and a worthiness to receive such devotion on the part of Guenever, aspects of the medieval concept of romantic love which involve humility and noble unswerving, lasting devotion on the part of the lover. The relationship as re-created by White, convincing as it is, is not at all the same.

He is not, however, attempting totally to up-date the story. White is genuinely trying to explain how it would have been, as it were. 'Why did not Lancelot make love to Guenever, or run away with his hero's wife altogether, as any enlightened man would do today?' he asks, with more than a touch of irony, when it has become overwhelmingly clear that they are in love with each other (OFK 383).[3] 'One reason for his dilemma was that he was a Christian', White explains, and so he 'put a higher value on chastity than is fashionable in our century' (OFK 384). 'His Church, in which he had been brought up – and it is difficult to escape from your upbringing – directly forbade him to seduce his best friend's wife.' Nevertheless he *did* seduce his best friend's wife, despite his Christian principles and bond of loyalty to Arthur. The mention of upbringing at this point is significant, for Lancelot is also restrained by 'the impediment of his nature. In the secret parts of his peculiar brain, those unhappy and inextricable tangles which he felt at the roots, the boy was disabled by something which we cannot explain.' Lancelot is created in White's own image in *The Ill-Made Knight*, and is no more able than his creator to escape from his upbringing.

ii. Lancelot and the 'Eternal Quadrangle'

In a letter to Potts of 9 April 1940, White wrote:

> You are quite wrong about Lancelot. He was an intensely *ugly* man, quite startling to look at, and he was distressed about this. When he took a nomme de guerre, he called himself Le Chevalier Mal Fait. He was also a sadist and very much muddled up psychologically. This was

3 See White's comments, quoted below (Chapter 10 and note), in *W/G L* pp. 274–5, on the binding nature of the 'solemn, voluntary oath' in marriage.

why he always had to be merciful etc. He was a romantic, and wanted to 'do miracles'. His Guenever trouble was not Arthur, but the miracles. But you will have to read my third volume, before you understand him. (Little boys still believe that they won't be able to bowl well in the 1st XI match tomorrow, if they abuse themselves today, and Lancelot was captain of the 1st XI. Guenever, whom he couldn't stop, was stopping his two main things – his bowling (feats of arms) and his miracles.) He was top of the battling averages . . . and he did manage to perform 2 miracles. (LF 111)

White clearly gave a great deal of thought to the delineation of Lancelot, in order to fill out and interpret for the modern reader the character presented by Malory. In his journal for 27 September 1939 he tabulated his perceptions:

Mallory's Lancelot is:
    1. Intensely sensitive to moral issues.
    2. Ambitious of true – not current – distinction.
    3. Probably sadistic, or he would not have taken such frightful care to be gentle.
    4. Superstitious or totemistic or whatever the word is. He connects his martial luck with virginity, like the schoolboy who thinks he will only bowl well in the match tomorrow if he does not abuse himself today.
    5. Fastidious, monogamous, serious.
    6. Ferociously puritan to his own body. He denies it and slave-drives it.
    7. Devoted to "honour", which he regards as keeping promises and "having a word". He tries to be consistent.
    8. Curiously tolerant of other people who do not follow his own standards. He was not shocked by the lady who was as naked as a needle.
    9. Not without a sense of humour. It was a good joke dressing up as Kay. And he often says amusing things.
    10. Fond of being alone.
    11. Humble about his athleticism: not false modesty.
    12. Self critical. Aware of some big lack in himself. What was it?
    13. Subject to pity. cf no. 8.
    14. Emotional. He is the only person Mallory mentions as crying from relief.
    15. Highly strung: subject to nervous breakdowns.
    16. Yet practical. He ends by dealing with the Guenever situation pretty well. He is a good man to have with you in a tight corner.
    17. Homosexual? Can a person be ambi-sexual – bi-sexual or whatever? His treatment of young boys like Gareth and Côte Male Tale is very tender and his feeling for Arthur profound. Yet I do so want not to have to write a "modern" novel about him. I could only bring myself to mention this trait, if it is a trait, in the most oblique way.

18. Human. He firmly believes that for him it is a choice between God and Guenever, and he takes Guenever. He says: This is wrong and against my will but I cant help it.

It seems to me that no. 12 is the operative number in this list. What was the lack? On first inspection one would be inclined to link it up with no. 17, but I don't understand about bisexuality, so cant write about it. There was definitely something "wrong" with Lancelot, in the common sense, and this was what turned him into a genius. It is very troublesome.

After this analysis, White goes on to list a number of 'people he was like':

1. Lawrence of Arabia,
2. A nice captain of the cricket xi,
3. Parnell,
4. Sir W.Raleigh;
5. Hamlet,
6. me,
7. Prince Rupert,
8. Montrose,
9. Tony Ireland or Um Simruniah or whatever,
10. Any mad man,
11. Adam.

This fascinating list would merit much explanation and explication if space permitted. It illustrates a remarkable range of potential heroes, who have in common one characteristic, their obsessive nature. Most of them were destined to a tragic end.

Item no. 6 in the list shows that White consciously identified with Lancelot while he was writing *The Ill-Made Knight*, whether or not he deliberately created a self-portrait. Lancelot's 'shame and self-loathing' which had been implanted when 'he was tiny, by something which it is now too late to trace', have their counterpart in White's childhood experience: he had himself been made to feel that he was 'horrible' by his mother, who had complained about the thickness of his lips when he was a little boy, and insisted that he should be made to hold them in. So with Lancelot:

> The boy thought that there was something wrong with him. All through his life – even when he was a great man with the world at his feet – he was to feel this gap: something at the bottom of his heart of which he was aware, and ashamed, but which he did not understand.
>
> (OFK 327)

Ray Garnett had provided this insight, quoted verbatim by White in Chapter X, 'It is so fatally easy to make young children believe that they are horrible' (OFK 383).

There is no basis in Arthurian tradition for the assumption that the 'best knight of the world', as Malory calls him, was either grotesquely ugly or ape-like, or aware of being so, as White must have known. On the contrary, Lancelot was outstandingly handsome, though Malory does not refer to this. But as White later explains, the title can be interpreted in other ways as well; it can mean the Knight Who Has Done Wrong, as well as the Ill-Starred Knight, the Knight with a Curse on Him (OFK 431). It is sad that White should have felt that such a title applied to him.

Lancelot was made to resemble the author in other ways, too: the integrity attributed to him in *The Ill-Made Knight* is seen in terms of White's own moral code. His letters and Sylvia Townsend Warner's biography reveal over and over again his moral scrupulousness and decency. Like his Lancelot he was, as he eventually told David Garnett, a sadist,[4] who struggled throughout his life to restrain the impulses which he believed derived from 'something which we cannot explain'. So Lancelot, knowing that his nature inclines him towards cruelty and cowardice, forces himself to be brave and kind. On the other hand, White does not seem to have had the highly developed spiritual nature that he attributed to Lancelot, who had been 'a very holy little boy' (OFK 399).

White indirectly suggests that there is an incestuous element, though unrecognised as such, in the relationship between Lancelot and Guenever. Guenever in *The Once and Future King*, as elsewhere in Arthurian literature, is in a sense a mother-figure, even though she is childless and represented as being about the same age as Lancelot. A strange tangle of relationships arises between the protagonists: White suggests that perhaps Guenever loved Arthur as a father, and Lancelot because of the son she could not have (OFK 498). Even in the traditional story, Launcelot's devotion to the superior quality of Guenever has something filial in it, as has most romantic love in medieval stories.

The tension between them is intensified by the sense of guilt about their relationship which torments Lancelot. His distress is explained in terms of the fear that he will be unable to do miracles because of his sexual guilt, guilt which seems to arise from something other than the realisation that he has committed adultery and betrayed his lord and best friend. At the beginning of the last chapter of *The Ill-Made Knight*, White concludes:

> Well, that is the long story of how the foreigner from Benwick stole Queen Guenever's love, of how he left her for his God and finally returned in spite of the taboo.   (OFK 539)

He refers to Lancelot's breaking of his taboo three times in this chapter, while at the same time he explains that 'God was Lancelot's totem' (OFK 540), commenting on how he had been trapped by Elaine 'on that terrible

---

4   White told David Garnett of his sadistic tendencies on the last occasion on which they met, some time after the publication of Garnett's *Aspects of Love* in late 1955. Garnett regretted that he had not known earlier, so that he could have better understood his friend.

evening so that he broke his taboo', and referring to it again just before the healing of Sir Urre. The conjunction of totem with taboo in this chapter constitutes an indirect reference to Freud's *Totem and Taboo*,[5] and for Freud, taboo meant incest with the mother. Although David Garnett in *The Familiar Faces*[6] says of White, 'it is impossible to imagine his mind being influenced by Freud or Proust', he was certainly conversant with the former, and in any case hardly any intellectual in the 1930s could avoid such influence. His library contained a large number of books on psychology, among them Freud's *Introductory Lectures on Psychoanalysis* (1923). It would have been strange if he had not read such books while undergoing psychoanalysis, omnivorous reader as he was, and while he had free access to libraries. At Stowe, J.F. Roxburgh had made a point of encouraging the study and discussion of psychology among both the masters and the sixth-formers. White refers to Freud a number of times in *The Once and Future King*, for example when Merlyn advises Palomides on how to deal with the love-sick Questing Beast:

"Psycho-analyse her," he said eventually . . .
"Just find out what her dreams are and so on. Explain the facts of life.
But not too much Freud."   (OFK 315)

White's identification with Lancelot and his representation of Guenever in terms often similar to those in which he depicted the Witch in the Wood, acknowledged to be a portrait of the mother whom he detested, together with the Freudian references, indicate the undercurrents which help to give tragic force to *The Ill-Made Knight*. The sterility of the guilt-ridden relationship turns the third book away from romance and towards tragedy. Instead of Malory's powerful and glamorised knight, White's Lancelot is a tormented figure, unable to resolve the conflict which the Eternal Quadrangle of his love for God, Guenever and Arthur arouses in him. He is unable to break away from Guenever the 'man-eating lioncelle' who will not let him go, to find an appropriate partner outside the family circle. Even his initial seduction by Elaine was in effect a seduction by Guenever, since he was under the illusion that he was going to the Queen's bed. His horrified realisation of what he had done derived its anguish, not from the fact that he had slept with Elaine instead of the Queen, but from guilt and fear – the fear that he had 'lost his miracles'. He had thus committed an act which had not only damaged his integrity and gone against his true nature, but which was, in so far as he had believed that he was with Guenever, in a sense actually taboo. Potts commented on this incident:

I wish you had followed Malory in making Lancelot's shame be for

---

5 Freud, S.: *Totem and Taboo. Resemblances between the Psychic Lives of Savages and Neurotics.* Authorised English translation. London, 1919.
6 Garnett, D.: *The Familiar Faces*, London, Chatto and Windus 1962, p. 175.

having threatened to kill Elaine rather than for having begotten
Galahad. This lifts him above Guenever, where he ought to be.

(LF 127)

In combining Malory's two Elaines into one composite and consistently
unattractive figure, White deliberately (though perhaps without full realisation of the implications of the decision) made additionally sure that
Lancelot could not break out of the tragic Oedipal pattern, since there was
no acceptable alternative to Guenever. *The Ill-Made Knight* is thus as much
concerned with Lancelot's personal tragedy as *The Candle in the Wind* is
with Arthur's. Although his quest is spiritual, Lancelot can never escape
from the grasp of Guenever who even denies him the right to his individuality by refusing to acknowledge or attempt to understand his religious
aspirations. Malory's Guenever does not understand or sympathise with
Launcelot's spiritual yearnings after the Grail quest, but he is not thereby
diminished: differences of focus and of emphasis give him a grandeur
largely, if unintentionally, denied him by White.

While *Le Morte Darthur* was the sole actual source for *The Ill-Made Knight*,
White also found in Jessie Weston's *From Ritual to Romance*[7] support for his
interpretation of Lancelot's character. His opinion of Jessie Weston was not
exactly high: in his copy of her book such contemptuous marginal comments as 'and you are a school marm and nought else' are not infrequent.
Where it is maintained that Lancelot is in no special way connected with a
spear or lance, White sneers:

> No, of course he never used a lance at all, did he? You might as well
> say that Bradman was in no special way connected with a cricket bat.

(The Australian Bradman was the most famous cricketer in the world in the
1930s and '40s.) However, he marked with three lines in the margin some
sentences relating to Malory's sources which evidently helped to suggest
the possibilities open to him at this stage in his epic. He refers to the two
main strands of medieval French prose romance about Lancelot. One is the
courtly *Lancelot* and the other is the *Queste*, written probably by a Cistercian
in the thirteenth century, which is fundamentally anti-chivalric and anti-
courtly and emphasises Lancelot's sinfulness:

> In the *Queste* Lancelot's conscience is sorely vexed, and his sin in-
> sisted upon. The compilers of the *Lancelot* have a very courtly respect
> for women – the author of the *Queste* despises them utterly. The interest
> of the *Lancelot* lies in the relation between the sexes – the respective
> duties of knight and lady – the theme which inspires the *Queste* is their
> abiding separation.

It was towards the *Queste* that his sympathies led him.

---

7 Weston, Jessie L.: *From Ritual to Romance*, Cambridge 1920.

iii. Guenever

About the time that White was meditating on the character of Lancelot, he was also thinking about women in general – presumably because he knew that he would soon have to 'explain' Guenever. In his journal he wrote:

> Women:
> Something uncanny about their hysteria. It seldom goes so far as to do their real interests a mischief. Does it ever?

After quoting Freud on the subject, he continues with the comment that women are much more jealous than men, and that they are peculiar in their incapacity for detachment: 'The two most intelligent women I ever met were neither of them able for abstract speculation. Everything must refer to themselves.' It is perhaps hardly surprising that he should have found it difficult to understand women and to create credible female characters since his experience of them was so limited, a limitation shared with many of his male contemporaries. Noel Annan, a pupil of White's at Stowe, in *Our Age: Portrait of a Generation*[8] draws attention to the extent to which the society in which he himself grew up was polarised: 'gentlemanly pursuits' tended to separate men from women, who were to be regarded as a potential snare and should be treated warily. In schools:

> Women in any shape, even that of mother and sister, were unwelcome visitors; and the only feminine shapes to entrance boys' eyes were the ample form of the matron and the housemaster's wife, who lived on the other side of the impenetrable green baize door.

Annan comments on life in an all-male society in his generation, which was also White's: it was easy to grow up without coming into contact with women. The strong emphasis on the desirability of repressing the emotions also tended to make it extremely difficult for young men to be at ease with women.

White's journal indicates that he turned from the contemplation of the character of Lancelot in September 1939 to the specific problem of Guenever in the following month. On 10 October he was asking himself:

> Much more important question than what sort of person was Lancelot is what sort of person was Guenever?
> She must have been a nice person, or Lancelot and Arthur (both nice people) would not have loved her. Or does this not follow? Do nice people love nasty ones? Arthur was hardly a judge of nice people, or he

---

[8] Annan, Noel G.: *Our Age: Portrait of a Generation*, London, Weidenfeld & Nicolson, 1990, p. 43.

would not have had a child by Morgause. And Guenever hardly seems to have been a favourite of Mallory's, whatever Tennyson may have thought about her.

She was insanely jealous of Lancelot: she drove him mad. She was suspected of being a poisoner: she made no bones about being unfaithful to Arthur: she had an ungovernable temper: she did not mind telling lies: she was hysterical, according to Sir Bors: she was beastly to Elaine: she was intensely selfish.

The analysis suggests how closely and with what deep engagement with the characters White read *Le Morte Darthur*. In effect he takes them as real people, almost as contemporaries. A few lines further on, he considers Guenever's good qualities. His characterisation of her suggests a deep ambivalence towards her, but he consciously does his best to be fair:

> Guenever had some good characteristics. She chose the best lover she could have done, and she was brave enough to let him be her lover: she always stuck to Arthur, although unfaithful to him, possibly because she really liked him: when finally caught, she faced the music: she had a clear judgment of moral issues, even while defying them, a sort of common-sense which finally took her into a convent when she could quite well have stayed with Lancelot now that her husband was dead.
>
> Was this a piece of clear-sightedness or was it cowardice? One way to put it would be to say that she grasped the best of two men so long as she profited by it, but afterwards betrayed them both. When there was no more to be got out of the Arthur-Lancelot situation she preferred the convent. The other way to put it would be to say that she finally recognised her ill influence and thought it best to shut herself up.
>
> She was brave, beautiful, married young by treaty. She had very little control over her feelings, which were often generous: c.f. her tears, weeping as though she would die, over Lancelot's recovery.

After some reflections on the character of Elaine which seem to apply in the main to Elayne the mother of Galahad, rather than to Elayne of Ascolat in Malory, he continues:

> It is plain that Guenever was a woman of character. She must have been a passionate lover.
>
> Could she be a sort of tigress, with all the healthy charms and horrors of the carnivore? Is she to eat Lancelot as Morgause ate Arthur? It seems to make him by so much less the man. Yet both he and Arthur were hero-worshippers. Do people hero-worship tigresses? Arthur looked up to Merlin, and Lancelot looked up to Arthur. Were they both lookers-up, who needed a tigress to look up to?

In the end she seems to be (but is not really, White suggests) 'a sort of man-eating lioncelle', a heraldic beast with royal associations, and thus more appropriate than the tigress.

After Ray Garnett had come to White's rescue as he was struggling with the character of Guenever, by suggesting that he should turn to the Russian novelists in order to improve his understanding of women, his reading of *Anna Karenina* in particular helped him considerably. At first he was not impressed by it: in Vol. I he wrote: 'Considering what a wonderful person he is, Tolstoy is strangely full of nonsense', listing the subjects of Christianity, women, sport and farming as most revelatory of his shortcomings. In the end-papers of the second volume, however, he commented, 'Among other things, Tolstoy was a first-rate psychologist', and marginal notes in the text indicate his increasing sympathy with the views of the author. Furthermore, he evidently saw a parallel between the situation of Anna (actually referred to in Chapter XVI (OFK 405)) and that of Guenever which was to help him in *The Ill-Made Knight*. Anna is more self-aware than White allows Guenever to be, but her meditation in the train probably provided the basis for White's analysis of Guenever's state of mind when Lancelot returns after the Grail quest:

> My love grows more and more passionate and selfish, while his is dying, and that is why we are drifting apart . . . And there's no help for it. He is all in all to me, and I demand that he should give himself more and more entirely up to me. And he wants to get farther and farther away from me. Up to the time of our union we were irresistibly drawn apart. And nothing can be done to alter it. He says I am insanely jealous; but it is not true. I am not jealous, but unsatisfied. . . . If I could be anything but his mistress, passionately caring for nothing but his caresses – but I can't, and I don't want to be anything else. And my desire arouses his disgust, and that excites resentment in me, and it cannot be otherwise. . . . If he does not love me, but treats me kindly and gently out of a sense of duty, and what I want is not there – that would be a thousand times worse than having him hate me. It would be hell! And that is just how it is. He has long ceased to love me. And where love ends, hate begins.[9]

In Anna's reflections, Tolstoy seems to have provided a parallel in modern terms for Guenever's dissatisfaction and jealousy, suggested but not fully explored by Malory, on which White could draw for his own purposes. Writing to Potts at about this time he asked:

> Have you found what a remarkable person Guenever was? She is an Anna Karenina, but her trouble is that she has no children. . . . Guenever is one of the *realest* women in literature: not a Dresden shepherdess or any stereotyped figure, but somebody with a frightful temper, enormous reality etc. etc. She lives on a different plane. I treat her with the greatest respect, like somebody handling a cobra. But I like and admire

---

9 *Anna Karenina*, translated by Rochelle Townsend, Vol. II, Chapter XXX, p. 311 in the Dent Everyman edition which White used. He refers to Anna Karenina by name in Chapter XVI of *The Ill-Made Knight*.

cobras. I hold her tightly by the head and unfold the coils with respectful wonder, studying their firm markings and wonderful strangeness.

(LF 112)

Potts could be a severe critic: in response to this, after declaring that he and
his wife Mary had enjoyed *The Ill-Made Knight* he wrote:

I agree with her [Mary] that Guenever will do, on the whole. Am I right
in saying you have concealed, even partly *conquered* your dislike of her
very creditably? I think her convincing throughout. (LF 127)

The Russian novelists, however, could not tell White all that he felt that
he needed to know. In a long postscript to the above letter, he asks whether
Potts or Mary had heard anything about 'what love feels like at 50, or about
whether a man of 50 can go on loving a mistress of the same age, with
whom he has been sleeping for 30 years'. He also asked Mary to give him
some information 'about love-making during the change of life' – 'will she
write me a brief monograph on the subject (and will it get past the censor?)'
(LF 114)

Despite all his difficulties, the portrayal of Guenever is one of the most
successful features of *The Once and Future King* because of the psychological
realism with which White coloured in Malory's outline. Although she is
seen almost entirely from the outside, Guenever is set before the reader as a
real-life figure, as someone known but not known intimately, and about
whom one can only speculate. Her actual thoughts are very seldom revealed. She is, however, presented from a number of different angles, and
she ages convincingly as her story proceeds. She appears only in the background to begin with, as Lancelot is introduced to her, with fearless blue
eyes and startlingly black hair, she is merely 'that woman' as far as he is
concerned (OFK 348). To Arthur, she is his 'rose-petalled Guenever', adored
for her dash, and later remembered by him as a bold girl (OFK 505); and
she adores her famous husband, even though he is so old – eight years
older than she, in fact. At twenty-two, she is seen in general terms – 'It is
difficult to imagine her', and so White hypothesises about her character.
These 'must have been some of Guenever's characteristics at twenty-two,
because they are everybody's' (OFK 396) he says, after making a long list of
the features of youth. A similar method of speculation about both her
superficial preoccupations and her deeper, unrealised anxieties brings her
closer as an individual when the rivalry of Elaine for Lancelot's attention
becomes apparent to her:

Probably she was not over-strained by Elaine's immediate problem.
Probably she had no real suspicion against that side of Lancelot. Yet,
with her prescience, she was aware of dooms and sorrows outside her
lover's purview. It would not be accurate to say that she was aware of
them in a logical sense, but they were present in her deeper mind. . . .
    Perhaps she was actually jealous, not of Elaine, but of the baby.

Perhaps it was Lancelot's love for Arthur that she feared. Or it may
have been a fear of the whole position. . . .   (OFK 406)

Our narrator, at least, knows her well, and can set out the possible undercurrents in her mind which may account for what follows: her restlessness,
her unreasonable behaviour, and her cruelty. Of her three great virtues he is
in no doubt: courage, generosity and honesty (OFK 407). The rest of the
story is concerned (among other things, of course) with the testing of these
'great virtues' in various ways, and it is the extent to which Guenever
succeeds in maintaining them, or fails to do so, that is significant in making
her appear 'a real person' to the reader. It must be said that in the aggre-
gate, the qualities to which White draws the reader's attention in Guenever
are almost entirely unpleasant, but perhaps it is this very fact that makes
her lifelike. It also gives a sense of the power of the love between her and
Lancelot, as indeed it does in *Le Morte Darthur*.

White varies the portrait by also showing Guenever from Lancelot's
point of view, on his return after two years from the Grail quest, setting the
remembered image of the young girl beside the older woman. He sees an
idealised Guenever:

> a condemned and innocent child, holding her indefensible position
> with the contemptible arms of hair dye and orange silk, with which she
> had – with what fears? – hoped to please him.   (OFK 483)

Meanwhile, however, a dialogue is going on in her mind: she knows that
her make-up is 'making a guy of her' (a guy in the old sense of a grotesque
figure), and hates it, while at the same time she is also saying to herself:

> I am not old, it is illusion. I am beautifully made up. See, I will perform
> the movements of youth. I will defy the enormous army of age.   (*ibid.*)

There is an effective interplay between the double vision of each which
intensifies the sadness and inevitability of ageing.

Guenever's worst qualities were those that White had earlier attributed
to Constance White, in particular her love of self-dramatisation and her
liking for making scenes. In Malory, after Lancelot has 'gotyn a chylde uppon
Elayne', Guenever is wroth, and 'gaff many rebukes to sir Launcelot and
called hym false knyght', until Lancelot had told her all, including 'how he
was made to lye by her, "in the lyknes of you, my lady the quene" ', at
which point 'the quene hylde sir Launcelot exkused' (Vin 485). In *The
Ill-Made Knight*, Guenever (to do her justice) tries not to make a scene when
she hears about the incident, but she is soon in a frenzy, telling Lancelot not
to touch her and to go away, plucking at the neck of her dress as if it were
too tight for her, and beginning to cry (OFK 402). Her anger and jealousy
take a still more dramatic form in Chapter XVIII (in the scene already
discussed earlier) when she finds out that Lancelot has again spent the

night with Elaine. Again, some years later when White's Guenever hears about Lancelot and the red sleeve, she is of course enraged, accusing him of treachery, to the indignation of Bors who shrugs his shoulders and turns his back on her as he leaves, thus showing what he thinks of women. But the Queen rushes after him. 'She was not going to be cheated of her scene as easily as that' (OFK 520).

The shadow of Constance White again falls over Guenever when she makes a half-hearted attempt to vamp Galahad on his arrival at court, as Morgause had tried to vamp Sir Grummore and King Pellinore in *The Witch in the Wood*. Malory provides no precedent for this particular elaboration of the story, but the motivation suggested by White – 'a strange mixture of curiosity, envy and horror' – is subtle, and throws some further light on the character of Guenever (OFK 459).

After the Grail quest, White does not allow Lancelot to 'resorte unto quene Gwenivere agayne', so that 'they loved togydirs more hotter than they dud toforehonde' (Vin 611) as Malory does. While her lover has been away, the Queen has been 'petulant, cruel, contradictory, miserable' (OFK 496 ff.). After his return she changes, and her ladies are sure that Lancelot has become her lover again, but 'This was not the case.' White gives no reason for his departure from his source, except for the implication that Lancelot's spiritual aspirations hold him back. There follows what is perhaps White's most extended analysis of the character of Guenever. 'She was beautiful, sanguine, hot-tempered, demanding, impulsive, acquisitive, charming. . . . But . . . she was not promiscuous'. 'She must have been generous, too. It is difficult to write about a real person.' And he goes on to point out that her 'central tragedy was that she was childless', she had 'been robbed of her central attribute', and 'she was not cut out for religion'. She humours Lancelot in his desire to convert her to God: her reaction is given in terms of the insincerity of Morgause in *The Witch in the Wood*. Lancelot 'was a darling. She had agreed with every word he said – was a regular convert already' (OFK 500), but she is soon furious with him, 'as the months of holiness added together. Holiness? Selfishness, she cried to herself' (*ibid.*). White's departure from Malory gives her additional reasons for frustration and allows her to grow 'madder every day'. So, just after the poisoned-apple incident, we have a long diatribe, looking back once again to *The Witch*, in which Guenever rails at Lancelot in reported speech with a vulgarity born of frustration as well as jealousy.

It is not until after the death of Elaine and at the time of the Meliagrance episode that she accepts her defeat and is prepared to let Lancelot be himself, love his God, and do whatever he pleases; and at this point her character changes back from the jealous, vengeful virago that she has been so long, to the 'young creature' of happier times. She renounces her 'possessive madness' and becomes all sweetness. But White is non-committal about what happens when Lancelot appears at the window of Meliagrance's castle with its iron bars:

Nobody knows what they said to each other. . . Probably they agreed
that it was impossible to love Arthur and also to deceive him. Probably
Lancelot made her understand about his God at last, and she made him
understand about her missing children. Probably they fully agreed to
accept their guilty love as ended.   (OFK 533)

Lancelot tears out the bars, and 'Later still, the whispers faltered, and there
was silence in the darkness of the room.' That is all that White is prepared
to tell us. Malory is rather more explicit:

So, to passe uppon thys tale, sir Launcelot wente to bedde with the
quene and toke no force of hys hurte honde, but toke hys plesaunce
and hys lykynge untyll hit was the dawnyng of the day; for wyte you
well he slept nat, but wacched.   (Vin 657)

White rejected the overtly sexual nature of the episode indicated by Malory,
perhaps because he still had young readers in mind, but also because
deliberately or unconsciously he did not want to have to represent a relationship other than platonic. He did not want Lancelot to be the Queen's
lover in the full sense of the word, engulfed by her demanding sexuality
and deprived of his 'miracles'. Malory, however, comes to the rescue with
his comments on love in the old days:

For men and women coude love togydirs seven yerys, and no ly-
coures lustis was betwyxte them, and than was love trouthe and faythefulnes. And so in lyke wyse was used such love in kynge Arthurs
dayes.   (Vin 649)

White sums up love in those days as 'chivalrous, adult, long, religious,
almost platonic' (OFK 538), and now 'Lancelot had given his God to Guenever, and she had given him his freedom in exchange' (OFK 539).

iv. Arthur

Although *The Ill-Made Knight* is the book of Sir Lancelot, White keeps
Arthur before the reader, interweaving his concerns with those of the
lovers, and subtly showing him ageing with the passage of two decades.
His rôle which might be seen as that of ineffectual king and cuckold is so
managed that neither respect nor sympathy for him are lost. He takes on a
more substantial personality than Malory could give him, and despite his
continuing concern with the progress of civilisation within the realm, with
Might and Right and Justice, he is more than a mere mouthpiece for
White's views. He is both a symbolic figure, representing England, even
humanity itself, and an individual growing in wisdom as in maturity.

On Lancelot's return from his self-banishment, early in the story, Arthur
has conquered the Dictator of Rome, and is Emperor of all Europe, but

what is the use of that, he asks, 'if the whole place is fighting mad?' He is a kind, conscientious, peace-loving fellow, 'who had been afflicted in his youth by a tutor of genius', and now, 'in an effort to impose a world of peace, he found himself up to the elbows in blood' (OFK 380). Nevertheless there is a deep ambivalence in his attitude to fighting, despite the efforts of the 'tutor of genius' whose high-minded notions were so patently unworkable. One afternoon when Lancelot remarks to him ' "We don't see many arrows thrilling in people's hearts nowadays," ' he replies, ' "Thrilling! . . . What a splendid word to describe an arrow vibrating, just after it has hit!" ' He soon adds gloomily, ' "We don't get much of the old fighting in these decadent days" ' (OFK 448). White slips into the traditional attitude to warfare, and inadvertently reveals how natural it is for men to fight. Arthur's belief that the failure of the Round Table to ensure peace was caused by its being a channel for brute force, and his conviction that Right can only be established by right (OFK 450) fails to take into account the fact of man's belligerent nature. Kind, just, generous, simple and affectionate though White insists that he is, he still yearns for the 'old fighting'.

Arthur is seen under two distinct aspects, as king, and as friend and husband. Time passes, and he becomes no longer the 'crusader of a future day, but the accepted conqueror of a past one' (OFK 442). He is seen as England itself, but he seems to lack the charisma of Lancelot, the 'great Dulac'. Even so, he can be stern, even terrifying 'in his royal rage' when confronted by Gawaine and Mordred, fresh from the scene of the murder of their mother and Lamorak. The problem of how to put an end to 'feud law' and to establish lasting peace is always with him, and the Grail quest is actually his idea, as a means of finding a channel for Might so that it could work for God. Arthur's enthusiasm for his project contrasts with what Malory tells us, of the king's 'grete sorow' at the departing of his knights on the quest (Vin 522). But the idea of the spiritual quest as a means of movement towards a higher degree of civilisation is important, since Arthur's rule notionally refers to what in fact were several centuries, involving progress from the anarchy of the early medieval period, through the crusades, towards the more ordered rule of the late fifteenth century. Arthur gropes his way to an ideal of justice for all, even though it involves assenting to the burning of his own wife whom he believes to be innocent. Though White always represents Arthur as a private person, rather than as both private and 'public', he makes it clear that the king had been intended not for personal happiness, but for 'royal joys, for the fortunes of a nation' (OFK 539). His rule represents positive progress; he is inventing 'Law as Power', and in the new law courts, now that Fort Mayne is over, the lawyers are busy as bees.

White solved the problem of explaining Arthur's position in his private capacity as a cuckolded husband without destroying his dignity by building him up as a personality. From the beginning his kindness, generosity and evenness of temper are stressed. The warmth of his friendship for

Lancelot is taken for granted, and accounts for his not wanting to know what is going on. He is 'only a medieval savage' says White ironically, who 'knew no better than to try to be too decent for the degradation of jealousy' (OFK 408), though as in Malory, he knew perfectly well, unconsciously, that Lancelot and Guenever were lovers. Mordred thinks him a hypocrite. But Arthur is not completely complaisant or indifferent: at the Westminster jousts he takes the opposite side to Lancelot in the *grand mêlée*, tries to hurt him and loses his temper. Just for that one moment of anger, Arthur was the cuckold and Lancelot his betrayer, says White (OFK 524). He trusts Lancelot and Guenever not to cause a scandal, not even to make *him* aware of their relationship, not out of weakness, but because of the power that he possesses:

> He had been in the position of a husband who could, by a single command, solve the problem of eternal triangles by reference to the headman's block or to the stake.   (OFK 539)

They are at his mercy, and so 'his generous heart had been determined to remain unconscious.'

v. 'The Two Elaines'

White had problems in writing *The Ill-Made Knight*, not only with the middle-ageing of Guenever, but also with the Elaines:

> Trouble number 2 keeps my heart in my mouth, but I have made my choice and I shall have to brave it out. To confess it in one word, I have run the two Elaines together into one person. In my reading of the matter, the maid who floats down to Camelot is the same as the one who gave birth to Galahad: a fat old matron, pathetic and abandoned: her son dead: no lily maid. In one way this is a sensible, economical step (almost the only place at which I have wandered from Malory) but in others it is a mistake. I did it largely because I thought that M. may have himself been muddling his sources in this matter – for Lancelot's mother was herself called Elaine, and it seems really too pathological to give him *two* mistresses of the same name. Also it keeps the plot neater to have a single Elaine as one of the main figures of its eternal quadrangle.

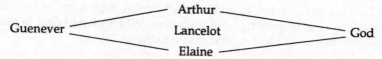

The objection is that Malory's *psychology* is better than my plot, when you reflect that most of the characters are about forty-five. It is just the

age at which Lancelot would seek a young girl, instead of the ageing
Guenever. And, by turning the 2 Elaines into one, I am eliminating the
young girl. It is a nasty problem.   (LF 114)

Given that White's intention in his third book was not, as he asserted, to
make a romance of it, but rather to re-tell Malory's story in terms of psychological realism, the running of the two Elaines together was a brilliant
inspiration. All the same, much was lost by the sacrifice of the 'lily maid':
Malory's Elayne of Ascolat dies of love for Launcelot with a touching
pathos. She is a charming youthful figure, whose unobtrusive but single-
minded devotion is a tribute to the charismatic nature of Launcelot, and her
death demonstrates the 'trouthe and faythefulnes' of the 'olde love . . . in
kynge Arthurs dayes' (Vin 649), and enhances the reader's awareness of its
power. She fades and dies like a flower. White's composite Elaine, though
she seems undemanding, indeed almost self-abnegating, gets Lancelot into
her castle and sets about destroying him in her own way. Her story, however, though it ends in the tragedy of suicide begins in the high comedy
characteristic of White's earlier books.

Lancelot is waylaid and made to visit the castle of Corbin, where in a
room so full of steam that he cannot see across it, he rescues from the magic
water, 'sitting shyly in the bath looking at him, a charming little lady, who
was – as Malory puts it – as naked as a needle.' When she has thus been
rescued she is handed over to the people outside:

> They had brought a dress with them, and the proper underwear, and
> the ladies of the village formed a circle in the gateway while the pink
> girl was dressed.
> "Oh, it does feel lovely to be dressed!" she said.   (OFK 386)

There follows the realistic comedy of Lancelot and the unctuous butler, the
episode which prepares for the begetting of Galahad, and another change
of tone, when Lancelot accuses Elaine of betraying him and stealing his
miracles. She is still the boiled girl, but gradually comes into focus more
clearly as an individual: 'She was eighteen, pitifully small in the big bed,
and she was frightened.' Unlike Malory's Elayne in similar circumstances,
however, she immediately goes on to alienate Lancelot: ' "I want to have
your baby," said Elaine. "I shall call him Galahad, like your first name" '
(OFK 393), causing Lancelot to turn on her in fury. White does not allow her
at this point the justification for her actions of the prophecy that must be
fulfilled.

White soon sets to work to make the 'charming little lady' of the magic
cauldron a very unappealing young woman. When he had first begun to
think about Elaine, he had been more sympathetic:

> Guenever was like most women, Elaine like most girls. Elaine never
> developed the adult feelings of the average woman: jealousy, pos-
> sessiveness, self-reference. She remained a poor little thing at the mercy

of her fate, like a child sent to bed by the governess when it was bed-time, and taken out of bed by the governess when it was time to get up. She could make little effort to control Lancelot's life. She managed to get a child by him . . . She did not – was not in a position to – demand anything in return. A girl and a beggar. A pathetic figure. She had nothing to offer him except love. He must have found her boring as a companion, but felt the flattered protective affection which men have for shooting dogs.

Guenever was not a girl, but a grown woman. She exercised control, demanded return, felt jealousy. The adult and the child: the difference between adolescence and adultery.

One cant imagine Elaine having a "change of life". Guenever could have it and did, and was extremely trying to everybody.

By the time that she is getting ready to come to Camelot, however, Elaine is presented in a harsher light. She does develop the 'adult feelings of the average woman', 'possessiveness and self-reference' if not jealousy, but although she has 'decided to meet Guenever on her own ground', to which end she has ordered gowns of the utmost magnificence and sophistication which only make her look 'the more stupid and provincial' (OFK 404), she remains a colourless character. What is added to Malory is merciless in its diminishing of Elaine: Lancelot's neglect of her when she arrives makes her sob helplessly, so that she looks repulsive, with her red nose. When she tries to throw herself into his arms, he pushes her off, in fear and exasperation. White follows Malory more closely in what follows, when Lancelot runs mad and Elaine, now proud and upright, reproaches the Queen for causing him to go out of his mind, with the result that she regains something of the dignity lost in the scene with Lancelot alone. But she is soon denigrated again; she has become a homely girl and 'done the ungraceful thing as usual', getting plump and walking with a clumsy action in the clothes of a novice. When she finds Lancelot, who has meanwhile run mad with misery and is now the unknown Wild Man, asleep in the garden she 'squats on her hams' – Guenever would never have been allowed to perform so undignified an action – beside him. White seems to try to be fair to her, however: he makes her weep for Lancelot in pity, and nurse him undemandingly back to health. There was something in her heart, he says, 'either decency, or pride, or generosity, or humility, or the determination not to be a cannibal – which spared him' (OFK 429). The implication is clear enough: women are normally cannibals, but Elaine in this instance, by making a special effort, managed not to be. She is presented as an exasperating woman all the same, insensitive as well as commonplace. As in Malory, King Pelles provides a castle for Lancelot and Elaine when he has recovered (dame Elayne is, incidentally, 'the fayryste lady in thys londe' in Le Morte Darthur), and Elaine goes wild with joy:

> "We will call it the Joyous Island," she said. "We shall be so happy
> there. And, Lance," – he flinched when she called him by the pet name

– "I want you to have your hobbies" . . .

"You will be able to attend to Galahad's education personally," she said. "You will be able to teach him all your tricks . . ."   (OFK 432)

White gives her an intolerably trivialising conversational style. As he remarks a little further on, 'she had never been clever' (OFK 433) – but Malory's Elayne is neither stupid nor repellent. Even though White says that his Elaine has a sensitive nature, he is so patronising about her (he speaks of 'the poor lady's simple hope'; and says that she had been 'picturing all the fights – almost certainly picturing them quite wrong' in OFK 518–9, for example) that he makes it hard to summon up much sympathy for her, even when she 'strikes the only strong blow of her entire life and commits suicide'. In the barge, it is not a Tennysonian lily maid of Ascolat who is seen, but a middle-aged woman with a stern, grey face. She is no more impressive in death than in life, totally unlike the image projected by the Victorian painters who found the subject appealing, or Malory's moving portrayal. White, in short, creates a gratuitous caricature in his Elaine. Guenever's reproach to Launcelot in Malory: ' "Sir, . . . ye myght have shewed hir som bownte and jantilnes whych myght have preserved hir lyf" ' (Vin 641) might well have been made to White.

Nevertheless the device of running the two Elaines together does work; it does keep the plot neater. The composite Elaine as she is here presented is both credible as an actual character and functional in the plot as a continual source of Guenever's jealousy and rancour against Lancelot. Such a presentation allows the story to be more convincingly updated in terms of psychological realism, though naturally it detracts from its potential as romance.

vi. The Grail Quest

David Garnett's son Richard, asked to read *The Ill-Made Knight* at an early stage, objected to the way in which the story of the Grail quest was told. White replied:

> When he complains that the Grail business is told in oratio obliqua he is paying me unintentionally the terrific compliment of assuming that it *could* have been told in oratio recta. In fact, I have 'sold' him the Grail, to a certain extent at any rate, by means of my oratio obliqua, and, when you reflect that the Grail story entails a personal meeting with Jesus Christ, you will realise what a hoax I have been hawking. Does he seriously expect me to start telling the public, in propria persona, that Lancelot met Jesus trapesing about with the wretched pot? Such things can only be said by one's characters, for whom one takes no responsibility whatever. And in the same way, he misunderstands my attitude to Galahad. Personally I consider that Galahad was a pain in the neck.

But I think that Lancelot was so nice that he would have been willing to apologise for him as well as he could.   (W/GL 100)

Just as White did not have much understanding of women, so his sympathy with the Grail quest was rather limited. The fascination with the story of the Holy Grail, apparent in the late nineteenth century with Wagner's *Parsifal* and Burne-Jones's designs, gathered new impetus in the early twentieth century with Jessie Weston's *From Ritual to Romance* and with many works of fiction. These accorded with the widespread interest in mysticism which found many different forms of expression in the years between the First and Second World Wars. To these trends White was clearly not attracted: his comments about 'the wretched pot' and Galahad reveal his general attitude. But in his journal for 2 May 1939 he wrote:

Part 3 in the Arthur story. The Grail. I had meant to leave it out. But if I could remember the feelings of the little chapel at Board's Mill, on a mission morning, and write them without spiritual pride, it would be a different matter. The beautiful voice of the old missioner speaking with consummate skill on Death: the congregation more and more hushed as it is most brought home to themselves. And, for the benediction, the darkening twilight, the candles gayly lit, the flowers arranged by Mrs This and Mrs That, the silhouettes of the congregation dark against the fluttering glow, the poor little modicum of incense just tingeing the air, and the Big Man (the priest at the head of the 3 who govern this parish) in his gold and white cope singing back to the choir and their harmonium – the choir slightly better than he was, but not much, and that was terrible. . . . The absolute piety and candle-glowing glory of the darkling scene, so difficult to give without condescention (sic) or mawkishness. . . . the candlelight. Kindness and belief. Grubby little choristers. The people on their knees, beads dangling, against the merry glow.

So 'difficult to give without . . . mawkishness': White could probably have mustered sympathy and understanding enough to allow him to give a serious account of the Grail quest, but the problem of blending that episode with the rest of the book would then have been acute. To many readers Malory's *Tale of the Sankgreal* is one of the less interesting and successful of his books. White's method of dealing with this part of the Arthurian story, though it is least successful where he takes the story most seriously (i.e. in Lancelot's account of his experiences) is most ingenious: Gawain, Lionel, Aglovale and Lancelot, on their return to Camelot, all report their adventures to Arthur and Guenever, and include those of Percival, Bors and Galahad, to whom Malory devotes separate chapters. Each tells his story in a very different way, according to his individual character.

The idea of the quest is introduced into *The Ill-Made Knight* as part of Arthur's continuing concern with the insoluble problem of Might versus Right, as he struggles to find acceptable outlets for the energies of his knights: 'While there were still giants and dragons and wicked knights of the old brigade, we could keep them occupied' (OFK 455). Chivalry has turned into Games-Mania, and the knights are obsessed with who has the best tilting-average, so that Arthur is afraid that his Table will go to ruin. There is feud and open manslaughter and bold bawdry as well. He decides that what is wrong is that the Table is based on a temporal ideal, and only by changing that to a spiritual one, can the Table be saved. Might must be given a channel so that it works for God, instead of for the rights of man (OFK 457). Thus the idea of the Grail quest originates from Arthur himself and his enthusiasm is quickly taken up by Lancelot, distinguishing this from many other versions of the story, notably Tennyson's. In these, Arthur deeply deplores the call which deprives the Round Table of many of his best knights, who set off on what seems a wild-goose chase from which they are destined never to return. For White on the other hand, the idea of the quest as it evolves in the conversation between Arthur and Lancelot is inclusive of all the idealisms he attributed to the Middle Ages: it might be a crusade, an attempt to rescue the Holy Sepulchre, a search for relics, for precious manuscripts – and finally, for the Holy Grail itself.

> If you want to read about the beginning of the Quest for the Grail, about the wonders of Galahad's arrival . . . and of the last supper at court when the thunder came and the sunbeam and the covered vessel and the sweet smell through the Great Hall – if you want to read about these, you must seek them in Malory. That way of telling the story can only be done once.   (OFK 459)

White goes straight on to the return of the knights from the quest, with Gawaine as 'the first reliable witness'. Reliable his account may be, but there is no doubt that it is also richly comic – a brilliant *tour de force*. He speaks in a Scottish accent: he is the only one of the Orkney clan who had refused to learn English correctly, which is just as well since too much dialect is usually very tiresome for the reader. But Gawaine's crabbed temper and roughness of manner are well sustained throughout his account, as he expresses his hostility to Galahad and his inability to understand quite why he has himself failed the test, as it were:

> "Bred in a nunnery," he went on furiously, "amidst a paircel of auld hens! I have news at me about his pairsonal quest from various who have fronted him – the holy milksop with his hairt of a cold puttock . . . But there, the chiel's an Englishman."   (OFK 460)

As well as the comedy, White's idiosyncratic way of updating his tale distinguishes it from other modern renderings: Gawaine, offered a drink by Guenever, appropriately asks for whisky. Lionel, the next knight to tell his tale – and also the story of Bors – does so in colloquial language somewhat reminiscent of P.G. Wodehouse. (White had wanted to get rid of any resemblances to Wodehouse in his earlier volumes.) Bors had been tempted by a dazzlingly beautiful lady, with twelve lovely gentlewomen, says Lionel, who had entreated him to save their lives by sinning with the lady. Guenever is shocked that Bors had refused. "Oh, they were only a collection of fiends, of course", replies Lionel casually (OFK 469). Later, Arthur is horrified to hear that Lionel had killed a defenceless hermit in the course of his quest:

> "I'm afraid that I was simply in a passion," admitted Lionel after a bit. "You know how you get. I wanted to fight, and I was going to have it. . . . You know how it is. It is like the sulks."   (OFK 471)

Despite such flippancies, the quest is nevertheless a serious matter. When Lionel ends his tale, they all sit silent, 'finding it difficult to talk about spiritual matters'. The uncomprehending worldliness of the little group of sophisticated courtly people comes across well through the different types of colloquial language allotted to them by the author.

The arrival of Aglovale takes up the unifying theme of the continuing feud between Arthur and the Orkney clan once again, the feud based on the 'law of the North' which Arthur hopes to make outmoded. His account includes the most important features of the story of Percival and of his sister, and White varies the form of the narration once again, by making him report the events as recorded in a letter. Even more than Lionel, Aglovale is another Bertie Wooster, in the style of his conversation: ' "Percy was the one in our family who took after Daddy most" '; and Percy is 'the poor old fellow', 'always keen on our Dumb Friends', who gets tempted by 'a perfectly delicious gentlewoman . . . with full camping equipment' (OFK 477). It is Aglovale's (and Percival's) sister, in whose hand the letter is found, who had given her blood to save the lady who had the measle and who had, he reports, 'died under the operation' (OFK 479).

Lancelot's return brings a very different mode of narration which works less well, White like his characters also finding it difficult to talk about spiritual matters. 'The great Dulac' is diminished, coming back 'out of a rainstorm, wet and small', and creeping up to his bed with a message to Arthur asking to be excused from waiting upon him until next day. Much of his tale is told awkwardly, for he has to speak of first-hand experience of the divine for which inevitably it must be difficult to find appropriate expression. The episode is nevertheless skilfully managed, in that White brings in, as Lancelot tells Arthur and Guenever of his experiences, the problem of the eternal triangle – or, in this case, quadrangle. Lancelot speaks first of how he had lost his 'Word' and his miracles, and then of his later humiliation in the course of the quest, in his loss of his prowess in arms. Then he tells them how he had gone to find a confessor so that he 'would not be wicked any more.' This time, he says, ' "I confessed everything." ' Tension mounts as he skirts around the sin on his conscience:

"Everything?" asked the Queen.

"Everything. You see, Arthur, I have had a sin on my conscience all my life, which I thought I could not tell to people, because – "

"There is no need to tell it to us," said the Queen, "if it hurts you. After all, we are not your confessors. It was enough to tell the priest."

"Leave her in peace," agreed the King. "At any rate she bore a fine son, who seems to have achieved the Grail."

He was alluding to Elaine.

Lancelot looked with sudden misery from one to the other, and clenched his fists. All three stopped breathing.   (OFK 489)

The moment becomes a cross-roads in Lancelot's life: 'Now was the time, they all knew . . . when he ought to have had it out with his friend and king – yet Guenever was thwarting him.'

While White's Lancelot is left with a sense of failure after the quest, in Malory, on waking from the long and deep trance into which he falls in the Grail chapel, he is assured: ' "Sir . . . the queste of the Sankgreall ys encheved now ryght in you . . ." ' (Vin 597ff). Soon after this, he experiences the coming of the Grail in the hall of King Pelles when 'hit befylle that the Sangreall had fulfylled the table with all metis that ony harte myght thynke', before returning to Camelot. There he finds Arthur and the queen and, says Malory, he 'tolde the kynge of hys aventures that befelle hym syne he departed.' Malory makes sure that, although he has not fully achieved the quest, no sense of personal failure remains attached to him. In *The Ill-Made Knight* White attempts a more difficult task in dealing with this episode by making Lancelot tell of his spiritual experience himself:

"Oh, Jenny, the beautiful chapel with all its lights and everything! You would say: 'The flowers and the candles.' But it was not these. Perhaps there were none.

"It was, oh, the shout of it – the power and the glory. It seized on all my senses to drag me in.

"But I couldn't go in. . . . a breath smote my face at the last door like a blast from a furnace, and there I fell down dumb."   (OFK 495)

The chapter ends here: there is no reassurance that 'the queste of the Sankgreall ys encheved now ryght in you' for White's Lancelot, no feast of 'all metis' to give a sense of fulfillment and completion. He is to remain torn between 'Arthur's Queen' and 'a wordless presence who had celebrated Mass at Castle Carbonek' (OFK 510).

Life at Camelot returns to its previous pattern after the Grail quest, which incidentally has done nothing to strengthen the ideals of the Round Table, but White follows Malory quite closely with the tales of the Poisoned Apple and the Knight of the Cart. Comedy reappears with Sir Meliagrance, 'a cockney knight . . . who had never been happy at court', and who kidnaps Guenever with whom he is 'desperately, hopelessly' in love. He is seen:

running up and down stairs with cries of "Yes, Ma'am, in 'arf a
minute" or "Marian, Marian, where the 'ell have you put the candles?"
or "Murdoch, take them sheep out of the solar this instant."

(OFK 529)

Like the story of the Poisoned Apple, this episode serves to glorify Lancelot, as he rescues Guenever from death at the stake in the nick of time,
overcoming Meliagrance against great odds; but both episodes bring all
three main characters further into the malign power of Mordred and
Agravaine. Still, their Indian Summer is before Lancelot and Guenever, and
Arthur, made for 'royal joys', finds these restored by Lancelot's two 'sensa-
tional victories' (OFK 539); meanwhile he banishes from his generous heart
consciousness of the lovers' relationship, not from reasons of cowardice,
but because of the extent of his power. Gossip is silenced, discourtesy put
down, and the Orkney faction can only grumble, but the calm is deceptive:
though Arthur's Gramarye is at peace, trouble seethes beneath the surface.

With the Healing of Sir Urre, the topic of Lancelot's sense of failure is
again raised. White returns to the concept of the Eternal Quadrangle. 'God
was Lancelot's totem . . . and now He chose the final moment to step across
the path.' For a quarter of a century, White tells us, Lancelot has remembered with grief 'that terrible evening' when 'trapped by Elaine' he had
'broken his taboo'. When the court musters for the attempt to heal the
wounded knight, Lancelot is hiding in the harness-room of the castle, contemplating suicide by hanging rather than face the test to which he will be
put if he confronts Urre. White explains it thus:

Do you think it would be fine to be the best knight of the world? Think,
then, also, how you would have to defend the title. Think of the tests,
such repeated, remorseless, scandal-breathing tests, which day after
day would be applied to you – until the last and certain day, when you
would fail. Think also that you know of a good reason for your failure,
which you have tried to hide, tried pathetically to hide and overlook,
for five and twenty years. . . .   (OFK 542)

He does not hang himself with the reins, but instead, 'ugly as ever' and
'ashamed', he walks down the ranks of knights gathered there, while
Mordred and Agravaine move forward like beasts ready to spring. He
kneels before Sir Urre and then the miracle of healing takes place, for by a
miracle he has been allowed to perform a miracle. Still kneeling when all
have left the field afterwards, he weeps 'as he had been a child that had
been beaten', while 'LIBER TERTIUS', as White calls it, ends like the books that
came before with wild celebration.

5

The Candle in the Wind
or, The Book of Sir Mordred

'I tried to write my fourth Arthur volume as a play, but all competent authorities, such as Noel Coward & R.C. Sheriff, assured me that it was childish, which it was', White wrote to David Garnett on 29 August 1941. In a letter dated 27 January 1939 Coward's actual comment had been:

> exquisitely written as I would have expected but theatrically speaking I am not so sure of it. I feel that some of the speeches are too long and I am a little doubtful of its sustaining powers. However, I could easily be wrong about this . . .

Whatever the strengths or weaknesses of the play were, the time when a straight Arthurian drama could be expected to be a box-office success was long past. Accepting the criticism of the 'competent authorities', White abandoned the earlier idea and transformed his fourth Arthur book into the narrative *Candle in the Wind*.

Although White's attempt to turn the last part of Malory's story into a play did not succeed, he was right in his belief that there was great dramatic potential in the events which led up to the death of Arthur. As these events are presented in *The Candle in the Wind* it is still possible to see the outlines of the original drama: his first conception of the story in this form helps to make his selection and presentation of key events in the last part of the story very effective.

White meant from the beginning that his fourth book should bring 'together for the final clash' the three tragic themes, which he had earlier defined as 'the Cornwall Feud, existing ever since Arthur's father killed Gawaine's grandfather', 'the Nemesis of Incest' and 'the Guenever-Lancelot romance'. In June 1939 when he had just finished his second volume, he commented 'Obviously the tone of the series has gradually got to change from sunshine to darkness', seeing the events culminating in the death of Arthur as 'a perfect Aristotelian tragedy'. In White's hands, the last part of the story becomes not just an account of how the tragedy happened, but a careful study of the psychology of Mordred, and of his relationship with his father. The form of prose narrative rather than stage play allowed him to differentiate and motivate the characters more fully, and so to avoid what might otherwise have seemed mere melodrama. The book begins dramatically, with Mordred and Agravaine plotting together, looking for opportunities to revenge themselves on Arthur and Lancelot. Agravaine is now a seedy middle-aged man, while Mordred, much younger, is determinedly vicious. Their conversation immediately indicates that the Indian Summer of the previous book is over.

The first chapter ends with a summary of past history, to make the first two tragic themes quite clear:

> The position was, and perhaps it may as well be laboured for the last time, that Arthur's father had killed the Earl of Cornwall. He had killed the man because he wanted to enjoy the wife. On the night of the Earl's killing, Arthur had been conceived upon the unfortunate countess. Being born too soon for the various conventions of mourning, marriage, and so forth, he had been secretly put to nurse with Sir Ector of the Forest Sauvage. He had grown up in ignorance of his parentage. . .
>
> (OFK 552–3)

In Malory's *Le Morte Darthur*, these events, contrived as they are by Merlin, are not seen to arouse horror or indignation in the minds of Mordred and his half-brothers. White modernises and rationalises the situation by suggesting that Arthur had been handed over to Sir Ector at birth in order to preserve the decencies and conform to the conventions of early twentieth-century middle-class society. He implies that it is Morgause's poisoning of her children's minds – and especially of Mordred's – that makes an ancient feud of Uther's act, and keeps their resentment smouldering. Although his summary also includes Arthur's seduction by Morgause and the birth of Mordred, subsequently brought up alone with his mother in the barbarous remoteness of the Outer Isles, he does not at this point tell the whole of Mordred's story.

White was not alone in seeing the story of Arthur as having similarities with classical tragedy. C.B. Lewis in *Classical Mythology and Arthurian Romance* (1932) had suggested that the Atrean legend (the story of Agamemnon and Menelaus) influenced the Arthurian, but it seems unlikely that White, widely read though he was, owed the idea to anything other than his own perceptions working in accord with his own education and the spirit of the age. As an undergraduate at Cambridge, he had read for the famous and influential Tragedy paper which was a compulsory part of the English Tripos. His tutor and life-long friend, L.J. Potts, translated Aristotle's *Poetics* which included his theory of tragedy.[1] The idea of

---

[1] L.J. Potts later published *Aristotle on the Art of Fiction: an English translation of Aristotle's Poetics*, with an introductory essay and explanatory notes, Cambridge: University Press 1963.

tragedy was in the air: 'Ours is essentially a tragic age', is the first sentence of *Lady Chatterley's Lover* (1928).

The first essential of Aristotelian tragedy is that it should arouse pity and fear. It should surprise the audience, and each step of the plot should arise out of what precedes it, a requirement which suggests the necessity for clear-cut sequential action, and the elimination of what may therefore seem irrelevant detail. So White begins with Mordred, as the unwanted product of incest comes to court looking and longing for revenge. It is virtually inevitable, therefore, that when he sees an opportunity to strike at his father through the Queen and Sir Lancelot, he loses no time in taking it. He knows well what must follow: Arthur, having striven to establish justice in the land, must implement it by condemning his own wife to a cruel death. White makes Mordred and Agravaine return again and again to their demand for justice (while in Malory it is Arthur who is determined that the Queen shall 'have sone her jugemente' (Vin 683)), emphasising the inescapable consequences of the setting up of Arthur's judicial system. There are then further unavoidable consequences, the first of which is that Sir Lancelot will rescue the Queen, the second that the deaths of Sir Gareth and Sir Gaheris will precipitate war, which will in turn lead to the downfall of the Round Table and the death of Arthur. The events of the story as related in White's source fit closely into the Aristotelian pattern, but in retelling them he intensified the dramatic effect by sharpening up the plot, eliminating such details as seemed irrelevant and emphasising those that might help to tighten the causal sequence.

For those not familiar with the complex sequence of events that traditionally led up to the Last Battle, *The Candle in the Wind* is full of surprises: the foiled attack of Mordred and Agravaine, the Queen's sudden rescue from burning and its tragic aftermath in the deaths of Gareth and Gaheris, Lancelot's return with her to Arthur's court, and Mordred's proposal to marry her. The crisis of the unfolding drama, the intended execution of Guenever, brings about the reverse of what the agent, Mordred, intends, in that she is rescued by Lancelot, while his half-brothers Gareth and Gaheris are killed in the process. Their accidental slaughter sets in train all the subsequent events. To each of them, White gives dramatic impact. He elevates into a complete scene what is merely a brief statement in Malory, that Mordred intends to marry Guenever. He evokes pity for the predicament of Arthur in particular by enhancing his humanity and his individuality, so that he is at the same time the noble king and the loving husband, friend and father. He arouses fear by emphasising the remorseless hatred and cruel vindictiveness of Mordred, and also by showing how easily evil ideas can spread and how readily they are taken up by the growing numbers of Mordred's followers, the Thrashers. Guenever's intended execution is made horrifying by the gloating of Mordred and the vivid evocation of every detail of the proceedings by means of the dialogue of the onlookers.

In another respect, too, White tried to bring the action of *The Candle in the*

Wind into greater conformity with Aristotle's theory of tragedy, by the revelation at the beginning of the book of the relationship between Arthur and Mordred. This relationship, though it is critical to the motivation of the plot, is not made apparent before this point in *The Once and Future King* as a whole, and is indeed unsuspected until Mordred's vicious revenge is imminent. However, White drew back from fulfilling the final demand of tragedy, that it should end with the deaths of the protagonists: 'Pendragon can still be saved'. As everyone familiar with the story of Arthur knows, we know even as he awaits the morning and with it the Last Battle, that he must die, but that is enough. White completed his story in *The Book of Merlyn*, discussing the various theories about the death of Arthur, and relating what subsequently happened to Guenever and Lancelot, but it is in hope for the future rather than with the darkness of tragedy that he chooses to end *The Candle in the Wind*.

White expanded his source to make Mordred not only the mainspring of the action in this fourth Arthurian book, but also an individual. In consequence, he virtually dominates the book, even though its subject is the tragedy of Arthur's downfall. Where Malory merely mentions Mordred's origins and barely outlines his actions White, in one dramatically realised scene after another, places him in the forefront of the action. Demanding that Arthur implement his 'famous justice' so that the lovers may be trapped and punished, and inciting Gawaine to demand vengeance even more insistently, Mordred remorselessly presses on to his goal of overthrowing the Round Table and revenging himself on his father.

He first appears briefly in *The Ill-Made Knight*, as a 'thin wisp of a fellow, so fair-haired that he was almost an albino' (OFK 453). He is clean-shaven, with a skeletal, pink face, and eyes into which you cannot see, but which look far and deep with an irony that may be mistaken for humour. Behind the description lies the suggestion of the death's head, and the association with death is carried further in *The Candle in the Wind* in which he is always seen dressed entirely in black, or as a 'ghostly creature' (OFK 617). While Marion Bradley in *The Mists of Avalon*[2] makes Mordred explain that his name means 'something like to "Deadly counsel" or even "Evil counsel" ' (800), White suggests that he is, as it were, death personified. He is also the conventional bastard, like Edmund in *King Lear*, determined to be a villain, totally opposed to all that Arthur has worked for throughout his life. White further suggests a resemblance to Richard III – one shoulder is higher than the other – making him 'halt and hunched' like Tennyson's Modred in *Guinevere*.[3] His violent and subversive tendencies are indicated by reference to political movements, medieval and modern. White sees him, in one of his notebooks as:

---

2 Bradley, Marion Z.: *The Mists of Avalon*, London, Michael Joseph, 1983.
3 Tennyson, Alfred: *Guinevere* (1859), line 41.

urged along almost helplessly now, by numbers of people whom you could not count: people who believe in John Ball, hoping to gain power over their fellow men by asserting that all are equal, or people who see in any upheaval a chance to advance their own might. It seems to come from underneath. His men are the underdogs seeking to rise. . . . It is a meeting of the Haves and Have-Nots in force, an insane clash between bodies of men, not between leaders.

By 1941, as White was becoming increasingly disenchanted with Ireland where he had never come to be accepted, he looked back through history, and commented bitterly on 'the savagery and feral wit of the Pict' (OFK 548), seeing Mordred as a member of the race:

> now represented by the Irish Republican Army rather than by the Scots Nationalists, who had always murdered landlords and blamed them for being murdered . . . the race which had been expelled by the volcano of history into the far quarters of the globe, where, with a venomous sense of grievance and inferiority, they even nowadays proclaim their ancient megalomania. (*ibid.*)

Despite his tribal loyalties, Mordred is shown as the very incarnation of treachery even when he is with his half-brothers: Gareth catches him in the act of trying to stab Gawaine, when the brothers quarrel about the plot to trap Lancelot and Guenever together (OFK 557). It is he who has stabbed Lamorak in the back; in the end, he indirectly brings about the deaths of all his brothers as well as his father. Soon, as Arthur's fortunes decline, Mordred becomes a leader of the popular party, dressing with 'dramatic simplicity' in what becomes a uniform for his followers, reminiscent of the blackshirts of the Fascism of the 1920s and '30s:

> Their aims were some kind of nationalism, with Gaelic autonomy, and a massacre of the Jews as well . . . There were already thousands, spread over the country, who carried his badge of a scarlet fist clenching a whip, and who called themselves Thrashers.   (OFK 628)

Finally he comes almost to be identified with Hitler:

> there are all these speeches about Gaels and Saxons and Jews, and all the shouting and hysterics. I heard him laughing last week, by himself. It was horrible . . .

says Agnes, Guenever's lady-in-waiting (OFK 645). He has always been given to putting on an act (as his mother, Morgause, is also alleged to have been) but by this time, we are told, he is actually mad and has 'ceased to be real'.

Mordred is not only a murderous fanatic, but also an obsessive character, embittered not merely because he is a bastard, and hump-backed as well, but above all because Arthur had tried to have him drowned when he was a baby. White makes him frequently refer to this incident, mentioned very early in the first chapter of *The Candle in the Wind*, when he is discussing with Agravaine his hostility to Arthur, in a scene which itself returns again and again to the attempted drowning. Mordred begins by merely alluding to it:

> "It may have happened long ago, but that doesn't alter the fact that Arthur is my father, and that he turned me adrift in a boat as a baby."

A few moments later he reiterates his grievance even more vehemently:

> "I could shout that my mother was his sister, and that he tried to drown me because of that."   (OFK 550)

It is 'the sin of Arthur with his half-sister which had ended in an attempt to murder the bastard who had resulted' that adds fuel to the fire of the Orkney clan's original grievance, but Agravaine points out that the wrongs of a bastard could not be expected to elicit much popular support. A 'son could hardly raise his illegitimacy as a banner under which to overthrow his father' (OFK 550). It is from Agravaine that the proposal of a plot against Lancelot and Guenever originates, as a means both of finding an outlet for his own enmity against Lancelot, and enabling Mordred to revenge himself on Arthur. As realisation of the inherent possibilities of the scheme dawn on Mordred, he reverts again to his obsession: ' "It means that I could revenge myself on the man who tried to drown me as a baby. . ." ' (OFK 552). It is only after this (in Chapter IV), when Arthur realises what is happening, that he makes his confession to Lancelot and Guenever in order to warn them of the treachery that he suspects is being plotted against them. The lovers are together, and Lancelot is trying to persuade Guenever to come away with him to Joyous Gard, to stop deceiving Arthur and so eventually to die in peace. But 'without eavesdropping for a second', Arthur has come in, seen them together and sensed the gravity of the situation now facing them all. The tone changes gradually as he insists on telling them first of his own birth 'at rather an awkward date', and then of the begetting of Mordred. The same ground as at the end of the first chapter is thus gone over again, but this time it is for the benefit of Lancelot and Guenever, so as to make sure that they know of the growing threat from the Orkney faction. Arthur's last dreadful revelation, that he had tried to drown Mordred and the other babies, frightened by the horrible prophecies of nothing but sorrow to come from his unwitting incest with his sister, thus confirms Mordred's grounds for hating his father.

Mordred is soon accusing Arthur to his face of having intended to drown him, when he and Agravaine are demanding justice, and Arthur appeals to Agravaine for mercy. Mordred is quick to comment, to Arthur's ' "I suppose it is no good reminding you that there is such a thing as mercy?" ':

"The kind of mercy . . . which used to set those babies adrift, in boats?"
(OFK 590)

His obsession with his grievance against Arthur appears once more in his conversation with Guenever towards the end of the story in his scornful question: ' "I suppose he didn't know that I was his son, when he put us out in the boat?" ' (OFK 650)

In giving both individuality and motivation to the character of Mordred to an extent that few other writers have attempted, White's emphasis falls once again on the importance of upbringing. Mordred has been brought up in isolation from his half-brothers, who had all left home for Arthur's court while he was still a little child. As a result he had had the undivided and deeply corrupting attention of his mother. White comments:

> It is the mother's not the lover's lust that rots the mind. It is that which condemns the tragic character to his walking death. It is Jocasta, not Juliet, who dwells in the inner chamber. It is Gertrude, not the silly Ophelia, who sends Hamlet to his madness . . . Desdemona robbed of life or honour is nothing to a Mordred, robbed of himself – his soul stolen, overlaid, wizened, while the mother-character lives in triumph, superfluously and with stifling love endowed on him, seemingly innocent of ill-intention. Mordred was the only son of Orkney who never married. He, while his brothers fled to England, was the one who stayed alone with her for twenty years – her living larder. Now that she was dead, he had become her grave. She existed in him like the vampire. (OFK 647)

His education has taught him only how to hate, and in particular to loathe and despise his father and all he represents (such as 'Sport . . . the Done Thing and the Best People' (OFK 548)).

Though we are not shown the 'enfances' of Mordred, the care with which White portrayed and motivated his character suggests a special interest, since Mordred is the son of Morgause, who had been openly acknowledged as being drawn from White's mother (even when she was completely recast in *The Queen of Air and Darkness*). Mordred's family situation had not been unlike White's; he was in effect an only child, alternately neglected and suffocated with affection, and brought up (as White appears to have been) without contact with his father. Mordred's resentment against Arthur perhaps owes something to the relationship that must have left White feeling unwanted, abandoned even, by his own parent. White, himself never to marry, specifically makes the point that, unlike his half-brothers, Mordred is unmarried. His proposal to marry Guenever does not, of course, succeed: he remains a 'have-not', the tragic character condemned to a walking death, finally 'robbed of himself'.

'Confused between the loves and hatreds of his frightful home', he had been a party to his mother's assassination, with typical treachery, even though he loved her. When he comes to Arthur's court, he finds that his father has been considerate enough to hide the story of his birth, and that he is lovingly treated by the 'King-father whom his mother had taught him to hate with all his heart' (OFK 553). As crippled and twisted in mind as in body, he is gloatingly to propose to marry his father's wife, as well as to kill his father to carry out the Oedipal pattern that White discerns behind his story. Arthur is too decent, too loving to understand Mordred's true vileness: he sees him as ambitious, it is true, but also quite mistakenly as fond of honour, brave, and loyal to his own people.

White's mode of narration in *The Candle in the Wind* suggests once again a divided self. In *The Sword in the Stone* he seems to identify both with Merlyn and also (though to a lesser extent) with the Wart. His sympathies now appear to lie with the older Arthur far more than they did with the younger. There is a weariness in the ageing King which probably developed out of White's growing weariness with Ireland and his isolation there, with all the frustration that his abortive attempts to contribute to the British war-effort caused him, and with his increasing despair of human nature.

There is a sense in which Mordred is Arthur's *alter ego*. Mordred is complementary to Arthur, embodying the ruthlessness in which Arthur is so signally and so increasingly deficient. Arthur, unremittingly (and to his son, infuriatingly) kind, gentle, patient and tolerant, is everything that Mordred is not. Trapped by his own system of justice which his ideals force him to implement, Arthur is ready to temper justice with mercy. Mordred insists on justice, but pursues it as retribution, exploiting the new system for his own ends. Yet, ' "I can see myself in him" ', says Arthur of his son, proceeding to find similarities and sympathy while Lancelot's solution to the problem that Mordred poses is to ' "Cut the sniveller's head off and have done with him" ' (OFK 579). Arthur's horrified reaction to this seemingly sensible suggestion draws attention to the strong contrast between father and son.

It is probable that White also to some extent identified with Mordred, since in terms of family situation, he saw a similarity between himself and the figure of Mordred. He also attributes to him the sadistic tendencies which, late on in their friendship, he mentioned to David Garnett as having been his own lifelong problem. These tendencies underlie the cruelties of *The Queen of Air and Darkness*: the boiling alive of the cat and the killing of the unicorn. In *The Candle in the Wind* they can be seen in one form in Mordred's tormenting of Arthur, and more overtly in the scene when Guenever is brought to the stake. Mordred, watching from the window as Guenever is about to be executed, gloatingly comments:

> "It will be a cruel death . . . They are using seasoned wood, and there
> will be no smoke, and she will burn before she suffocates."
>
> (OFK 607)

He is carefully portrayed as sadistic well before he is to be thought of as mad. His cruelty is a different matter altogether from the thoughtless, instinctive cruelty of the primitive society in which he and his brothers grew up. The preparations for Guenever's execution reveal something much more conscious and refined:

> "I understand," continued Mordred, in what was almost a soliloquy, "that our liege lord himself must watch the execution from the window."
>
> Gareth lost his temper completely.
>
> "Can't you hold your tongue about it for a minute? Anyone would think that you enjoyed watching people being burned."
>
> Mordred replied contemptuously: "So will you, really. Only you think it is not good form to say so. They will burn her in her shift."
>
> "For the sake of God, be silent."   (OFK 607).

Mordred is no villain of melodrama, but a completely convincing figure. White could simply have assigned to him the straightforward part in the plot that he has in Malory. Instead, he made him both a more prominent and a fully motivated principal in the last scenes, embodying some of his own personal bitterness which had resulted in his early emotional crippling and life-long loneliness. In developing Mordred's character and bringing him into the foreground of the story as he did, however, White makes the downfall of the Round Table and the death of Arthur very much more Arthur's personal responsibility, and so an Aristotelian tragedy, than Malory had made it. Here, it is not so much the divided loyalties of Lancelot, torn between his duty to his king and his devotion to his lady, that bring about the ultimate disaster, but Arthur's sin of incest – unwitting though it was – and his subsequent attempt to obliterate its consequences.

ii.

By thus making Mordred's hatred of Arthur and desire to punish him through those he most loves the main feature of *The Candle in the Wind*, White gave an entirely new slant to Malory's narrative. As Mordred is moved into the foreground and his relationship with his father made of prime importance to the action, Arthur too is presented with greater psychological realism. White's portrayal of the ageing king is convincing, indicating as it does his attitudes and responses to the course of events in which he is involved in much greater detail than Malory is able to offer. While Mordred with his bitter contempt and hostility towards Arthur is a vile figure, he is nevertheless not unreasonably provoked, not only by the King's endless patience and forbearance, but also by his lack of perception and his genial tactlessness. At his first entrance, just when Agravaine and Mordred have been devising their treacherous plan of action, and the savage quarrel between the brothers has broken out, Arthur moves across the cloister to 'kiss Mordred gently, smiling upon them all' (OFK 558). He is unable even to begin to understand Mordred's bitter resentment: just before the accusation against Lancelot and Guenever is made, Arthur says blandly:

"These spring nights are too beautiful for us to worry with unpleasant things, so why don't the two of you [Agravaine and Mordred] go off and make it up with Gawaine? You could ask him to lend you that clever goshawk of his for tomorrow. The Queen was mentioning just now, how she would enjoy a nice young leveret for dinner."

(OFK 587)

After treating Mordred and the fifty-five year old Agravaine as if they were schoolboys, he adds insult to injury by drawing attention not only to Mordred's deformity, but also to his physical cowardice and lack of martial prowess:

"It is not as if you would have to fight the Queen's champion in your own person, Mordred. You could plead infirmity and hire the strongest man you knew to fight for you . . ." (OFK 588)

He still misjudges Mordred's character – 'Mordred is ambitious and fond of honour', he has earlier remarked to Lancelot and Guenever – while being fully aware of the young man's embitterment resulting from his 'weak body' and failure in what he terms 'our sports'. To the very end he is unable to see him as he really is, defending Mordred to the injured Gawain on the grounds that he has had an unhappy life: ' "You may depend upon it there is a regular fire of love inside him" ' (OFK 655).

Arthur is introduced as a 'quiet old man' who looks older than his age, a man who has 'done his best for so long', and who is markedly aged by the effort and the burdens that he has borne. Malory's Arthur is not burdened by the weight of guilt that White's Arthur feels on account of the drowning of the babies, a deed that continues to haunt him throughout his life. He is surprised when Lancelot and Guenever both assure him that he is not a wicked man on account of this incident. But despite his weariness and his sense of guilt, he retains a certain grandeur. He is indeed, as Agravaine, 'exulting in his cold mind, thought: "Hoist with his own petard!" ' (OFK 589) when the brothers insist that Lancelot and Guenever should be brought to justice, but it is with royal dignity and in the power of his integrity that he dismisses them:

He looked at them from an immense distance, seeming to weigh truth, justice, evil and the affairs of men.
"You have our permission."

His eyes came back from the distance, fixing them personally with a falcon's gleam.

"But if I may speak for a moment, Mordred and Agravaine, as a private person, the only hope I now have left is that Lancelot will kill you both ... And I may add this also, as a minister of Justice, that if you fail for one moment in establishing this monstrous accusation, I shall pursue you both remorselessly, with all the rigour of the laws which you yourselves have set in motion."   (OFK 591)

If White's Arthur is very different from Malory's in the extent to which he is individualised and motivated, he is also strikingly different from Tennyson's stern King. Guenever is spared the reproaches of her husband who remains unfailingly affectionate and patient in *The Once and Future King*, only blaming himself with regard to Mordred and the babies, instead of reproaching his wife for starting the rot that has undermined and virtually caused the overthrow of his kingdom. The way in which he has come to terms with the love-affair between Lancelot and Guenever had earlier been explained in *The Ill-Made Knight* (Chapter XVI), so that his acceptance of the situation is well prepared for. His confession is made in the intimate and informal setting of his own fireside, in a scene that is as different as possible from the dramatic last meeting between King and Queen in Tennyson's *Guinevere*, in which the King's self-righteousness finds its exact counterpart in the Queen's self-abasement. White's king and queen are in fact thoroughly modern liberals, he in his imaginative humanity and she in terms of the lively spirit which would brook no such accusations as those of Tennyson's Arthur. But then White's characters are meant to be real people and not quasi-allegorical figures.

iii.

White's portrayal of his characters as real people and the original dramatic form of the book both led to an increase of dialogue as opposed to narration, which parallels Malory's own increased use of dialogue at this stage of the story. White attempts on the one hand to give a colloquial modern tone to the exchanges between his characters, sometimes to the verge of bathos, while on the other he sometimes makes use of Malory's 'High Language' ('for in those days there were two kinds of speech like High and Low Dutch or Norman French and Saxon English') when greater formality is needed, or for moments of intense emotion. He sometimes achieves an astonishingly successful if precarious balance in telling the story, with real pathos and a true sense of a painful human situation, both historical and yet contemporary. The last part of the story as Malory tells it also includes much dialogue as a result of the conflicts that ensue from the enmity of Agravaine and Mordred, and when Arthur, Gawayne and Launcelot express their grief as the tragedy unfolds. White reduces or eliminates or expresses in more dramatic form, almost all of the long formal speeches in his source which, noble as they are, are more in keeping with late medieval convention than with modern taste.

White's dialogue is thus for the most part naturalistic. As elsewhere in the book as a whole, he solves the problem posed by the historical novel in this respect by simply adopting modern modes of discourse. They are now inevitably somewhat dated but they are vigorous if rather stilted at times. The speakers are reasonably well differentiated; extensive use of sarcasm distinguishes Agravaine and in particular Mordred from the other brothers, while Gawaine is characterised by his constant use of dialect. (In *The Queen of Air and Darkness* White indicates that Gawaine and his brothers speak Gaelic, but actually makes it sound like Irish English, while at Arthur's court in later life Gawaine speaks with a Scottish accent.)

In *The Candle in the Wind*, dialogue has the important function of clarifying the plot as well as of revealing character and motivation. What Malory often passingly mentions as fact or motive, White explores and makes explicit by means of dramatic interchanges between the characters. So we overhear the plotting of the conspirators, instead of merely being told of their enmity. Mordred's constant reference to his father's attempt to drown him reveals his obsession. Arthur makes a full confession to Lancelot and Guenever of his sins of the past, including the drowning of the babies, thus enlarging our understanding of him as a private person. Lancelot and Guenever, alone together, discourse intimately, calm and happy for almost the last time until Arthur introduces the note of warning of the threat now hanging over them. Gareth's subsequent warning to Lancelot, in contrast to Bors' more limited attempts at persuasion in Malory, of the danger of going to the Queen, is built up into an extended dialogue which creates suspense and expresses personal feeling. The fact that Lancelot later accidentally kills Gareth adds poignancy to this scene.

Most effective in this book is the episode in which Arthur and the 'Gawaine clan' look on, as the Queen is brought out for execution, since to the reluctance of sir Gawayne in *Le Morte Darthur* to see Guenever burnt to death, White adds through expressive speech the reactions of Arthur as a private person, which Malory does not represent. He brilliantly sets forth the differing responses of the onlookers, while at the same time describing the mode of procedure: 'There was nothing dingy, at any rate, about a legal murder in the Age of Darkness' (OFK 613). The dialogue clarifies the attitudes and emotions of the participants in the scene, fluctuating between apprehension and enormous relief on the part of the King and Gawaine, and the horror that ensues when the deaths of Gareth and Gaheris are revealed. The reporting of their killing is done with masterly skill: Mordred's dreadful echoing of others' words until the tragic truth dawns is entirely consistent with his mocking character, yet also reveals his genuine horror at what has happened.

White was less successful, however, when it came to representing, earlier on, Lancelot and Guenever alone together on the night of Mordred's attack. Malory had no such problems: he merely remarks that:

> . . . as the Freynshhe booke seyth, the quene and sir Launcelot were togydirs. And whether they were abed other at other maner of disportis, me lyste nat thereof make no mencion, for love that tyme was nat as love ys nowadayes.   (Vin 676)

White makes the mistake of recording the elderly lovers' trivial conversation, as Lancelot brushes Guenever's grey hair for her. The scene develops into something of a summary of past history, ingeniously preparing for the dramatic moment when the door handle is seen to be moving and the knocking begins, but there follows an uncomfortable blend of the flaccid modern with the 'language of chivalry' into which Lancelot slips. The twentieth-century colloquial discourse fails embarrassingly to rise to the necessary heights:

> "Jenny, I am going to call you my most noble Christian Queen. Will you be strong?"
> "My dear."
> "My sweet old Jenny. Let us have a kiss. Now, you have always been my special good lady, and we have never failed before. Do not be frightened this time. If they kill me, remember Sir Bors. . ."
>
> (OFK 602)

Elsewhere similar problems arise, as for example when Lancelot hands the Queen over to Arthur again at the instigation of the Pope, in a scene which is very formal in Malory, but which White has to present in modern terms. Once again there is an awkward blend of ancient and modern: the switch from Lancelot's formal:

> "It repents me to the heart . . . that you should think so, my lord sir Gawaine, for I know that while you are against me I shall never more be accorded with the King"   (OFK 634)

to the Bishop of Rochester's:

> "Gawaine, cannot we leave this wrangling to another time? The immediate business is to restore the Queen"   (OFK 634)

to Lancelot's use of 'the simple tongue'. His:

> "Can't we be forgiven? Can't we be friends again? We have come back in penitence, Arthur, when we needn't have come at all. . ."
>
> (OFK 635)

adds to the pathos, perhaps, but diminishes the dignity of the scene.

It might be thought that the tragedy is by this time too far advanced for touches of humour to be appropriate, but White attempts it in the dialogue between Guenever and Agnes in the castle at Carlisle:

"Would that be what they call a nervous shakedown, madam?"

The malapropism and the comic-servant device perhaps serve to lighten the sombre tone of the scene, as well as to underline the isolation of the Queen, alone in her castle with only her maid to look after her, and so entirely at the mercy of Mordred. He, too, brings touches of comedy to the dialogue with his sardonic remarks:

"One has to come through a door somehow, madam. It is more convenient than coming through the window – though, I believe, some people have been known to do that."   (OFK 647)

In the final chapter, White begins with straightforward narration and ends with dialogue, thus giving a dynamic quality to the end of the story. In his long vigil before the Last Battle, Arthur unremittingly continues to try to grapple with the baffling problems both of his reign and of human life in general, but it is his dialogue with Tom of Warwick that provides the solution through the handing on of the torch, as it were. So the last glimpse is of an Arthur, concerned as always for the well-being of his subjects and his kingdom, 'refreshed, clear-headed, almost ready to begin again', on the morning of the battle.

iv.

In *The Candle in the Wind* the concept of justice becomes of ever-increasing importance, as Arthur struggles to demonstrate its existence in his realm in ever more difficult situations. Justice was the primary attribute of the medieval king, symbolised by the sword laid on the altar at the coronation, as it was also the primary function of kingship to establish it. In this respect White fully appreciates the essence of the medieval concept. Arthur has not only to inculcate the concept of justice, but to decide the terrible problem of how it should be administered in the case of his own wife. His life-long struggle against the forces of anarchy culminates in the situation with which he is faced by Mordred's demands. White's characters are modern people caught in a medieval trap – yet the idea of justice is also fully modern, so that it is easy to feel the bitterness and horror of their situation.

White had already structured the last part of the story of Arthur into a series of encounters which move the action forward with dramatic force before he rewrote it in narrative form. The plotting of Agravaine and Mordred was brought into the foreground, to intensify the feeling of approaching disaster. To simplify the staging, in its original form as a play, these scenes were intended to be enacted in sets which could easily be constructed and changed. Each has a quite precise location which helps to reduce the complexities of Malory's narrative at this stage of the story, in contrast with the unvisualised settings for the action in *Le Morte Darthur*. All the scenes take place indoors: the cloisters, the solar, the Justice Room, bedrooms in the castle, the hall at Joyous Gard, and finally the tents, of Gawaine and then of Arthur. All are precisely suggested as settings that increasingly confine and constrain the lives of their occupants as fate seems to close in on the actors in the tragedy, while the tents perhaps also indirectly suggest the impermanence of human life. The varied use of lighting would, in the theatre, have offset the practical necessity of restricting the number of sets, and this in the novel turns into the symbolic imagery of light as daylight changes everything, or the candles flicker in the night wind. The movement towards the darkness of tragedy is thus suggested through the use of evocative images.

The first 'scene' takes place in daylight, in the cloisters, where Mordred openly voices his grievances and Agravaine points the way to revenge. The next scene moves to the solar of Arthur's castle, where the lovers are together, looking out over Arthur's England, 'under the level rays of sunset' but also at the same time, 'over the sundown of chivalry' (OFK 570). As the light leaves them, their profiles against the window become black like silhouettes; darkness falls as the King approaches and sends for candles, then tries to illuminate them by telling them of past events and hinting of future danger. As they face the onset of night together, the image of the tower suggests that they are already prisoners, beleaguered by Agravaine and Mordred. The coming of night, the dim light of the candles and the very nature of the location symbolically suggest the actual situation. We have come a long way indeed from the bright morning sunlight of *The Sword in the Stone*.

The dominant theme of justice is emphasised by the setting of several scenes in the Justice Room itself. At first it is claustrophobic: 'you felt you were in a box: you had the strange feeling of symmetrical enclosure which must be known by butterflies in killing bottles' (OFK 583). The walls seem to be crowding in on the occupants. They are hung with tapestries which tell the story of David and Bathsheba, and of Susannah and the Elders[4] – narratives from the Old Testament chosen in each case for their symbolic undertones. The story of David and Bathsheba has both sexual and political significance: it tells of the seduction by King David of Bathsheba, the wife of Uriah the Hittite, but it is also concerned with the later struggle for the throne. It has indeed been seen as having similarities with Arthur's own birthtale. The story of Susannah and the Elders is about a false accusation

4   For the story of David and Bathsheba, and of her husband Uriah the Hittite, see the *Second Book of Samuel*, Chapter 11. The story of the subsequent struggle for the throne is told in the *First Book of Kings*, Chapters 1 and 2. The story of Susannah and the Elders is told in the *Apocrypha*, in *Daniel and Susannah*.

of adultery: the beautiful wife of the virtuous Joakim was lusted after by two elders of the community, who foiled of their plan to seduce her, accused her of adultery with a young man. She was saved from death by the quick-wittedness of Daniel who ingeniously uncovered the lies of the accusers. Together the tapestries suggest the themes of political ambition and unjust accusations brought against the virtuous. What follows upon the description of the tapestries is Mordred's and Agravaine's request that a trap should be set for Lancelot and Guenever.

A week later the Justice Room is seen again, but no longer as 'the kind of arras trap which tempted Hamlet's rapier to prick about for rats'. The tapestries are still there, but now the reader's attention is directed to the details of the David and Bathsheba scene. Bathsheba is in her bath, exposed to the view of David on the roof next door, while Uriah is tumbling from his horse, cleft in two in battle: 'a lot of realistic vermilion worms were gushing out of the wound in a grisly manner . . . intended to be his guts' (OFK 606). The picture thus evoked looks forward to the events about to be enacted: Arthur and Gawaine are inside the Justice Room looking out at Guenever exposed in the market place in her shift, fastened to the high stake for execution. Then Lancelot comes to the Queen's rescue, incidentally and accidentally hacking Gareth and Gaheris to death. White makes dramatic use of the indoor viewpoint for this scene: what happens in the room is of less importance than what is going on outside, as Arthur and Gawaine watch helplessly the proceedings in 'the foreshortened market-place under the window'. It is a birds-eye view so distanced that it gives a sort of nightmare unreality to the sequence of events, which allows them to fit plausibly into what otherwise is a novel of psychological realism.

It is in the Justice Room that the 'final pageant' takes place, but in this scene the room has ceased to be the claustrophobic box that before could scarcely hold five people. Justice, perhaps, has expanded as the Pope has intervened to bring about reconciliation. The tapestry is still there, but now it reveals nothing, hidden behind 'bald-faced ladies in head-dresses which looked like crescents or cones or the astonishing coiffure worn by the Duchess in *Alice in Wonderland*' (OFK 631). Though the Justice Room is not seen again, the tapestry accompanies Arthur on campaign, and reappears in his pavilion at Salisbury before the Last Battle, making it sumptuous. Finally, in the tapestry Uriah alone is noticed, 'still in the article of bisection' (OFK 665): only wounds and death are to be expected now. This imagery is supplemented by the 'great wind of sorrow' blowing outside the tent as Arthur looks back on his life and prepares for the end; and by the darkness fitfully illuminated by the 'flashing candles'.

The darkness has already closed in on Gawaine, earlier shown lying seriously wounded in the darkness of his tent, relieved only by 'a flat pan of charcoal which lit it dimly from below'. As finally he tries to rise and follow Arthur, he sways in the dim light while his shadow moves grotesquely round the tent pole.

Still other locations are so described as to add to the sense of approaching doom. When Lancelot is getting ready to go to the Queen's room just before Agravaine and Mordred attack, it is dark in his bedroom 'except for the one light in front of the holy picture' (OFK 592), and from this dim light he presently steps out into the unlighted passage. White evidently chose the source of light advisedly: Lancelot's religion gives him little illumination at this point. He turns his back on it, and steps out into the total darkness on his way to the Queen.

Guenever's room by contrast is full of golden candlelight, reflected, causing sparkles of light and silvery and golden gleams, the artificial light of the last happy moments left to the lovers before Mordred's attack. In the next chapter the scene changes to Benwick, to Lancelot's castle, Joyous Gard, where he and Guenever have taken refuge, but though it is a bright day, it is winter and the sun is low in the sky. Although White speaks of the 'joyful castle', it offers no joy to its occupants now, as the winter of their lives sets in. But it is light, contrasting with the Queen's Chamber at Carlisle, in which it grows darker and darker as Guenever and Agnes sit together, in a gloom which makes a suitable setting for Mordred's visit.

Later, round Benwick Castle, now no longer called Joyous Gard as it had been when Lancelot and Guenever were together there, the wind of sorrow blows, while everything is seized with numbing, deadly cold: 'even the fire seemed frozen' (OFK 660). Though it is not yet night, it is dark in the castle: Lancelot has to carry his letter to the window to read it, the letter written by the dying Gawaine, now cold in his grave. It is the wind that is the most powerful symbol here, however: sounding like 'some monstrous, elemental being, wailing its damnation' as the last stages of the tragedy are enacted.

Finally in Arthur's tent, once again it is dark except for the fitful illumination of the 'flashing candles'. Throughout the 'deep night', Arthur wrestles for the last time with the unsolved problems of a lifetime. At last he hits on the only solution: young Tom (Malory) of Newbold Revell near Warwick must carry the candle as Arthur himself has done, 'with a hand to shield it from the wind', bearing the message of the justice and decency which Arthur has sought with only partial success to bring to England, and which Malory's book will repeat down the ages. The device of introducing the young page Thomas Malory focusses attention on *Le Morte Darthur* as an element of continuity in the long struggle for civilisation. By implication, it praises and justifies Malory's masterpiece not only as White's main source, but as a great civilising adventure story.

Just as White makes use of the imagery of darkness and light, savage cold and violent wind to create atmosphere for the last scenes of the tragedy, so he also uses animal imagery effectively to suggest what is going on, at another level. The friendly animals of *The Sword in the Stone* are all gone, and in their place appear birds of prey. From the cloisters of the 'Orkney palace' at Camelot the hawks are seen; a jerfalcon, a goshawk, a falcon and her tiercel, and four little merlins – fierce birds waiting for the moment when they can strike, as Agravaine and Mordred are waiting too. More sinister is the 'enormous eagle-owl' which is sometimes used as a decoy. 'When he opens his eyes he is a creature from Edgar Allan Poe'. Sylvia Townsend Warner records in a letter a visit to the mews of J.G. Mavrogordato, with whom White corresponded, while she was writing White's biography:

> But the strangest thing was the eagle owls. There was a fierce screech-ing while we were in the mews, coming from a shed next door. When he said he would show us an eagle owl too . . . I expected to see the bird fly out. Not at all. It walked out, slowly, stumping, its feet spotted in beige feathers down to the talons, tall ears standing up on its head, enormous round fire-coloured eyes – and was exactly like a court dwarf in Velasquez: just about as tall, as erect, as burly, as intimidating. But the stare glowed like a furnace. He fed the furnace with a (dead) day-old chick.[5]

In *The Candle in the Wind*, the eagle owl's eyes are red, 'homicidal, terrific, seeming actually to give out light', and he is appropriately associated with Mordred, whose eyes open 'as the owl's had done' when Agravaine di-vulges his plan. As, later, Mordred slips behind Gawaine with a hand on his dagger to stab his own brother the shadows, it seems, are actually 'lit by the owl's eyes' (OFK 557). Even the gentler Gareth and Gaheris are associ-ated with the hawks too on the day of Guenever's intended execution: all the brothers are together (except for Agravaine, now dead) united by their membership of their clan. Gaheris is nervously fiddling with the braces of a leather hood for a hawk (OFK 606), while Gareth is itching to take over the job which he feels he can do better, suggesting the concern of these two to restrain their predatory brother. Hawk imagery appears again in the fal-con's gleam in Arthur's eyes when, after the challenge of Mordred and Agravaine, his old spirit momentarily returns.

v.

White diverges from Malory at the end of the story in what each writer sees to be of central importance. In *Le Morte Darthur*, the emphasis is on the tragedy of the destruction of the Round Table: after the rescue of the Queen from burning, Arthur swoons for 'verry pure sorow' when he hears of the death of his noble knights and especially of the deaths of Gareth and Gaheris.

> 'Alas, that ever I bare crowne uppon my hede! For now have I loste the fayryst felyshyp of noble knyghtes that ever hylde Crystyn kynge

---

5   See Maxwell, William ed., *Letters: Sylvia Townsend Warner, op. cit.*.

togydirs. . . . And much more I am soryar for my good knyghtes losse
than for the losse of my fayre quene; for quenys I myght have inow, but
such a felyship of good knyghtes shall never be togydirs in no company. And now I dare sey,' seyde kynge Arthur, 'there was never
Crystyn kynge that ever hylde such a felyshyp togydyrs.'   (Vin 685)

Since White is reinterpreting the story in terms of modern personal relationships and naturalistic motivation, his emphasis falls upon Mordred's
part in the tragedy. He is much more individualistic than Malory and does
not sense so keenly the loss of the chivalric fellowship. At the same time, for
all his antifeminism, or because of it, he gives more prominence to Guenever's place in the tragedy. Similarly he pays less attention to the more
'public' issue of the ensuing war between Lancelot and Arthur. The loss of
the Round Table as institution and its knights as upholders of it grieves
White's Arthur less than his personal sense of failure and bewilderment,
and his distress at having to condemn the Queen to death, with its consequence in his alienation from Lancelot.

To the very end of *Le Morte Darthur* it is the figure of Launcelot that
represents the chivalric ideal. He is the noblest of the knights, his death
brings to an end 'the hoole book'. White's dominant interest in the internal
stresses of the Arthur:Mordred:Guenever triangle led him to concentrate
on Arthur and therefore he cut out or simplified much that concerned
the hostilities between the King and Lancelot. His original conception of
this part of the story as a stage-play also forced the reduction of much
that in Malory takes the form of a narrative, to dramatic encounters between the protagonists. At the same time, he streamlined the action so
as to reduce the number of characters involved and the events that take
place. In this way he gives pace and impact to the tragic dénouement of
the story.

In his handling of the plot at this stage, a significant innovation is his
replacement of Lancelot's cousin Sir Bors by Gareth, to warn Lancelot of
the danger of answering the Queen's summons while Arthur is away on
the hunting party. By this means White focuses the reader's attention on
the 'Orkneys', reducing one's awareness of Lancelot's extensive following,
which though important for Malory, would here have been a distraction.
The tensions between Mordred and Agravaine on the one hand and Gawaine, Gareth and Gaheris on the other are enhanced and so add to the
suspense of these chapters, as Gareth takes it upon himself to try to foil his
brothers' intentions. Although Sir Bors does play a small part in *The Candle
in the Wind*, he is nowhere the close friend and confidant of Lancelot as he is
in Malory. Somewhat similarly, White makes 'Agravaine of Orkney' instead
of Collgrevaunce of Goore the first to fall victim to the might of Lancelot
when Mordred and his followers attack him at the door of the Queen's
bedchamber.

Just as he has warned Launcelot about Mordred's plot, Malory's Bors is active after the attack in organising the plans for rescuing the Queen if and when she is to be burnt. The emphasis is on the loyalty of Launcelot's followers:

> 'Sir,' seyde sir Bors, 'all ys wellcom that God sendyth us, and as we have takyn much weale with you and much worshyp, we woll take the woo with you as we have takyn the weale.'   (Vin 679)

He insists that he and all Launcelot's supporters will be ready to rescue the Queen, and himself proposes that she should be taken to Joyous Gard, where Trystram had earlier kept La Beall Isode for 'nere three yere' (Vin 681).

For the modern reader, White's handling of the scene in which in Malory 'the quene was lad further withoute Carlyle, and anone she was dispoyled into he[r] smokke' (Vin 684) is especially effective. Guenever is distanced – he does not attempt to tackle the impossible task of describing or even indicating what her feelings might have been. Instead, he focuses on Arthur, his nephews and Mordred as they watch the scene, which is set not outside Carlisle but appropriately in the town square, outside and beneath the Justice Chamber. By this means he is able to suggest credible reactions on the part of those who are watching while remaining close to what he selects from his source. Much of what follows in Malory is cut in favour of the scene in Joyous Gard in which White presents Lancelot and Guenever together, and by their conversation makes clear what the situation now is. Lancelot is deprived of the long speech in which he answers Arthur from the battlements of the castle, asserting the Queen's innocence and justifying his own action in saving and now protecting her. He begins to be diminished, in comparison with Malory's Launcelot, here and when in accordance with the Pope's bull he brings the Queen to Carlisle. Malory writes:

> Than sir Launcelot purveyed hym an hondred knyghtes, and all well clothed in grene velvet, and their horses trapped in the same to the heelys, and every knyght hylde a braunche of olyff in hys honde in tokenyng of pees. And the quene had four-and-twenty jantillwomen folowyng her in the same wyse. And sir Launcelot had twelve coursers folowyng hym, and on every courser sate a yonge jantylman; and all they were arayed in whyght velvet with sarpis of golde aboute their quarters, and the horse trapped in the same wyse down to the helys, wyth many owchys, isette with stonys and perelys in golde, to the numbir of a thousande. And in the same wyse was the quene arayed, and sir Launcelot in the same, of whyght clothe of golde tyssew.
>
> (Vin 693–4)

White paints a very different picture, in which the Queen is presented with harsh and unsympathetic realism:

There was something pathetic about their grandeur, as if they were dressed up for a charade but not quite fitted. They were in white cloth, of gold tissue, and the Queen, no longer young or lovely, carried her olive branch ungracefully. They came shyly down the lane [of court-iers], like well-meaning actors who were not good at acting. They kneeled in front of the throne.   (OFK 633)

Lancelot is also diminished as he says farewell both to Arthur and to Guenever at the end of the scene, though he makes her 'bloom again . . . into the Rose of England', lifting her to 'a crest of conquest'. He himself, however, is once more 'the gargoyle', as he addresses his last words to the assembled company: ' "My King and my old friends, a word before I go . . . if any danger may threaten you in future, then one poor arm will come from France to defend you – and so let all remember" ' (OFK 638). The trivial conversational tone draws attention to the difficulty that White had in dramatising moments of strong emotion and high seriousness, for which he often quotes directly from Malory. The inspirational speeches of earlier centuries would have been incompatible with the psychological realism in terms of which he had chosen to tell his story. Lancelot's parting speech is perilously reminiscent of the kind of banality White had so effectively parodied in Sir Ector's Christmas speech in *The Sword in the Stone*. It is a far cry from Malory's Launcelot's 'Moste nobelyst Crysten realme, whom I have loved aboven all othir realmys!' and the speeches that follow in which he says goodbye to the Queen 'in hyryng of the kynge and hem all:

'Madame, now I muste departe from you and thys noble felyshyp for ever. And sytthyn hit ys so, I besech you to pray for me, and I shall pray for you. And telle ye me, and if ye be harde bestad by ony false tunges, but lyghtly, my good lady, sende me worde; and if ony knyghtes hondys undir the hevyn may delyver you by batayle, I shall delyver you.'   (Vin 697)

He leaves defiantly, throwing out a final challenge as he says 'all opynly':

'Now lat se whatsomever he be in thys place that dare sey the quene ys nat trew unto my lorde Arthur, lat se who woll speke and he dare speke.'

Malory is drawing here on an entirely different ancient concept of truth and justice and might, which no modern writer could, nor would White have wished to convey. But though he differs from Malory in presenting Lance-lot as humiliated rather than defiant as he begins his journey to Dover 'in the felon's way "ungirt, unshod, bareheaded, in his bare shirt as if he were hanged on a gallows" ', he does not allow him to depart without remarking that 'People felt tawdry in the Justice Room when the old soldier had left it' (OFK 639). White has responded to the outmoded magnificence he has not recorded, and implies a sense of its absence.

The next significant change in the mode of telling the story, originally dictated to some extent no doubt by dramatic necessity, is the introduction of the scene in which Guenever, attended by Agnes, is visited by Mordred at Carlisle Castle. This replaces Malory's chapter, 'The Siege of Benwick', dealing with the progress of the war between Arthur and Launcelot and the first combat between him and Gawayne. White very effectively uses this scene to summarise the general situation by means of the conversation between the two women, as well as to add to his reader's knowledge of Mordred's character. In addition, the sense of the approaching end is put across vividly by means of images of cold, darkness and isolation. Agnes puts the commonsense view of what is happening in the wider world, thus drawing attention to the seeming inanity of the conflict between Arthur and his best friend. Her terror of Mordred when Guenever orders her to open the door suggests, as Malory does not choose to do, how sinister and dangerous he is. Mordred himself then communicates his intention of wedding his 'owne fadirs wyff', the enormity of which is in Malory only suggested by the Archbishop of Canterbury, who when savagely threatened quickly and prudently departs, to curse Mordred in 'the moste orguluste wyse that myght be done' (Vin 708).

Despite its title, Malory's great work is in the end as much the story of Launcelot as of Arthur. Towards its close, Arthur seems almost to slip away, after he has slain Mordred and been mortally wounded by him, almost been cheated of his last wish by Bedivere, and finally been borne away by the weeping queens to his mysterious destination. About this, Malory will only commit himself so far as to say, 'here in thys worlde he chaunged hys lyff'. In leaving Arthur in *The Candle in the Wind* with his last battle still to fight, and the tales of Lancelot and Guenever unfinished (except for the mere mention that 'it was Lancelot's fate and Guenever's to take the tonsure and the veil', White made it possible for his story to bear the sense of continuity suggested by Malory's REX QUONDAM REXQUE FUTURUS (the Once and Future King). Outside the King's pavilion (White keeps the archaic name for the great tent from which Arthur is conducting his campaign), before the Last Battle, while the 'wind of sorrow' blows, inside 'there was a silent calm'. Arthur, with the royal tapestries still depicting the death of Uriah, looks back over his whole life, his successes and the failures with which they had been followed, the insurmountable difficulties and insoluble problems with which he had grappled throughout his reign. Still wholly intractable is the problem of why men fight. But young Tom of Newbold Revell finally leaves him with hope, the hope that a better world may come about through culture: 'If people could be persuaded to read and write, not just to eat and make love, there was still a chance that they might come to reason.' In keeping the candle burning, in keeping the story of Arthur alive, Tom can give him immortality and perhaps save future generations from the hell on earth of war. So there is both a grandeur and a hopeful finality in White's ending:

The cannons of his adversary were thundering in the tattered morning when the Majesty of England drew himself up to meet the future with a peaceful heart.

EXPLICIT LIBER REGIS QUONDAM REGISQUE FUTURI

THE BEGINNING

6

Comedy in
The Once and Future King

i.

Comedy pervades *The Sword in the Stone* and contributes quite substantially to the second and third books of *The Once and Future King*. Even the last book is not without it. White's mode of telling the story is very much in contrast with Malory's, whose seriousness seldom admits of humour anywhere in *Le Morte Darthur*. The comedy is appropriate in *The Sword in the Stone*, in Merry England: instead of running counter to the 'poetry' which it was intended should characterise the book, it enhances it. Though the childhood years and early adolescence of the Wart naturally have their sorrows, his childhood is and is meant to be idyllic, contrasting with the problems, frustrations, troubles and sorrows of his adult life. His education, under the care of an eccentric teacher, naturally offers opportunities for comedy: to the young, teachers are often funny in every sense of the word, and Merlyn is rightly so, although he is also an impressive figure, and one not to be trifled with. He is the prime source and centre of an immensely varied range of jokes, verbal and practical, and of White's remarkably ingenious and original vein of fantasy. The comic element, so dominant at the beginning of Arthur's story, is continued as White shows us the upbringing of Morgause's sons far away in Orkney, tutored in bloodthirstiness by the rascally Irish 'saint', Toirdealbhach, the 'sort of guru . . . who gave them what little culture they were ever to get'. Inevitably, there is less comedy as the story moves towards its tragic conclusion, but like Dickens, White is always ready to mix comedy and tragedy.

The humour, particularly in *The Sword in the Stone*, arises from both situation and dialogue, appearing in the form of caricature and parody, in the absurd anachronisms and in authorial comment. The facetiousness can be tiresome, and the snobbishly patronising and racist jokes now seem in poor taste half a century later – White's sense of humour occasionally gave offence in his own lifetime, too – but it is probably for the humour more than for any other feature that the first half of the tetralogy is appreciated today. His astonishing inventiveness, particularly associated with the figure of Merlyn, never falters in *The Sword in the Stone*, nor does his ability to exploit conventional ideas about the past to comic effect. His intentions are often satirical: at the beginning of the story, Sir Ector is introduced with his friend (chosen for his rather absurd, but genuinely Malorian name) Sir Grummore Grummursum, and White manages to make fun both of the knights' exaggeratedly upper-class mode of discourse, and of popular notions about medieval education, in their first words:

> When they had got rid of the governess, Sir Ector said, "After all, damn it all, we can't have the boys runnin' about all day like hooligans – after all, damn it all? Ought to be havin' a first-rate eddication, at their age. When I was their age I was doin' all this Latin and stuff at five o'clock every mornin'. Happiest time of me life. Pass the port."   (OFK 3–4)

Similarly, popular ideas about the subjects of medieval romance are mocked next: Sir Grummore has had 'a rattlin' good day':

> "Found a chap called Sir Bruce Saunce Pité choppin' off a maiden's head in Weedon Bushes, ran him to Mixbury Plantation in the Bicester, where he doubled back, and lost him in Wicken Wood. . ."   (OFK 4)

Sir Grummore Grummursum, with King Pellinore, remains a figure of fun throughout *The Once and Future King*, while Sir Ector who begins as a comic parody of an Old Etonian hunting squire is also seen as a kind and wise father-figure at the end of *The Sword in the Stone*. The humour apparent in the presentation of these characters is very characteristic of the 1930s and '40s, as seen in *Punch* and in such radio programmes as *ITMA*, in which the comedy is based on the interaction of sharply-defined types. The stratified and class-conscious society of the inter-war years gave greater scope for genial caricature than is possible now: White shows no signs of 'liberal guilt' where his comedy is concerned. His humour is often typically prep- and public-school, as in his punning nickname for Arthur, 'the Wart'.

In the sequence in which, as part of his education, the Wart becomes a fish, parody contributes to the comedy of the episode. White is looking back to nineteenth-century children's fiction, and probably directly to Charles Kingsley's *The Water Babies* when the timid young roach asks for a doctor for its dear Mamma:

> "If you p-p-p-please, doctor," stammered the poor creature, . . . "we have such a d-dretful case of s-s-s-something or other in our family, and we w-w-w-wondered if you could s-s-s-spare the time? It's our dear Mamma, who w-w-w-will swim a-a-all the time upside d-d-d-down . . ."   (OFK 44)

Merlyn as doctor at once assumes the manner of a Victorian physician when he asks the patient: ' "and how is Mrs Roach today?" '(47) and his incantation recalls *The Water Babies* when the doctors prescribe:

> Metallic tractors.
> Holloway's Ointment.
> Electro-biology.
> Valentine Greatrakes his Stroking Cure

and so on, and so on, down to '*Maleficarum, Nideri Formicarium, Delrio, Wierus, etc.*'.[1]

Another kind of parody appears in the brilliantly funny account of Sir Ector's address to his family, friends and tenants on Christmas night. It begins with the absurdly well-worn cliché, 'unaccustomed as I am to public speaking", followed by a vivid parody of the kind of clumsy formal speech with which many older readers may be familiar:

> "it is my pleasant duty – I might say my *very* pleasant duty – to welcome all and sundry to this our homely feast. It has been a good year, and I say it without fear of contradiction, in pasture and plow. We all know how Crumbocke of forest Sauvage won the first prize at Cardoyle Cattle Show for the second time, and one more year will win the cup outright. More power to the Forest Sauvage. As we sit down tonight, I notice some faces now gone from among us and some which have added to the family circle...."   (OFK 140)

Not quite so successful are White's literary parodies, of the National Anthem to conclude this particular Christmas feast, for example; but the reader can nevertheless take pleasure in his variations on 'The Lincolnshire Poacher', and 'D'ye Ken John Peel' as sung by William Twyti the king's huntsman. The most amusing of these parodies is Palomides's sonnet (the most impeccable, we are told, of the whole sonnet-sequence) in honour of La Beale Isoud in *The Witch in the Wood*. Palomydes is in *Le Morte Darthur* the faithful but rejected suitor of La Beale Isoud (Isolde), and a 'Saracen'. White makes him into a caricature of an Indian clerk or official with a superficial English education, hence the 'Babu English' of both his speech and his literary composition:

> Hon. Madam! Kind regards! Immortal life
> Be yours henceforth from 18th ultimo
> Is prayer which Palomides sings to fife
> And tabor twice per diem. May you know
> Ten thousand offspring (male) legitimate,
> Each one well blessed with twenty thousand wives! ...[2]

and so forth (WW 119). This was cut when in the course of transforming

---

1 Kingsley, Charles: *The Water Babies*, Collected Edition, London, Macmillan, 1880. Vol. IX, p. 192.

2 See Sprague, Kurth ed. *op. cit.*, 'Palomides to La Beale Isoud', p. 53 for the complete poem.

The Witch in the Wood into *The Queen of Air and Darkness* White reduced the role of Sir Palomides from incompetent tutor to Gawain and his brothers, to that of one half of the pantomime Questing Beast. At the same time he regrettably also cancelled the very amusing episode in which King Pellinore tries to write a sonnet to Piggy and finds it impossible to understand about the rhyme-scheme. But the figure of Palomides, though much diminished, still remains an amusing, although a patronising caricature. In his affected language, a mixture of business and pedantic jargon, he refers to himself as 'yours truly', and calls the Questing Beast's tail an 'anal appendage', and its eye an 'optic'.

Parody takes another form when the Wart asks Merlyn to let him see a tournament – he 'can't think of anything more educational than to see some real knights fighting' (OFK 57) – and the magician kindly obliges with the ridiculous contest between King Pellinore and Sir Grummore Grummursum, making a mockery of the very idea of jousting. Sir Grummore is singing his old school song as he canters up, 'We'll tilt together'. White uses a variety of techniques in presenting this farcical incident. The fatuous conversation of the participants is followed by the absurd difficulties encountered in the arming of Pellinore, who has to be helped out of his helmet (quite a feat because he clumsily set its nuts and bolts on the wrong thread when getting up in a hurry in the morning) and into his helm, an enormous thing like an oil-drum. After presenting the process in modern terms, White immediately moves into the language of *Le Morte Darthur*. But when Grummore answers the King with ' "Be that as it may, I choose that thou shalt not know my name as at this time, for no askin' " ' (OFK 61), and Pellinore replies, ' "Then you must stay and joust with me, false knight" ', Grummore counters with: ' "Haven't you got that wrong, Pellinore? . . . I believe it ought to be 'thou shalt'." ' The joke becomes a matter of grammar, and a rather unusually perceptive realisation of the nuances between second person singular and plural in medieval English. Later, incongruity is piled upon incongruity: the Wart cries, ' "They're off!" ', as if at the races, while slowly and majestically, the ponderous horses lumber into a walk. Soon of course the two jousters are unhorsed and sitting side by side on the grass, prior to doing battle with their swords, on foot, and having difficulty in locating each other because of their limited vision. The tournament ends with a slanging match couched in the language of prep-school boys in the 1930s. The episode invites comparison with the experience of Perceval as related by Chrétien,[3] when the youth sees a party of knights and is so much impressed that he at once insists on leaving home to become a knight himself. White wants to make sure that the Wart is not overcome by the glamour of chivalry and all its trappings, and he returns him to Sir Ector's tilting ground where the sergeant is a caricature of a public-school cadet-

---

3 See Chrétien de Troyes: *op. cit.*, p. 374 ff.

force drill-sergeant, such as White would probably have encountered during his schooldays at Cheltenham. He is heard calling, ' "Nah then, Master Art, nah then. . . . Come aht into the sunlight 'ere . . . and see some real tilting." '

White's ear for dialogue enhances the comedy, in the first two books in particular. The Wart's return from his 'quest' with Merlyn in tow catches the breathless excitement of the small boy suggested by the outpouring of disconnected remarks:

> "Look who I have brought," he said. "Look! I have been on a Quest! I was shot at with three arrows. They had black and yellow stripes. The owl is called Archimedes. I saw King Pellinore. This is my tutor, Merlyn. . . ."   (OFK 32)

Later on, in Chapter XIII when the Wart has been 'confined to his chamber for three mortal days' with a broken collar-bone, a brilliantly banal conversation between patient and magician takes place through the key-hole:

> "Can't you . . . turn me into something while I'm locked up like this?"
> "I can't get the spells through the key-hole."
> "Through the what?"
> "The KEY-HOLE."
> "Oh!"
> "Are you there?"
> "Yes."
> "What?"
> "What?"
> "Confusion take this shouting! . . . God bless my blood pressure . . ."
> "Could you turn me into an ant?"
> "A what?"
> "An ANT. It would be a small spell for ants, wouldn't it? It would go through the keyhole?"

White similarly often reproduces convincingly the fatuous arguments of childhood (' "I don't snore . . ." " You do." "I don't." "You do. You honk like a goose." "I don't" ' etc.), still indulged in by King Pellinore and other adults from time to time.

The nurse belongs in the tradition of Dogberry and Verges, of Mrs Malaprop and all those now extinct comic housekeepers and old servants who abound in English literature. (We can no longer laugh at anyone's grammatical lapses and mispronunciations, of course, for fear of hurting people's feelings and seeming to appear intellectual snobs; though pedantry is still considered to be funny.) But the comedy associated with the nurse goes beyond malapropism because of the comic juxtaposition of medieval and modern:

> "there, there," she sobbed. "His loyal highness dead and gone, and him such a respectful gentleman. Many's the illuminated picture I've cut

out of him, from the Illustrated Missals, aye, and stuck up over the mantel. . . ."   (OFK 198)

But as so often, there are unexpected depths in White's comedy. Superficially this is a jest about a good-hearted uneducated nurse. It is also a genial but none the less strongly felt comment on the widespread vandalism of nineteenth-century scholars and collectors who destroyed so many precious medieval manuscripts precisely by cutting out the illustrated scenes and initials.

The discourse of Saint Toirdealbhach is music-hall Irishry, though with a flavour of the original with which White became familiar at Doolistown: ' "Glory be to God," remarked St Toirdealbhach. "It does be a strange story yer after wanting entirely" ' (OFK 243), and he refreshes himself when he has finished telling it with a fresh dose of whiskey, humming a few bars of 'Poteen, Good Luck to Ye, Dear' meanwhile. The contrast between the concept of the Irish saint and its 'fulfillment' in the person of this old reprobate never loses its comic effect. Just as many of White's characters are satirised through their comic dialogue, he even mocks himself in making fun of Merlyn as tutor with the kind of exasperated remarks, such as ' "Oh, go and put your head in a bucket" ' (OFK 239), which he probably addressed to the more tiresome of his pupils at Stowe.

Since White's humour is often satirical and is generally based on anachronism and parody, its appreciation depends upon a certain amount of general knowledge. Despite his obvious understanding of young boys and ability to establish a rapport with them, *The Once and Future King* is full of jokes that could hardly have been appreciated by child readers, even given the much more extensive quantity of general knowledge often acquired by intelligent and well-taught children fifty or sixty years ago. But in aiming the humour at adults rather than children, he was writing in the well-established tradition of earlier authors – Thackeray, Kingsley and Kipling, for example – and even nearer contemporaries such as Kenneth Grahame and A.A. Milne. All these writers, as well as some even today, used perhaps only half-consciously the pretence of writing for children, while really addressing adult readers at least much of the time. The most obvious parallel in modern times is the work of J.R.R. Tolkien. It seems a particularly English literary trait, intensely disliked by some sophisticated readers, though many enjoy what is in fact a rather subtle mixture. Merlyn's testimonials signed by Aristotle, Hecate and the Master of Trinity, and Sir Ector's explanatory asides as Merlyn displays his magical powers are typical examples. ' "He had 'em up his sleeve" . . . "They do it with mirrors" . . . "It's done by hypnotism" ' (OFK 34)), as if Merlyn was a twentieth-century conjuror. Similarly, the exuberant entrance, trident in hand, of Neptune (not actually named) with a loud blowing of sea-shells, conches and so forth is very amusing for an adult reader but its full absurdity would probably be lost on a child: 'He had an anchor tattooed on his stomach and a handsome mermaid with Mabel written under her on his chest', and he is chewing tobacco like the old sailor of nineteenth-century popular tradition.

A similar technique of parody and anachronism is used with the many literary allusions and quotations from Shakespeare and the English poets, as in the episode when the Wart is turned into a hawk. When he becomes a badger and meets the hedgehog, also referred to as a hedge-pig, urchin and 'porpentine', White alludes to the line in *Hamlet* 'Like quills upon the fretful porpentine' (I.v.15) to suggest the poor animal's alarm at the threat of being eaten. The learned old badger subsequently ends his parable of the embryos with the ingenious joke based on the concept of God as Three in One:

> " 'We were only going to say,' said God shyly, twisting Their hands together. 'Well, We were just going to say, God bless you'."

White's comic genius is at its best in Chapter XXII of *The Sword in the Stone* when King Pellinore arrives for 'the important week-end' of Kay's knighting. His fatuous exclamations which eventually culminate in the announcement that Uther is dead are followed by the absurd formality of Sir Ector, who stands up respectfully and takes off his cap of maintenance,[4] while over-reaction to the news is taken still further as everyone else stands up, the nurse bursts into tears, and then launches into her exquisitely ridiculous series of malapropisms and anachronisms.

Pellinore tries to enhance the solemnity of the moment by parodically declaring, in terms of a school history lesson, 'Uther the Conqueror 1066 to 1216'; while Kay makes his mundane suggestion, derived from old-fashioned social custom on the occasion of a death in the family, that the curtains should be drawn. A burst of activity follows, as the cockney sergeant's: ' "Nah then, one-two, special mourning for 'is lite majesty" ', is followed by 'the flapping of all the standards, banners, pennons, pennoncells, banderolls, guidons, streamers and cognizances which made gay the snowy turrets of the Forest Sauvage.'

The next joke is a literary one: like the Red Cross Knight in Spenser's *Faerie Queene*, King Pellinore has been 'pricking' through the purlieus of the forest, and has met a 'solemn friar of orders grey', a familiar figure in the ballads. Pellinore is admirably chosen to make a mysterious happening – the appearance of the sword in the stone – even more baffling and mysterious:

> "Well, there has appeared a sort of sword in a stone, what, in a sort of church. Not in the church, if you see what I mean, and not in the stone, but that sort of thing, what, like you might say."
> "I don't know what the Church is coming to," said Sir Grummore.

---

[4] Cap of maintenance: 'A kind of hat or cap formerly worn as a symbol of official dignity or high rank, or carried before a sovereign or a high dignitary in processions.' Earliest example c.1485. (*O.E.D.*)

"It's in an anvil," explained the King.

"The Church?"

"No, the sword."

"But I thought you said the sword was in the stone?"

"No," said King Pellinore. "The stone is outside the church."

"Look here, Pellinore," said Sir Ector. "You have a bit of a rest, old boy, and start again. Here, drink up this horn of mead and take it easy."

When Pellinore gets round to saying that there are words written on the sword, Sir Grummore characteristically assumes that they are 'Some red progaganda, no doubt', but in fact they turn out to be the actual words used by Malory at this point in *Le Morte Darthur*. The piling up of anachronisms, malapropisms, incongruities, social satire and parodic elements in this episode is brilliantly successful.

The interplay of humour and seriousness, of incongruity and appropriateness, and of human and animal which makes White's technique so elusive is particularly apparent in the list of coronation gifts that Arthur receives. Just as often in real life in the twentieth-century, these gifts are more representative of the resources of the donor than appropriate to the recipient: Little John sent 'a yew bow, seven feet long, which he was quite unable to draw. An anonymous hedgehog sent four or five dirty leaves with fleas on them', for example. But 'Cavall [the dog] came simply, and gave the Wart his heart and soul.' The splendour of the occasion is indicated, not by any description of the ceremony, but by the list of presents sent by the Wart's friends, as well as by the unspecified gifts of the various 'barons, archbishops, princes, land-graves, tributary kings, corporations, popes, sultans, royal commissioners, urban district councils, czars, beys, mahatmas, and so forth' (OFK 211–12).

One of White's favourite devices is to create an incongruous effect by contrasting the 'High Language' (as he calls it) used by Malory, with modern colloquial language. When at the beginning of the second book, Morgause's sons are recounting the family history, there is an amusing blend of childish argumentation, authentic Malorian language, false archaism and comical invention:

> "When King Uther Pendragon learned what had happened in the morning, he was wonderly wroth."
>
> "Wood wroth," suggested Gareth.
>
> "Wonderly wroth," said Gawaine. "King Uther Pendragon was wonderly wroth. He said, 'I will have that Earl of Cornwall's head in a pie-dish, by my halidome!' So he sent our Grandfather a letter which bid him to stuff him and garnish him, for within forty days he would fetch him out of the strongest castle that he had!"
>
> "There were two castles at him," said Agravaine haughtily.
>
> "They were the Castle Tintagil and the Castle Terrabil."   (OFK 219)

White's incongruous juxtapositions sometimes make serious points at the same time as they create comic effects: the sadism of the young 'Orkneys' with their donkeys is ironically described as an 'Eden-like scene', but before the reader has had time to reflect on the topics of childhood innocence and primitive barbarism, there enters a magic barge somewhat absurdly 'draped with white samite, mystic, wonderful' (echoing Tennyson's *Idyll*, 'The Passing of Arthur', line 312) carrying three knights and a seasick brachet. They are the love-sick Pellinore and his friends.

The action itself becomes more farcical when Sir Palomides and Sir Grummore fabricate their own Questing Beast. The episode begins with the Saracen knight as the funny foreigner, contrasting with Sir Grummore at his most inhibited and decent English upper-class (' "Well, thanks, Palomides. I must say, I think that's demned decent of you." ' [OFK 276]) Soon the two are having difficulty in getting their act together at the start, but eventually manage to prance, bound and bay all at the same time without bursting the buttons that hold their costume together. The arrival and subsequent infatuation of the real Questing Beast again shows White's comic invention:

> The Questing Beast . . . was staring up at Sir Palomides with her soul in her eyes. Her chin was pressed to the foot of the cliffs in a passion of devotion, and occasionally she gave her tail a wag. . . . Then, feeling that she had been too forward, she would arch her graceful serpent neck and hide her head beneath her belly, peeping upwards from the corner of one eye.   (OFK 298)

The literary jokes that follow are much more successful than White's parodies in the first book. The knights have eventually escaped from the cliff on which they had taken refuge from the Questing Beast, and returned safely to the castle:

> "Hoots!" cried various auld wives who were in the castle delivering eggs. Some of the castle circle could speak English after a fashion, including St Toirdealbhach and Mother Morlan.
> "Wee sleekit, cow'ring, timorous Beastie," said the drawbridge man.
> "Oh, what a panic's in thy breastie!"
> "Aroint us!" said the bystanders.
> "Bonnie Sir Palomides," said a number of Old Ones who had known of their plight on the cliff ledge all night . . . "is going to lay him doon and dee." . . . "Ah, the puir churl," they said compassionately. "The sassenagh! The sable savage! Will he no' come back again? Gie him anither drappie there. Ah, the braw splash!"   (OFK 300–1)

Here literary pseudo-dialect mingles with quotations from Burns's 'To a Mouse', as well as from Elizabethan drama and from the ballad 'Bonnie Charlie's Now Awa'.

White deliberately made farce dominant in *The Queen of Air and Darkness* in order to make a transition to and to offset the seriousness of Arthur's incest with Morgause. Potts, asked for his comments on and criticism of the book in its early stages, wrote: 'As for the farce, it is holy and sublime, and right at the root of what you are trying to say' (LF 121). He goes on to say that he 'couldn't *write* the book', and so does not feel very confident about telling White how to: interesting comments from a man who was himself to publish a book on comedy only a few years later.[5] As usual, the technique of up-dating is used to great effect in the lively account of the double wedding of King Pellinore and Piggy and St Toirdealbhach and Mother Morlan in the last chapter. Here, hyperbole plays an important part in an account of the proceedings, enlivened by the clichés of a modern news-paper report: the cathedral of Carlion had been booked for the wedding, 'and no trouble was spared that a good time should be had by all'; 'the church was packed'. But, 'As for the Latin, it was talked at such a speed that the rafters rang with genitive plurals', and 'Even the Pope, who was as keen as anybody that the thing should go with a swing, had kindly sent a number of indulgences for everybody he could think of.'

In *The Ill-Made Knight* comedy still plays a large part, even in the chapters relating to the Grail quest, and here White's main technique is up-dating. Drawing directly on Malory for several of the episodes, he exploits their comic potential. The scene in Chapter VII, in which Lancelot is carried off to the castle of Morgan le Fay under an enchantment, and then confronted by Morgan with three other queens who demand that he should choose one of them as his mistress, is particularly successful. White's humour is deadpan as usual, fantasy blended with mundane realism to great effect. The four queens all know that Lancelot is in love with Guenever, since 'Nothing travels quicker than scandal, especially among supernatural people', but they propose to ignore the fact and argue about which of them should have him for her magic. Morgan handles the tense situation in a brisk and businesslike manner: ' "We need not quarrel . . . I will put an enchantment on him" '. This contrasts effectively with the 'Judgement of Paris' scene which follows when next morning the queens, after a gracious introduc-tion, make stately curtseys to Lancelot, and are introduced. Then Morgan truculently and rather contemptuously addresses him:

> "Now . . . we know about you, so you need not think we don't. You are Sir Lancelot Dulac, and you are having a love affair with Queen Guen-ever. You are supposed to be the best knight in the world, and that is why the woman is fond of you. Well, that is all over now. We four queens have you in our power, and you have to choose which of us you will have for your mistress. It would be no good unless you chose for yourself, obviously – but one of us you must have. Which is it to be?"

With considerable ingenuity White keeps very close to Malory in telling

---

5 Potts, L.J.: *Comedy*, London, Hutchinson's University Library, 1957. Potts makes no mention of White or his writings in this book.

this story (Vin 151ff.), making it amusing by mixing modern banalities with direct quotation from his source.

White brings out the comedy inherent in the situation most effectively when Lancelot has a fight with a man in whose pavilion he has unwittingly been sleeping:

> "You have cut open my liver," said the man accusingly.
> "Well, I can't do more than say I am sorry, even if I have."
> When he had got the man to bed, and stopped his bleeding, and discovered that the wound was not a mortal one, a beautiful lady appeared in the opening of the tent . . . and immediately she began screaming at the top of her voice. . . .
> "Do stop howling," said the man. "He is not a murderer. We just made a mistake."
> "I was in bed," said Lancelot, "when he came and sat on me, and we were both so startled that we had a fight. I am sorry that I hurt him."
> "But it was our bed," cried the lady, like one of the Three Bears. "What were you doing in our bed?"   (OFK 362–3)

White here follows *Le Morte Darthur* fairly closely in outline, though in fact he slightly bowdlerises the story. Malory's 'man', thinking that his 'lemman' (the lady) was in the bed:

> leyde hym adowne by sir Launcelot and toke hym in his armys and began to kysse hym. And whan sir Launcelot felte a rough berde kyssyng hym he sterte oute of the bedde lyghtly, and the othir knyght after hym. And eythir of hem gate their swerdys in their hondis . . .
>
> (Vin 153–4)

Malory tells a funny story with complete seriousness; White treats it in a different way and succeeds in making it even funnier.

He uses a similar method with the 'boiled girl' episode. The interplay of the romantic and the prosaic, the 'High Language' and the modern and colloquial, the serious and the humorous is extraordinarily effective. For Lancelot what happens at the castle of Corbin is a strange adventure 'which he remembered for many years with awful grief', but for the reader much of this adventure is richly comic. On arrival, Lancelot is solemnly greeted by the people of the enchanted village who exclaim:

> "Welcome, Sir Lancelot Dulac . . . the flower of all knighthood! By thee shall we be holpen out of danger."   (OFK 385)

Realism then takes over briefly as he gropes his way through the steam-filled room until he hears a squeak, given by 'a charming little lady, who was – as Malory puts it – as naked as a needle' (OFK 386).

The comedy of the scene in which King Pelles's odious butler makes Lancelot drunk in order to bring about the conception of Galahad is more complex. White first uses his favourite technique of updating: Lancelot is compared to the 'young men who might still be undergraduates or jet-pilots if they were in England today'. King Pelles's butler 'would have made an excellent college butler', but when he pours the wine for Lancelot, he pours 'another horn', jerking the reader back into the Middle Ages. White follows this up with his ingenious use of the terminology of the wine-connoisseur: ' "A nice vintage, sir" '; ' "Observe the crust, sir" ', as the butler launches into his gross flattery of Lancelot. His obsequious pestering then makes Lancelot feel guilty: he ironically wonders if he has been discourteous to the butler, who perhaps 'had troubles of his own'. Lancelot is at the same time too noble and too drunk to be suspicious – his speech becomes hopelessly slurred – so that he falls easy prey to the plot that has been devised to get him into Elaine's bed under the impression that it is Guenever's (OFK 389–91).

Inebriation contributes extensively to the comedy when King Pelles celebrates the knighting of Castor, 'regrettably, by making too generous a use of the cellars over which dame Brisen's husband presided' (OFK 423). Malory merely provides a hint: 'And whan sir Castor was made knyght, that same day he gaff many gownys' (Vin 499). White develops it superbly by bringing medieval and modern into sharp juxtaposition:

> "Wossle," cried the King.
> "Drink hail," replied Sir Castor, who was on his best behaviour.
> "Everybody gotter gown?" shouted the King.
> "Yes, thank you, Your Majesty," replied the attendants.
> "Sure?"
> "Quite sure, Your Majesty."
> "Thas alri, then. Goo' ole gown!"
>
>   *   *   *
>
> "Warrabout the fool?" inquired the King suddenly. "Fool gotter gown? Where's the pore fool?"

Later, in Chapter XLII of *The Ill-Made Knight*, in a scene in which the comedy arises from false expectations and social contrasts, we see Guenever kidnapped by the 'cockney knight', Sir Meliagrance. In contrast with the old Etonian, fox-hunting knights of *The Sword in the Stone* he is 'not out of the top drawer', vulgar, ill-bred and cowardly, the complete opposite of the usual image of the knight, since he is neither noble nor aristocratic. White conjures up a lively scene of wild confusion in his castle, as his servants are making boudoirs for the Queen:

> taking the tapestries out of his bachelor bedroom to go in hers, and
> polishing the silver, and sending to the nearest neighbours for the loan
> of gold plate.

Meanwhile Meliagrance is 'running up and down stairs with cries of "Yes, Ma'am, in 'arf a minute" or "Marian, Marian, where the 'ell have you put the candles?" or "Murdoch, take them sheep out of the solar this instant" '.

White sees the implications of the various features of Malory's story – for example the cowardice of Meliagaunt – and develops them in his own way. The episode is a fine *tour de force*, its comedy deriving partly from its well-managed incongruities. White imagines the situation in terms of the present day but with authentic medieval details woven into it, and then adds the linguistic jokes represented by Meliagrance's ungrammatical speech.

Updating is the means by which White is able to make even the Grail quest manifest bright gleams of comedy. Gawaine's report of his experiences to Arthur and Guenever suggests his dislike of Galahad, arising from a narrow-minded and strongly-felt prejudice against what he sees as eccentricity:

> "What has Sir Galahad been doing wrong?"
> "Thing a bit. The man's a vegetarian and teetotaller, and he makes
> believe he is a vairgin. . . ."   (OFK 461)

Equally amusing are the comments expressed by other knights on the subject of Galahad, who is clearly not popular: Lionel for example complains of his 'insufferable self-confidence', a remark probably suggested by Tennyson's once very well-known poem 'Sir Galahad', in which the knight declares that his strength is as the strength of ten because his heart is pure.

Such comedy would not have been appropriate in *The Candle in the Wind*. The sadness of the approaching end of the story curbed even White's ebullience. Only in Chapter III does he manage a flicker of humour in reverting to the old 'Comic History of England' technique of Book I, as he describes 'the fabled Merry England of the Middle Ages', Arthur's Gramarye (OFK 561). The scene is evoked with great gusto, as in Chapter III White observes 'the coruscating mixture of oddities who reckoned that they possessed the things called souls as well as bodies, and who fulfilled them in the most surprising ways': the alchemist, the palmer with his relics, Joly Joly Wat, and some of Chaucer's more disreputable characters. White's magpie collection of books as well as objects – some of them listed in *The Book of Merlyn*, Chapter III in the Combination Room to which Arthur is taken to meet the animals – suggests the great range of his interests. It is often difficult to separate historical fact from fantastic invention, as in the authentic-sounding list of dubious medieval cocktails: 'Huffe Cap, Mad Dog, Father Whoresonne, Angel's Food, Dragon's Milke, Go to the Wall, Stride Wide, and Lift Leg' (OFK 565). While the medieval alchemist tried his best to turn base metals into gold, White frequently succeeded in turning the ponderous substance of the old history books into the pure gold of his fantasy.

For White, comedy was a tool, a means to an end. As a schoolmaster, he must have made frequent use of it to engage the attention of his pupils. In *The Book of Merlyn* we are told that Merlyn had 'always clowned on purpose. It had been a means of helping people to learn in a happy way' (BM

8). White's jokes are often intended to make information more memorable and so more easily assimilated, while at the same time they frequently depend upon knowledge already acquired – they are in-jokes, for the well-informed, the adult reader, the upper-middle classes. Even when they have dated, they are still funny. Many of them originate from the traditional nineteenth-century comic view of the past, the other side of the coin from Victorian solemnities, while others have their counterpart in the various forms of social comedy prevalent in the thirties. But the man who produced them did so not out of happiness and high spirits but from 'a troubled heart', as his epitaph records.

7

The Figure of Merlyn
and *The Book of Merlyn*

i.

Merlyn is not only the source of much of the comedy in *The Sword in the Stone* but also almost as much its hero as the Wart. Though it is Arthur's story, for most of the book he is just a fairly typical young boy, eager, lively, sensitive, and well brought-up, conforming to the contemporary ideal. He is too young to have much individuality: as in fairy-tales, so in White's fantasy, we see that it is the rôle of the young protagonist rather than his character that is important. Arthur's character is not yet formed, even though he has some individual traits. He is therefore in a sense a foil to Merlyn, affording his tutor the opportunity of putting forward his most cherished ideas – the ideas of the author himself.

Though other modern writers have also made Merlin the central figure in their fictions, White's nigromancer is unique for the blend of seriousness and comedy with which he is presented. David Garnett in *The Familiar Faces* said of White:

> he has a split mind ... For while Tim 1 is pursuing his occupation with
> terrific seriousness and concentration, Tim 2 is making notes of the
> comic side of Tim 1 whom he will hold up to delightful ridicule later.
> (FF 176)

So, while Merlyn's activities are frequently amusing, he is also capable of displaying an awe-inspiring sternness when he sees fit, as when he rebukes Kay: ' "Kay," said Merlyn, suddenly terrible, "thou wast ever a proud and ill-tongued speaker, and a misfortunate one. . . ." ' (OFK 34). He is not to be trifled with, but it is the force of his personality rather than his magical powers that make him formidable.

When the Wart first encounters him Merlyn is seen simply as a fairy-tale wizard, indeed a Disneyish figure, in his flowing gown and pointed hat and wand, with his long white beard and long white moustaches. 'Close inspection showed that he was far from clean.' He is thus on his first appearance seemingly very different from the dashing young master who made such an impression at Stowe in his black Bentley and his riding habit. But the bird-droppings with which Merlyn is liberally covered serve to show his affinity with nature and his love and understanding of birds and animals, a characteristic also shared with his creator. The similarity between White and the wizard appears again in the interests and attitudes attributed to Merlyn. Like White, he knows all about falconry, for example, and he grumbles about athletics: the very idea of tilting makes him tired, and he claims that the craze for games is the ruin of scholarship (OFK 52). He seems less successful at knitting, at which White claimed, in a letter to Garnett, to be very accomplished (W/G L 76). His cottage in the wood is clearly an idealised version of White's at Stowe Ridings, full of objects dear to the author's heart, such as the six live grass snakes and the guncase, rod-box and salmon flies which form part of the extraordinary mixture of articles in his 'marvellous room'. Fantasy here improves on reality as the breakfast things wash themselves up, in the cottage which like White's has neither electricity nor running water, while White's comic invention devises for Merlyn in *The Sword in the Stone* a splendid variety of spells. He is seen practising a forgotten spell, for instance, and thus making the drill-sergeant's moustaches uncurl and his ears flap. Sometimes he gets his spells wrong, alarmingly turning himself into a condor with a wingspread of about eleven feet. Worse still he loses his temper and swears:

> "Castor and Pollux blow me to Bermuda!" he exclaimed, and immediately vanished with a frightful roar.   (OFK 86)

Fragments of Latin from the schoolroom mixed up with French as well as assorted bits of mumbo-jumbo are deployed in his spells on other occasions by this 'magician of known probity and international reputation with first-class honours from every European university', as he grandly describes himself (OFK 55).

Merlyn's most important characteristic is that he lives 'backwards' in time, which is as it were a version of White's own feeling for historical periods, or of what he thought ancient times were like. David Garnett's comment, that he 'seemed to be unaware of the modern world. He was, and still is, an anachronism', is illuminating (*FF* 175). White's passion for the past, and especially for the Middle Ages, took him back in time from the twentieth century to the land of Grammarye (the 'Old England' of *The Sword in the Stone*). Merlyn's education of Arthur in *The Sword in the Stone* is therefore, Garnett suggests, 'not a piece of fanciful writing, but full of his own experience' (*ibid.*), culled not only from his study of history and his imaginative identification with medieval life, but from his practical experience of such medieval activities as the training of hawks.

White nevertheless very sensibly allows himself considerable licence in his treatment of medieval times. Merlyn does not offer the conventional instruction considered appropriate in the Middle Ages, which the Wart finds more stultifying than illuminating. Merlyn provides instead the child-centred education of the second half of the twentieth century, aware as he is that stereotyped instruction is not necessarily the best or only method of teaching. ' "That is the way to learn, by listening to the experts" ' (OFK 71) he says to the Wart, before sending him to spend the night with the hawks. And his famous pronouncement, ' "The best thing for being sad . . . is to learn something. That is the only thing that never fails" ' (OFK 185) represents the wisdom that White had himself acquired in a hard school.

White 'explains' the tradition that Merlyn could foretell the future by the device of having him live backwards. He conforms to tradition, too, in the account of Merlyn's parentage in *The Queen of Air and Darkness*.

> "Did you know," he [Merlyn] asked rather wistfully, "that I was one of the Old Ones myself? My father was a a a demon, they say, but my mother was a Gael. The only human blood I have comes from the Old Ones." [OFK 236])

Merlyn is, as customary, always benevolent. White departs from convention in not depicting him as a shape-shifter, except in his contest with Madame Mim in the first version of *The Sword in the Stone*, and when he briefly becomes a fish in the first of the Wart's excursions into the animal world. He takes on a variety of different guises, appearing at the boar-hunt in running shorts, in battle in his habergeon, and in North Humberland equipped with rucksack and enormous walking-boots. Even so he is always recognisably himself. That he is living backwards in time and so knows and is able to predict what is for ordinary mortals the future, because it is for him the past, is used to very great effect. His knowledge intensifies the sense of inevitability in Arthur's history, and White handles it dramatically, particularly when Merlyn is unable to remember what it is that he ought to have warned Arthur of – the vital information about his parentage – before Morgause comes to court and seduces him.

Merlyn's repeated attempts to recall what it is he should have mentioned enhance the suspense towards the end of the second book. Arthur's attitude to Merlyn's absent-minded foreknowledge, as to his inability to remember what it is he has to convey, carries a weight of irony: ' "I don't like knowing the future anyway. I had much rather you didn't worry about it, because it only worries me" ' (OFK 294). Arthur is unable to imagine that any particular danger threatens him, and his concern is only to think of 'something to prevent Nimue', that is, prevent her from imprisoning and killing Merlyn according to Arthurian tradition. In the ordinary way, Merlyn's knowledge of the actual past lets him advise and direct Arthur – to try to avoid the mistakes of his father, King Uther, for example – but at the crucial moment his forgetfulness takes over. Thus he represents the intersection of the comic and the tragic from which much of the dynamism of White's story derives. Though he is gifted with backsight, with foresight and with insight, his confusion about time and the human failing of forgetfulness render all his powers useless in the moment of greatest need. White's conception of Merlyn's unique role and his failure at this most crucial point in Arthur's life constitutes an imaginative and poignant commentary on the forces of chance and destiny.

At the beginning of *The Queen of Air and Darkness*, however, Merlyn is still in appearance the comic magician of convention with long white beard, horn-rimmed spectacles and conical hat. He is also still the young Arthur's mentor, constantly striving to make his erstwhile pupil think for himself. Now he is concerned to eradicate from the young king's mind the idea that fighting is fun, a task which he finds 'heartbreaking, uphill work', and to guide Arthur into the ways of peace, against the natural aggression of the young adolescent male. He is still trying to get Arthur to bring his ideas more into line with the pacificism of the 1930s. As Arthur struggles to grasp a concept in advance of his time, he tries it out on Merlyn in the form of a question: 'Might isn't Right, is it, Merlyn?'

> "Aha!" replied the magician, beaming. "Aha! You are a cunning lad, Arthur, but you won't catch your old tutor like that. You are trying to put me in a passion by making me do the thinking. But I am not to be caught. I am too old a fox for that. You will have to think the rest yourself. Is might right – and if not, why not, giving reasons and draw a plan."   (OFK 229)

The parody of the examination question with which Merlyn's speech ends suggests that Arthur is barely out of the schoolroom. Whereas at this point in *Le Morte Darthur*, Merlin's role is to help Arthur to win the battle of Bedegraine by bringing up a very large army, and by devising strategies which will outwit and defeat the enemy, in *The Queen of Air and Darkness* he is seen somewhat differently as the mouthpiece of the views on war which White was anxious to inculcate in his readers. Eventually he succeeds in changing Arthur's ideas: the concept of the Round Table – the means of harnessing Might so that it works for Right – develops out of Merlyn's teaching, while the nigromancer with a flash of the old magic directly supplies the formula, $2\pi r$, for working out the actual dimensions of the table. Arthur's idealism also slowly develops as a result of Merlyn's influence: by the end of *The Queen of Air and Darkness* he has begun to 'set a value on heads, shoulders and arms – their owners' value, even if the owner was a serf'. His vision, now embodied in the concept of the Round Table and communicated to his men, is altruistic: it involves 'something about doing a hateful and dangerous action for the sake of decency',[1] even

---

[1] 'Decency' is the single word in which White summed up his ideals. In 1961, after the death of L.J. Potts, White wrote of him that he was 'the most noble gentleman I have ever met. . . . he was the only man I have known to try to live up to his own rigid rules of decency and to behave himself. He also taught me to behave and think.' Quoted by

though his soldiers 'would get nothing but the unmarketable conscience of having done what they ought to do in spite of fear' (OFK 308). By the end of *The Queen of Air and Darkness*, when the battle of Bedegraine has been fought and won, Merlyn is represented as an old man, 'tired and muddled with his backsight' as well as forgetful, so that his magic is no match for the evil power of Morgause. White's organisation of his material in the final version of *The Queen of Air and Darkness*, rewritten so many times, is remarkably effective: by alternating the scenes in which Morgause and her children appear with those which concentrate on Merlyn and Arthur, he was able to hint at the unforeseen but ineluctable convergence of opposed forces, later to impinge upon each other with disastrous consequences.

Following Malory, White could find no place in his narrative for Merlyn after the end of *The Queen of Air and Darkness*, apart from his brief farewell appearance with Nimue near the beginning of *The Ill-Made Knight*. This visit on the part of Merlyn and Nimue to the castle where the eighteen-year old Lancelot is diligently preparing himself for his knightly career serves to link the two books, besides contributing some delightful social comedy:

> "My dear Merlyn," exclaimed the Queen, "but surely you will stay the night?"
> "No, no. Thank you. Thank you very much. We are in a hurry just now."
> "You will have a glass of something before you leave?"
> "No, thank you. It is very kind of you, but really, we must be off. We have some magic to attend to in Cornwall."   (OFK 339–40)

He thereupon vanishes with Nimue for 'a sort of honeymoon' in Cornwall:

> ... in a couple of spins they were both gone.
> Their bodies were gone, but the magician's voice remained in the air.
> "That's that," they could hear him saying in a relieved tone.

The story now leaves Merlyn, who is never to be seen again in *The Once and Future King*. White's idea of ending his Arthuriad with *The Book of Merlyn* must have appealed to him not only because it afforded him an outlet for the thoughts uppermost in his mind concerning man's incorrigible belligerence, but because as well as 'saving Pendragon', it would allow him to save Merlyn. As tutor, Merlyn's original objective in introducing the Wart to the animals had been to make him think about the problem of Might as Right, as part of his preparation for kingship. As king, Arthur's growing preoccupation with man's seemingly unnatural aggressiveness originates in Merlyn's condemnation of warfare, which becomes increasingly splenetic as time goes by. In *The Book of Merlyn* the old nigromancer

Sylvia Townsend Warner, *op. cit.*, p. 35, who describes White as 'a very moral young man.'

loses his zest and his hopefulness, and speaks of himself as having been 'a third-rate schoolmaster in the twentieth century' (BM 9). White, sad and disillusioned as he later seems to have become, was here in identifying with Merlyn, by implication belittling himself absurdly. At Reigate, he had considered himself a good teacher, and he was remembered by his former pupils at Stowe as an outstanding one. Although as a schoolmaster he must sometimes have been constrained by the demands of the syllabus that he had to teach, against his conviction that greater freedom to allow his pupils to find out for themselves would have produced better educational results, his sense of failure in *The Book of Merlyn* stems from his despair of human nature. At the very end of the whole story, on the other hand, he allows Arthur to look back with deeper understanding to Merlyn's methods and rôle as his teacher, when for example the old king realises that Merlyn 'had always clowned on purpose. It had been a means of helping people to learn in a happy way' (BM 8). Like any good schoolmaster, Merlyn had varied his techniques: he had 'saved his pupil from misery before, by being nasty to him when he was a young boy called the Wart' (BM 9). The implication is that in real life the teacher is required to be a protean figure, a magician, if he is to meet the needs of his pupils adequately. He must also be wise, and Merlyn can be seen in the first two books of *The Once and Future King* as a mentor who can explain the unfairness of life and help to make it acceptable, and who can give a perspective on fame ('only fools want to be great' [OFK 183]) useful for a future king.

In *The Book of Merlyn* we now see Merlyn in the Combination Room, rather as in the cottage in the wood of *The Sword in the Stone* where the Wart had first encountered him. In this dreamlike episode the Combination Room (the term refers to a common-room in a Cambridge college), underground in the badger's sett, seems also to be Merlyn's study. Here he is surrounded by 'thousands of books lying open to mark significant passages' (BM 21), amongst which Geoffrey of Monmouth, Giraldus Cambrensis and the Saxon Chronicle rub shoulders with *The Comic History of England*, suggestive of White's immensely wide-ranging reading. On the floor can be seen the 'debris of the magician's passing crazes', and on the table a microscope among the skulls of men, apes, fish and wild geese, all in 'indescribable confusion' (*ibid.*) – a description obviously based on White's own room in real life. Merlyn again resembles his creator in being a great talker: early on in the story, he is prepared to tell anybody about anything (OFK 239), whether they want to hear it or not. In *The Book of Merlyn*, he finds it quite impossible to hold off when it comes to talking (BM 25), and although from the beginning the Wart had found his tutor loquacious, it seems that by the time White had finished his last Arthurian book in 1941, his isolation at Doolistown had only enhanced his talkativeness, and Merlyn's with it. He is always ready to leap on his hobby-horse, and gallop off in all directions (BM 29), so much so that he has to be reproved by the animals for making Arthur miserable by throwing his weight about and exaggerating and prattling 'like a poop!' (BM 39). He has by this time, it seems, become a 'staunch conservative – which was rather progressive of him, when you reflect that he was living backwards' (BM 26).

Merlyn's rôle changes between *The Sword in the Stone* and his final appearance in *The Book of Merlyn*. As magician and tutor at the beginning he introduces the Wart to political ideologies by means of the transformations that extend his experience. In *The Book of Merlyn*, however, he has acquired other titles: Arthur now calls him Master, with a respect which was not displayed in the earlier books, when the Wart was even able to tease him. Although White can still be playful, in making Arthur smell Merlyn's skullcap with its dead mouse and frog to assure him that he is not dreaming his current experience, and by showing the nigromancer 'in the sulks' (BM 24), Merlyn has now become a more dignified figure, reminiscent of conventional notions of an aged don or the slightly decrepit master of a Cambridge college. He has become a scientist, who must follow the only thing of importance, Truth (BM 5). This is a more serious Merlyn from the superficial polymath of *The Sword in the Stone*, who has learnt 'to know a thing or two about pathology', as well as about analytical psychology and plastic surgery (OFK 118). Arthur now speaks of how he has been goaded by the conscience of 'that old scientist' who had fastened on his soul in youth, and of the enormous moral burden that his tutor had forced him to carry. In *The Book of Merlyn*, he is also seen as a philosopher, whose business it is to open new ideas, offering a faint hope of progress. Arthur insists that it was Merlyn who made him invent both Chivalry and the Round Table. In realistic terms one might question whether Merlyn's earlier uncompromisingly pacifist views are not largely responsible for Arthur's downfall, making him unduly reluctant to exert himself against the threat posed by Mordred and his supporters at the end of the story. That would be to forget that we are dealing with a traditional story, but it suggests how effectively White imagined himself into his characters and conceived their motivation. White's own eventual uncertainty about the pacifist creed that he had embraced for so long, and a degree of ambiguity towards his former fictional counterpart are suggested by Arthur's reaction against Merlyn at the end of the story, in *The Book of Merlyn*:

> "Everything which you helped to do was wrong. All your teaching was deception. Nothing was worth doing. You and I will be forgotten."
>
> (BM 4)

In *The Book of Merlyn*, the aged Arthur's visit to the geese, in the episode later transferred to *The Sword in the Stone*, concludes as the old king is 'dragged down into the filthy funnel of magic', just after he has proposed 'marriage' to a beautiful young goose, so that he is drawn back into the 'real' world (BM 96). Paradoxically, at this point Merlyn's magic brings him back to 'reality', and now for the first time, it is not appreciated. Merlyn is later further demoted from his high position as scientist and philosopher

when his *Libellus Merlini, The Prophecies of Merlyn*,[2] with its ridiculous pro-
nouncements, is brought in. White's disillusionment may have been personal in origin but it leads to greater complexity in the figure of Merlyn in
the book.

Merlyn's identification with White in *The Book of Merlyn* seems further
reflected in his ageing: he has lost his gaiety, and he recognises that now he
has finished his tutorship, he will 'not be able to rant any more, or to
twinkle and mystify with the flashing folds of his magic cloak'. He feels
'ancient and ashamed' (BM 125), an old man with hands that shake like
leaves, yet he is still a joker. The antidote to war that he now proposes – an
idea meant to provoke thought rather than to be taken seriously – is to have
an international fair, but there is a touch of despair in this silly suggestion.
'The difficulty about living backwards and thinking forwards is that you
become confused about the present. It is also the reason why one prefers to
escape into the abstract' (BM 102). White's epic ends with Merlyn, now an
anarchist ('like any other sensible person' [BM 124]), baffled and impotent
in the face of man's unending desire to make war. All his theories and
propositions and recommendations have proved useless, and he can only
fade away into despairing obscurity while White concludes the story in line
with tradition. The idealistic liberal intellectual of goodwill and rational
decency is defeated by the cruelty and irrationality of most of humankind.

It is White's special relationship with Merlyn that makes this a unique
interpretation. Through Merlyn he mocks himself; through Merlyn – particularly in his last book – he achieves an almost Dickensian blend of
comedy and pathos. Although he seems to have known of Merlin's background in English and French tradition, White takes Malory's figure as the
basis of his own, but where Malory's Merlin can be seen as a tragic figure
whose great achievement in establishing Arthur's kingdom is undermined
by a humiliating and destructive passion for a woman (Nimue), White only
allows him to age. His imprisonment remains in the future. As for later
interpretations, White obviously had no desire to take as a model Tennyson's Merlin with his 'great melancholy', in which he sees 'Death in all life
and lying in all love'. The 'Great Enchanter of the Time' of the *Idylls*[3] has
nothing in common with White's except for his shaggy eyebrows and 'the
hoary fell/ And many-wintered fleece of throat and chin'. Other more
recent writers have presented him very variously. John Cowper Powys in
Porius[4] follows Geoffrey of Monmouth, making him a mad sorcerer. As
Myrddin Wyllt, he is a weird shape-shifter, a wild man of the forest, but:

---

2 *Libellus Merlini, The Prophecies of Merlin*: White is referring to *Seven Several Strange
   Prophesies . . . some whereof are accomplished in this year 1643* by an unknown author.
3 Tennyson, Alfred: *Merlin and Vivien*, 1859, lines 838–9.
4 Powys, John Cowper: *Porius: A Romance of the Dark Ages*, London, Macdonald 1951.

nothing could conceal the jet-black sheen of his glossy Africa-thick hair; nothing could conceal the green-black enormity of his cavernous eyes; nothing could disguise the ape-like lowness of his primeval forehead or alter the sub-human manner in which his skull bulged out so monstrously behind his immense ears.   (89)

He emits a 'mortality-smell of fungoid vegetation' and an ice-cold breath; he is a towering figure reeking of 'thousands upon thousands of earth-chasms full of the black leaf mould of the original planetary forests', and to him all nature seems to belong. This Merlin is representative of what is frightening and sinister in the primeval, grotesque but not comic.

Mary Stewart's Merlin in *The Crystal Cave*[5] and its sequels, though possessed of magical powers, is likewise an entirely serious figure, but in no way grotesque. Like Cowper Powys, she sets the scene in the Dark Ages, but the story is retold with historical realism as first-person narration, and the characters are portrayed in terms of modern psychology. Merlin's magical powers take the form of visions which come to him in agonising trances, and his special powers are derived from the application of exceptional intelligence: he performs no conjuring tricks.

Very different from these earlier interpretations of the figure of Merlin is Robert Nye's *Merlin*,[6] based on Robert de Boron. Here, it is the fact that Merlin is the son of a devil and of a virgin that is all- important; it enables Nye to represent what he sees as the demonic side of sexuality. His Merlin has special powers which have enabled him to watch his own conception, and he suggests sadistic fantasies (Nye maintains that the early Arthurian stories contain an element of sadism) to Arthur. He claims that in this book he has 'stood the medieval world of chivalry on its head and . . . explored in a modern way the dark unconscious side of the Arthurian myth', an approach probably suggested by *The Grail Legend* of Emma Jung and Marie-Louise von Franz.[7] These authors claim that the unconscious mind is symbolically represented by the figure of Merlin, thus suggesting a new relevance for the myth. They claim that Merlin's story offers a means of dealing with the conflict that arises between the conscious and the unconscious. Man has in the past struggled to identify himself with the good, but now the real need is to recognise 'the dark instinctive side' of his nature, and instead of repressing it, to allow it freer play, and by so doing give life to the more archaic part of the self. According to such thinking the resulting liberation of the unconscious is only a part of what the figure of Merlin can effect: his 'painstaking attention to the divine' during his forest years, by means of which he acquired wisdom and understanding in the early stories

5   Stewart, Mary: *The Crystal Cave*, London, Hodder and Stoughton, 1970. See also the sequels, *The Hollow Hills; The Last Enchantment; The Wicked Day.*
6   Nye, Robert: *Merlin*, New York, Putnam 1979.
7   Jung, E. and von Franz, M.L.: *The Grail Legend*, translated by A. Dykes, London 1971.

concerning him, is also to be emulated at the present time. White's Merlyn, however, cannot be enlisted for these ends: he stands too firmly on the side of early twentieth-century liberal idealism, altruism and self-control to play the part of a liberator of the unconscious. Perhaps it would have been better for White if it had not been so.

ii. *The Book of Merlyn*

In January 1941 White wrote to David Garnett: 'My Death of Arthur is going to end up as a treatise on war' (W/G L 80). He had earlier written: 'So far as I can see, my fifth volume is going to be all about the anatomy of the brain. It sounds odd for Arthur, but it is true' (W/G L 76). When in the course of time David Garnett was sent the finished draft of *The Book of Merlyn*, he had some sharp comments to make on what he saw as White's facile discussion of man's belligerence, which he found superficial and irritating. It seemed as if White, away in Ireland, was entirely out of touch with what was going on elsewhere, and totally unable to realise the gravity of the situation in Europe, and the absolute necessity of combatting Hitler. Garnett probably also felt that White was unable to understand that his compatriots were not heedlessly indulging in warfare for the fun of it, but were deliberately and voluntarily laying down their lives in a war that had to be fought, if civilisation was to survive. Against such a background, White's preoccupation with the nature of the brain in various creatures must have seemed merely frivolous. But in his enforced isolation, deprived as he was of reliable information about the course of the war, a mere onlooker with no chance of intelligent or informed conversation, it was hardly surprising that he should turn his troubled mind to the question of what it was that made man seemingly so different from the animals in terms of aggression.

Interesting as *The Book of Merlyn* is, it would have made a strange ending to the story of Arthur, had its author been able to carry out his original intention of concluding his epic with it as a fifth book. For what reader, after reaching the tragic end of the story, when Arthur, old and defeated, faces death at the hand of his own son, really wants to attend a Privy Council of animals, including the sentimental and sentimentalised hedge-hog, for another dose of polemic and facetious humour before the end? Such a conclusion could only detract from the sadness and grandeur of the traditional ending, particularly as related by Malory, and the continued debate about man's belligerence could only seem an irrelevant after-thought. It is nevertheless sad that White had to abandon *The Book of Merlyn* since the idea of it meant so much to him: 'The last book, number five, is, I hope, the crown of the whole', he wrote to Garnett on 8 June 1941 (W/G L 86). But although *The Book of Merlyn* might seem to represent

White's last word on the subject of Arthur, since it was not published until so long after the rest, his final revision of *The Candle in the Wind* before the tetralogy eventually appeared in 1958 enabled him to end it more judiciously and with more decorum. So, although it was not until November 1948 that White at last decided that he would have in effect to discard *The Book of Merlyn* and that he would insert the visits to the ants and to the geese into *The Sword in the Stone*, in doing so he surely made the right decision. In making these experiences part of the Wart's education for kingship, he allowed them to take their proper place structurally among the metamorphoses of his first book, and among the learning-situations in which his young hero is placed.

As an independent if imperfect work (since White never revised it) *The Book of Merlyn* is a different matter altogether, particularly interesting for the earlier drafts of the episodes of the ants and the geese, a fuller version of White's views on war, and his unique handling of the end of the story of Arthur, Guenever and Lancelot. The starting point of the book is a variant of the folk legend found in various parts of the country and on which Masefield's poem 'Midsummer Night'[8] is based, that Arthur with all his knights still live underground in a 'hollow hill', and once a year can still be seen. In his diary for 14 November 1940, White in alluding to 'the legend of him going underground at the end' decided to take Arthur back to the badger's sett to discuss with Merlyn war 'from the naturalist's point of view. . . . Now what can we learn about the abolition of war from animals?' White's apparent belief in the importance, indeed the omniscience of the naturalist led him to classify Hitler himself as merely 'a bad naturalist' (BM 115). As conclusion to the great and poignant story of Arthur and the downfall of the Round Table, the naturalist's point of view as expressed through the medium of the animals' conversation seems particularly trivial and inappropriate. It also has the effect of making apparent how flimsy and unworkable White's political theories and notions were.

Arthur's return to the Privy Council in the hollow hill – or cave, or burrow, or badger's sett (as White variously refers to it) – at the end of his life does however have the symbolic resonance of the descent to the underworld of folklore and mythology. By such experience, usually undergone in fear and peril, the hero brings back essential knowledge and enlightenment. In *The Book of Merlyn* the old king, though harassed by his problems and battered by Merlyn's seemingly endless harangues, does gain understanding. The source of Arthur's enlightenment and spiritual renewal at the end of his life, which allow him to confront the horrors awaiting him in the Last Battle with courage and energy, is to be found in the affirmation of the imperishable value of human altruism and of the restorative power of nature, in the visionary experience to which his guide the hedgehog leads

---

8   Masefield, John: *Midsummer Night and Other Tales in Verse*, London, Heinemann, 1928.

him. By the hedgehog he is persuaded to turn his back on the hell of insoluble human problems and to look up to the stars.

The return to the animals at the end of Arthur's story is ingenious, too, in that it creates a circular pattern, somewhat similar to that in older Arthurian tradition, in which the appearance of the Lady of the Lake with Excalibur marks the beginning of Arthur's career as king, while the return of the sword to her at the end signals its close. The interaction of the human and the animal in *The Book of Merlyn* parallels that in *The Sword in the Stone*, involving movement between the primary world of human affairs, the secondary one of the friendly animals in the badger's sett, and its further extension in the episodes of the ants and the geese, allowing White to pose questions relating to his desire to make the story of Arthur profoundly relevant for the modern reader. Whether the now old King Arthur is merely dreaming, or whether his experience is 'real', he is made to contemplate the problems of humanity in terms of the modern world as well as of his own time, often to his bewilderment. In the badger's sett the animals all behave as if they were human beings. Among them Arthur receives the kindness, consideration and affection sadly missing from his everyday life. With Merlyn they are able to join in the argument about human beings: the badger ('who always took the kindly view of everybody, even of Karl Marx') is able to question Merlyn's judgment:

> "Surely that is hardly fair to actual communism? I would have thought that ants were more like Mordred's fascists than John Ball's communists . . ."   (BM 64)

When Arthur is sent off to live amongst the ants and geese, the fantasy takes a different direction, confronting him with forms of animal life seen predominantly from a political point of view. As in the Wart's metamorphoses into fish, insect, bird and animal in *The Sword in the Stone*, his bodily form becomes animal while his mind remains human.

When Merlyn reappears in *The Book of Merlyn*, not having been seen since the beginning of *The Ill-Made Knight*, it is his voice that is heard throughout. He dominates the book, despite White's intention of saving Pendragon (i.e. Arthur) by taking him back to his animals, which suggests that he meant Arthur to be the central figure. As Merlyn takes up again the argument against war which had been begun in the early days of Arthur's reign, his usual volubility is greatly increased so that the animals – apart from the hedgehog – hardly get a chance to speak. White now strives to make his retelling of the Arthurian myth relevant to the modern world more explicitly, as he struggles with the problem of why men fight. Here again, particularly at the end of his story, as in *The Once and Future King* as a whole he is still able to communicate a sense of decency and altruism which we now often shrink from expressing overtly.

In the first chapter, Merlyn's eloquence and special powers enable him to give a spirited resumé of Arthurian literature from Nennius to T.H. White

himself. Intended to comfort the aged and despairing King when he expresses the fear that they will both be forgotten, it at the same time provides
a context for White's version as it reminds the reader of the great number of
different ways in which the story has been interpreted through the centuries:

> "Forgotten?" asked the magician. . . . "There was a king," he said,
> "whom Nennius wrote about, and Geoffrey of Monmouth. The Arch-
> deacon of Oxford was said to have had a hand in him, and even that
> delightful ass, Gerald the Welshman. Brut, Layamon and the rest of
> them: what a lot of lies they all managed to tell! Some said that he was
> a Briton painted blue, some that he was in chain mail to suit the ideas
> of the Norman romancers. Certain lumbering Germans dressed him up
> to vie with their tedious Siegfrieds. Others put him into plate, like your
> friend Thomas of Hutton Coniers, and others again, notably a romantic
> Elizabethan called Hughes, recognised his extraordinary problem of
> love. Then there was a blind poet who tried to justify God's ways to
> man, and he weighed Arthur against Adam, wondering which was the
> more important of the two. At the same time came masters of music
> like Purcell, and later still such titans as the Romantics, endlessly
> dreaming about our king. There came men who dressed him in armour
> like ivy-leaves, and who made all his friends to stand about among
> ruins with brambles twining round them, or else to swoon backward
> with a mellow blur kissing them on the lips. Also there was Victoria's
> lord. Even the most unlikely people meddled with him, people like
> Aubrey Beardsley, who illustrated his history. After a bit there was poor
> old White, who thought that we represented the ideas of chivalry."
>
> (BM 4)

The passage well illustrates White's extraordinary versatility as he successfully introduces into a tragic story this comprehensive, succinct and witty
summary. Elsewhere, Merlyn can still give rise to some flashes of his former humour despite the over-insistent argument; in trying to convince
Arthur that he is not dreaming, he asks him if he has ever dreamed of a
smell:

> "Come, come. You have dreamed of a sight, have you not? And of a
> feeling: everybody has dreamed of a feeling. You may even have
> dreamed of a taste. I recollect that once when I had forgotten to eat
> anything for a fortnight, I dreamed of a chocolate pudding: which I
> distinctly tasted, but it was snatched away. The question is, have you
> ever dreamed of a smell?"
> "I do not think I have: not to smell it."

Merlyn then convinces Arthur that he is awake by exclaiming ' "Then smell
that!" ' as he snatches off his skull-cap and presents it under Arthur's nose
(BM 10). A more pleasing fragrance is released when the badger searches
among many scattered slips of paper for one of Merlyn's spells: one says
briefly ' "Half a rose noble each way on Golden Miller" ' while the third:

which smelt strongly of Quelques Fleurs, and was not in Merlyn's hand, said: "Queen Philippa's monument at Charing Cross, seven-thirty, under the spire." There were a lot of kisses on the bottom of it, and, on the back, some notes for a poem to be addressed to the sender.

(BM 43)

As the book circles back to the old pupil/teacher relationship between Arthur and Merlyn, although Merlyn can still instruct, Arthur can only momentarily become the Wart again. The burden of the years of kingship and of his age oppress him, to be lightened only by his contact, under the hedgehog's guidance, with nature and with his country, a contact which at last restores to him, if only briefly before the end, his vigorous and impressive kingship. Arthur is England, and Merlyn pressing on without remorse in the pursuit of 'the only thing of any importance, Truth' (BM 5), insists that Arthur – and England – shall pursue it too. Merlyn has gone on 'believing and trying with undaunted crankiness, spite of ages of experience' to get his lesson across (BM 8). The only way, he argues in the badger's sett, in which the human condition can be improved is by increasing the stock of ideas (BM 11), hence the importance of education. White's interest in the structure of the brain now comes into play: man's is unique, his cerebrum developed in a way that no animal's is. It therefore seems to follow that capitalism is also man's speciality, 'a jewel in the crown'. Nevertheless the term 'homo sapiens' is inappropriate; 'ferox' (savage) would be a much better adjective than 'sapiens' (wise) for the Inventor of Cruelty to Animals, though it seems that Archimedes the owl has proposed 'stultus' (stupid) as more accurate. The badger, however, has suggested the label 'impoliticus' (unpolitical) because man solves his problems either by force or by argument, rather than by thinking. It will take a million years, therefore, before man can justly be described as a political animal.

Arthur is greatly distressed by this thorough-going condemnation of man, and has to be consoled by the weak argument that the human race is redeemed by its love of pets. Shortly after this, he consents to visit the ants. Merlyn tells him that he had forgotten to show them to him when he was small, and that unless he sees them now, 'we shall get no further'. The horrible experience quite properly results in fury on Arthur's part rather than the wisdom proverbially supposed to ensue from such contemplation.

On Arthur's return to the Combination Room after this visit, the discussion moves on to the subject of Karl Marx, 'a bad naturalist' because he subscribed to the Égalité Fallacy which is equally abhorrent to nature: 'You might just as well insist that all the people in the world should wear the same size of boot', insists Merlyn (BM 67). When the badger begins to say something about 'Liberty, Equality and Fraternity', he is promptly shouted down by Merlyn, who changes it to 'Liberty, Brutality and Obscenity', insisting that that is what such slogans really entail, and instancing the Spanish Civil War in the 1930s as an example. Exhaustion overcomes the aged monarch at this point, and as he shuts his eyes he slides back 'into the real world from which he had come, his wife abducted, his best friend banished, his son at his throat' (BM 69). His animal friends wake him nevertheless and make him visit the geese in order to experience a better social system, before his next bout of indoctrination with Merlyn's political theories.

Next we see White propounding the idea that it is 'communal property' rather than the ownership of private property that leads to war. Nationalism is the curse of man, and for this Merlyn has a simple, easy solution to propose. All you have to do is to abolish nations, 'tariff barriers, passports and immigration laws, converting mankind into a federation of individuals' (BM 101), and tolerating no unit larger than the family. All the badger's arguments against this programme are again briskly swept away by Merlyn, who agrees that it will mean economic revolution. He sees it as the only chance of survival, for man has now to choose between being liquidated and 'being manly', by which he presumably means acting intelligently, in accordance with the 'sapientia' (wisdom) that he has claimed for himself. There is hope for mankind, he seems to think, if only in the far-distant future.

He continues his championship of the rights of the individual by reference to another part of the human brain, the neopallium which is 'concerned with memory, deduction and the forms of thought which result in recognition by the individual of his personality', and makes him conscious of himself as a separate being. Thus any form of pronounced collectivism in politics is contrary to man's unique nature; and Merlyn claims that his attempts to persuade Arthur (as a young man) that Might is not Right and to believe in justice rather than in power, were based on this fact about mankind. He insists that 'the Individual is more important than the State', and so once again, every effort must be made to abolish the power of the state. Merlyn looks back upon the efforts he had made to persuade the young Arthur of the evil nature of war, of the contempt due both to the 'Games-Maniac' and to the proponents of Fort Mayne, as well as of the need to believe in justice rather than power, but in doing so he cannot put his arguments without recourse to the language of war. He has 'waged his little war', he has investigated the causes of 'the battle we are waging', he has engaged in a 'crusade' (BM 116): once again it would seem that the concept is so deeply embedded in human consciousness as to be ineradicable, still inadvertently thrusting up in the form of metaphor in White's own arguments against war.

Merlyn finally puts forward some arguments in favour of war, though they are hardly serious ones. It is one of the mainsprings of romance: without it, there would be no 'Rolands, Maccabees, Lawrences or Hodson's Horse'. (White condemns Shakespeare, however, for apparently being in agreement with the Germans on the subject of war, asserting with iconoclastic fervour that *King Henry V* is the most revolting play he knows, and Henry the most revolting character.) War keeps down the population and provides a vent for the pent-up ferocity of man, thus answering a real need, and finally, as the animals would argue, it 'is an inestimable boon to creation as a whole, because it does offer some faint hope of exterminating the human race'. In the end, the whole discussion – or perhaps harangue would be a more appropriate word – fizzles out as it creeps to the final conclusion, that 'man is a slayer by instinct'. War 'is due to national property, with the rider that it is stimulated by certain glands.' At any rate, there is something in the physical make-up of man that is responsible, so 'perhaps the root of war is removable, like the appendix.' Unhelpfully, Merlyn at the last declares himself an anarchist; he can offer no solution to man's problems, while Arthur must go back to the world to do his duty as well as he can. The only hope for the future of the human race, it would appear, lies in 'that strange, altruistic, rare and obstinate decency which will make writers or scientists maintain their truths at the risk of death' (BM 112). White himself is not only writer but also scientist in this sense, proclaiming the noblest of human ideals and values with fervent conviction. After all the naive muddle and superficiality of the discussions in the badger's sett, he at last comes to a human, and humane, if necessarily non-rational conclusion. His insistence on the value of individualism strikes an authentically modern, non-medieval note. But here as elsewhere he seems to have been embarrassed by his own idealism, and so swiftly lowers the tone of the passage with the re-introduction of the hedgehog with its banal remarks and sentimental songs.

White's struggle with the problem of why men, unlike animals, fight other members of their own species was long continued. In an Appendix to his Journal 1945–7 he wrote: 'It is certainly true that war is only caused by boundaries'. He instances the United States of America as a successful example of the peaceful co-existence of 'different cultures, different industries, . . . different internal laws', and goes on to ask explicitly the question which already underlies the visit to the geese in *The Book of Merlyn*: 'What must you give up? Only three things:- passports, immigration laws, tarriffs (sic).' As Lyo-lyok the goose explains to Arthur, there is no need to sacrifice private property 'within very wide limits'.

The nature of the animal-fantasy changes as *The Book of Merlyn* progresses. The animals first of all constitute a sort of chorus, lovingly welcoming Arthur (though the point is soon made that all animals fear man) and doing their best to console him when he is cast down by Merlyn's diatribes. Apart from this, they have little to say: the arguments are really Merlyn's, although some points are occasionally attributed to the badger and to Archimedes. They are brought together in a harmony which is humane rather than characteristic of the animal kingdom, acting as human beings at their best, in fact. Their interaction with human beings, with Arthur and Merlyn, so that they can discuss human problems with them (as with their previous appearances in *The Sword in the Stone*) distinguishes them from the animals in, for example, such works as *The Wind in the Willows*, or in

George Orwell's *Animal Farm*, or Richard Adam's *Watership Down* where the characters are all animals. It is the old intermingling of animals with men of folktale, or of Masefield's *Midnight Folk* and *Box of Delights*. The animals are differentiated not only by their natural characteristics as animals, but also by the human ones attributed to them, which imply an intellectual and social hierarchy. The badger, a donnish if muddled character (sometimes referred to nevertheless as 'it' rather than as 'he') has some Marxist notions, while Balin the hawk is clearly upper-class and the patriotic hedgehog is lowly and uneducated. Cavall the dog remains truly dog-like throughout.

The return to animal fantasy at the end of the 'epic' mustered a host of witnesses to what seemed to White the inexplicable, the apparently unnecessary savagery of man. As he first conceived the work, before the visits to the ants and geese had to be transferred to *The Sword in the Stone*, he must have felt that the point of man's difference from the animals, in habitually making war on his own kind as virtually no other creatures do, had not been made strongly enough. His final book becomes fable, as he tries to show that we ought to be able to learn from them. Yet since that seems impossible, some explanation must be found to account for so remarkable a difference between the animal and the human: science at any rate should be capable of shedding light on the matter, if as seemed likely to him, it is a significant difference in the structure of the brain that accounts for our lamentable propensity.

Some of the ideas which formed the basis of *The Book of Merlyn* had their counterpart in a work by Freud which it is probable that White knew, given his interest in psychology. In *Civilisation, War and Death* published in 1939, Freud asks: 'Why do animals, kin to ourselves, not manifest any such cultural struggle?' (as human beings do) and he goes on to consider the 'state institutions' of bees, ants and termites. His comments are the more interesting for his attitude towards such 'institutions':

> we should not think ourselves happy in any of these communities of the animal world, or in any of the roles they delegate to individuals.[9]

His comments look forward to Arthur's/the Wart's visit to the ants. When Freud turns specifically to the subject of war he takes, like White, the relations between Might and Right as 'assuredly the proper starting-point for our inquiry'; and he sees hope only in 'a strengthening of the intellect' and in 'man's cultural disposition'. Just as at the end of *The Candle in the Wind* White looks to culture as the only source of hope for the future, so Freud similarly emphasises that 'whatever makes for cultural development is working also against war.'[10]

9 Freud, S., ed. J. Rickman: *Civilisation, War and Death: Selections from 3 Works by S. Freud*, London, Hogarth Press 1939, p. 56.
10 *Ibid.*, p. 97.

The main source of White's practical and theoretical interest in ants, which also inspired the idea of Arthur's visit to them, was almost certainly a book in his library, *The Social World of the Ants Compared with that of Man*, by Auguste Forel, first published in 1928. In it the author gives a very attractive account of how as a child of five he became fascinated by ants and subsequently made them his life-long study. One of the things that particularly intrigued and puzzled him was their habit of fighting ants from other colonies, and like White he made comparisons between them and human beings. In a passage which White marked, he said:

> We men are fierce beings, family-loving individualists, endowed with a great brain and a desire to command and oppress weaker folk. Our sentiments of sympathy and devotion are as a rule very exclusive and scarcely social at all. But at the present time we cover the surface of the whole globe *with a single true species*, for all our living races and varieties can produce fertile cross-breeds between them. Thanks to modern means of transport, therefore, we can achieve something which the little ants, with more than 3,500 distinct species, each possessing its fixed instinct, are unable to establish – a world federation of races. That is our only means of taming ourselves to any reasonable extent, and of putting a definite end to our wars, as the United States and the Swiss Cantons have done among themselves. When such a state of affairs becomes universal, we shall never repeat the horrible tragedy of the World-war of 1914–1918. But we shall still be oppressed by the age-long tragedy arising from the very fact of our individualistic nature, which makes us revolt against any social organisation that restricts our liberty, and so demands communal laws. We shall see whether the social war begun in 1919 will be able to triumph gradually over our egotism in its fiercest manifestation – organised war between states. (p. xxxviii)

Forel experimented extensively with colonies of ants, as well as simply observing them. He set up a battle between the inhabitants of three different nests, for example, seeing it in terms of Homeric battle, and again finding a close parallel with human behaviour in the wars of the ants. He ends his chapter on this experiment with a comment on his observations of 'collective spite' between the various colonies of ants which he had found 'so poignantly reminiscent of our wretched human society that they cannot but wring the heart of every man with moral – that is, social instincts'. This chapter ('Ordinary Wars Among Ants') undoubtedly interested White deeply: he marked it and put a note in the end-paper of the book relating to Forel's experiment. It is characteristic of him: 'I do not think it is fair to "observe battles" which have been artificially provoked by man', though he also goes on to suggest that these battles are not scientifically valid, since 'a true battle must be spontaneous'.

The passage must also have made a deep impression on him, as he reflected on Forel's comment that after only two decades the 'horrible tragedy of the World-war of 1914–1918' was in process of being repeated, 'organised war between states', with the additional horror of the Holocaust in Europe. It is not difficult to understand why, despite the depth of his interest, all White's reading, observation and experimentation never resulted in either the affection or the admiration for ants that inspired Forel's life-long study. They seem only to have aroused an intense dislike, which found expression in his vision of their social organisation as symbol of a totalitarian regime.

As well as Forel's two-volume work, White also possessed Julian Huxley's much less comprehensive and less thought-provoking book on the subject, *Ants* (1935) in the end-papers of which he drafted a letter asking for the author's advice:

> I am trying to write a book about the politics of animals, for the Pelican sixpenny's – if they will take it, and I am stuck in a chapter on war, for lack of true examples except the Harvester ants. You seem to suggest in your book on ants that other examples (species v. same species) could be found. Can you tell me of any? Bees?

The draft letter continues with the theory that 'our opposible fingertips and stereoscopic vision have developed out of proportion to the neopallium'. As a result, he impractically suggests that we have now got to 'examine the politics of older animals, give our ingenuity a compulsory rest, abolish national property as such, and concentrate on letting our brains catch up with our fingers'.

White was able to make more of the episodes of Arthur's visits to the ants and to the geese when they took place at the end of his life, in *The Book of Merlyn*, instead of forming part of his youthful education. He had necessarily to modify them when they were transferred to *The Sword in the Stone*, since here the Wart is too young and inexperienced to be able to understand the full significance, in human terms, of the different social systems they represent. As a boy, he reacts strongly against the ants' regime, it is true, in contrast to his response to the free and happy way of life of the geese, but he obviously cannot appreciate all the political implications.

White's obsession with the possibility of learning how to abolish war by studying animals, though it seemed ridiculous to some of his friends, at least sprang from a very deep horror of the terrible inhumanity of the Nazis and its implications for the future of mankind. The ants manifest all the worst features of the totalitarian régime in their utter denial of the rights of the individual. In *The Book of Merlyn*, Arthur's reaction when confronted with their forces is desperate: as the Red Army marches to war, Arthur as ant/man 'suddenly faced about in the middle of the straw like an insane creature, ready to oppose their passage with his life' (BM 62). The animals in the badger's sett, watching anxiously as he is rescued in the nick of time, soon discover that he is 'furiously angry'; he finds the ants 'horrible creatures', 'the walking dead', 'not human, but like humans, a bad copy'.

Arthur's visit to the geese is closer in tone to the Wart's earlier transformations: while the aged Arthur experienced it, 'All the sorrow of his thoughts about man . . . fell from him for the moment in the glory of his wings' (BM 77), an image perhaps suggested by White's early experience of piloting an aircraft. The whole episode also looks back to the happier days before the outbreak of war when he had gone wild goose shooting on the Norfolk coast, which resulted in an unfinished novel (begun before he left England for Ireland) called *Grief for the Grey Geese*. Sylvia Townsend Warner in her Introduction to *The Book of Merlyn* speaks of the 'intense physical excitement' of this period of White's life:

> He was alone, he was in the intimidating sea-level territory of the Wash, he was pursuing a long-ambitioned desire, intricately compounded of sporting prowess and sadism – to shoot a wild goose in flight. The theme is significant. The geese are warred on by the goose shooters. Among the goose shooters is a renegade who takes sides with the geese, deflecting their flight away from the ranks of the shooters. White plainly identifies himself with the renegade, while bent on shooting a wild goose.   (BM xiii).

The aged Arthur's metamorphosis into the wild goose introduces him to an idealised society. As with the visit to the ants this episode, too, includes material which was not incorporated into *The Sword in the Stone*, as Arthur enquires about the attitudes of the geese to such matters as nationalism, state-control, individual liberty, property and so forth, and the conclusion is reached that it is territorial boundaries that are the cause of war. But where at the end of the episode in *The Sword in the Stone* the Wart skims on down-curved wings and wakes up beside Kay, who accuses him of snoring and honking like a goose, Arthur in *The Book of Merlyn* is 'dragged down into the filthy funnel of magic' by Merlyn's dark hand, his dream of lasting happiness among the geese shattered. The utopian world of the geese is based on anarchy, but it works because there is no need for the geese to extend their territory, or to possess themselves of the territory of other creatures, since there is always enough space and food readily available for them. Their social system is therefore not necessarily transferable to human societies.

The visit to the geese in its first form in Chapters 12 to 15 of *The Book of Merlyn* turns out to be more than a utopian fantasy, for it is not merely their way of life and political system (or lack of it) that appeals to Arthur. He comes to love his companion, Lyo-lyok, and bizarre as it seems proposes marriage to her, being able at the same time to compare her very favourably with 'the women he had known', in a remarkably revealing passage. He finds a warm feeling for her in his old heart, 'even if there was little passion', first because she is not only as healthy as himself, but also because she had never 'had the megrims or the vapours or the hysterics'. She is as strong as he, but in addition she is 'docile, prudent, faithful, conversable', 'a

great deal cleaner than most women', and more beautiful because not
disfigured by paint, and possessed of a more natural shape (BM 94). Finally,
'She would be a loving mother': White's old wound would, it seems, never
heal. This daydream, originating in the tormenting conflict of longing and
loathing with regard to women which he could never resolve, is oddly
touching in its naive sincerity – and despite its strangely old-fashioned
references to paint and natural shape, not intrinsically so very absurd.

When after this idyllic episode, the old king returns to 'reality', it is the
grubby little hedgehog, with his fleas and dirty paws and bad language full
of outrageous mispronunciations and malapropisms, who is the creature
best able to console him and to reconcile him with the life that he is so soon
to give up. Not even Cavall the dog, for all his devotion, can help Arthur to
accept both humanity in general and himself with all his failures. The
urchin (which is a dialect or archaic term for a hedgehog as well as for a
mischievous little boy) invites the King to come out into the night with him:

> "Nay, Measter," he said. "Tha hast been within too long. Let thee
> come art along of a nugly hurchin, that tha mayest sniff God's air to thy
> nostrils, an lay thy head to the boozum o' the earth.
> "Teak no thought fer them bougers," he continued. "Lave 'un fer to
> argyfy theirselves inter the hy-sterics, that 'ull plaze 'un. Let thee smell
> a peck of air wi' ter humble mun, an have thy pleasure of the sky."
>
> (BM 105)

This Lawrentian prescription works, enabling Arthur to forget the intoler-
able problems which beset him, and to identify with his native land. The
chapter begins in a low-key and confidential tone which recalls the early
twentieth-century nature writers whom White admired – Richard Jefferies,
Edward Thomas, Kenneth Grahame, Henry Williamson, D.H. Lawrence
and the rest (and who in the polluted air of modern Britain will say they
were wrong?):

> There is nothing so wonderful as to be out on a spring night in the
> country; but really in the latest part of night, and, best of all, if you can
> be alone. Then, when you can hear the wild world scamper, and the
> cows chewing just before you stumble over them, and the leaves living
> secretly, and the nibblings and grass pluckings and the blood's tide in
> your own veins: when you can see the loom of trees and hills in deeper
> darkness and the stars twirling in their oiled grooves . . . when the
> dogs' chains rattle at the farms, and the vixen yelps once, and the owls
> have fallen silent: then is a grand time to be alive and vastly conscious,
> when all else human is unconscious, home-bound, bed-sprawled, at
> the mercy of the midnight mind.   (BM 108)

As the moon rises, Arthur looks out over his England and feels 'the
intense sad loveliness of being as being, apart from right or wrong' and he
begins 'to love the land under him with a fierce longing, not because it was

good or bad, but because it was'. This vision of his realm, and of the natural world with its own harmony, brings reconciliation and enables him to contemplate the integrity, altruism and heroism of which man is capable, and to understand the importance of Truth. His Englishmen:

> might be stupid, ferocious, unpolitical, almost hopeless. But here and there, oh so seldom, oh so rare, oh so glorious, there were those all the same who would face the rack, the executioner, and even utter extinction, in the cause of something greater than themselves. Truth, that strange thing, the jest of Pilate's. Many stupid young men had thought they were dying for it, perhaps for a thousand years. They did not have to be right about their truth, as Galileo was to be. It was enough that they, the few and martyred, should establish a greatness, a thing above the sum of all they ignorantly had.   (BM 112)

White's tribute to those who were prepared to lay down their lives for their perhaps unformulated ideals, and who were doing so at the very time that White was writing it, is also Arthur's consolation and inspiration, enabling him to face the future as 'England' personified. From the identification with nature of many writers, from the Wordsworthian sense, apparent here, of a moral or spiritual power in nature which can both console and uplift, White at last seems to find a means of acceptance of and reconciliation with humanity. But he soon feels the tone to be too lofty; the feeling generated has to be transposed into the hedgehog's rendering of 'Home Sweet Home' and Blake's 'Jerusalem'. Then Arthur returns to the committee to say goodbye: 'But it was England who came in' (BM 115). When he eventually leaves the badger's sett after the Council, it is in full knowledge that he is going to his death. The grass-snake, T.natrix, with the wisdom of the serpent, looks forward to the trivial event that precipitates the final catastrophe, the killing of the adder, with words that augment the sense of impending doom:

> "You will fail because it is the nature of men to slay, in ignorance if not in wrath. But failure builds success and nature changes . . . and so, strong courage to Your Majesty, and a tranquil heart."

At this point, both inspirational vision and serious argument dissolve in facetiousness and sentimentality again as Arthur and the hedgehog say goodbye. White gives the last word to Tiggy: ' "Say not farewell" ' . . . ' "Orryvoyer", whispered the urchin. "Orryvoyer" ' (BM 128).

Since *The Book of Merlyn* was rejected by Collins and only published posthumously, White never revised and rewrote it in the way that he did his other books. After salvaging the ants and the geese for *The Sword in the Stone* he abandoned it. One's impatience with Merlyn's long-winded ranting in the Privy Council of the animals is therefore, perhaps, unreasonable: there is much in the book that is successful, not least the alternative ending to the story of Arthur which White discarded in favour of the episode with which he concludes *The Once and Future King*. This alternative ending includes a brief but dignified and often moving account of the Last Battle itself, and of the fate of Guenever and Lancelot. Throughout the book Arthur, despite his age, his baffled impotence and his sadness, is still an imposing figure, through whom White movingly reveals his own feeling for England once again. When he goes forward to the battle, to be beaten at last by the fact 'that man was a slayer by instinct', the final conflict is succinctly, splendidly described. Arthur struggles to the last

> against the flood of Might which had burst out all his life at a new place whenever he had dammed it, so the tumult rose, the war-yell sounded, and the meeting waters closed above his head.

White follows Malory in summarising the last sad events which lead to the death of Lancelot and Guenever, but with some interesting modifications. Guenever 'knew that Lancelot did care for God most passionately, that it was essential he should turn in that direction' (BM 132), whereas in Malory she refuses to accept that Launcelot has a true religious vocation: ' "But I may never beleve you . . . but that ye woll turne to the worlde agayne." ' (Vin 720). White at this point decided to simplify – rightly in terms of the focus of his narrative – rather than to involve himself with the complexities and subtleties of the relationship between the Queen and Launcelot after the death of Arthur. He has lost sympathy with the Ill-Made Knight by this time, trivialising him by showing him climbing the convent wall 'with Gallic, ageing gallantry' (BM 132). As a hermit, Lancelot 'even learned to distinguish bird-songs in the woods, and to have time for all the things which had been denied to him by Uncle Dap. He became an excellent gardener' (BM 132). Reputed to be a saint, he dies in the 'Odour of Sanctity' which White transmutes into the fragrance of new hay, of spring blossom, of the clean sea-shore. Sir Ector's lament for his dead brother is quoted direct from Malory, but its grandeur is devalued in White's description of it as his 'keen, one of the most touching pieces of prose in the language' (BM 133).

After a brief mention of the surviving members of the Round Table, White characteristically switches back to the comic mode in the course of expounding the theories held by a whole series of authorities as to the fate of Arthur after the Last Battle. Just as Merlyn's survey of the Matter of Britain in the first chapter displays White's extensive knowledge of Arthurian literature, so this passage shows his awareness of Arthurian scholarship. He begins by mentioning the views of the fifteenth-century Robert of Thornton, and of Adam of Domerham, then alludes to the 'tale . . . that our hero was carried away to the Vale of Affalach by a collection of queens in a magic boat'. And 'Then there are the Irish, who have muddled him up with one of the FitzGeralds and declare that he rides round a rath, with sword upraised, to the "Londonderry Air" '. Soon in this catalogue he has reached 'an irascible scholar called Dr Sebastian Evans', and his own 'bête noir', 'A

Miss Jessie L. Weston' who, he claims contemptuously, 'mentions a manuscript which she pleases to call 1533, supported by *Le Morte d'Arthur*, in which it is stated that the queen who came to carry him away was none other than the aged enchantress Morgan', a view not shared by Dr Sommer and 'A lot of people called Wolfram von Eschenbach, Ulrich von Zatzikhoven, Dr Wechssler, Professor Zimmer, Mr Nutt and so forth' who 'either scout the question wholly, or remain in learned confusion'. Chaucer, Spenser, Shakespeare, Milton, Wordsworth, Tennyson and 'a number of other reliable witnesses' meet with White's approval since they agree that Arthur is still on earth, 'while Tennyson is of the opinion that he will come again to visit us "like a modern Gentleman of stateliest port," possibly like the Prince Consort' (BM 136). He manages to end his survey with a fine tribute to Malory, 'that great man who is the noblest source of all this history', who 'maintains a discreet reserve' about the ultimate fate of Arthur. His own view is that his 'beloved Arthur of the future' is still alive somewhere 'in the Combination Room of the College of Life'.

Effective though this ending is, White ultimately devised for *The Once and Future King* a far more satisfying and elegant conclusion. Though in it there is some loss in the omission of the account of the Last Battle and of the end of the story of Lancelot and Guenever, all of which Malory movingly relates in *Le Morte Darthur*, the passage with which White finally concluded *The Once and Future King* is in keeping with both the sadness and the splendour of the traditional story. At the very end he was able to take a longer view, worthy of his great subject, and in contrast with his inappropriately personal comment at the end of *The Book of Merlyn*, that he is voluntarily laying aside his books to fight for his kind. The war was over, of course, when he put together the final version of *The Once and Future King*, enabling him to take a different and a larger perspective: 'The fate of this man or of that man was less than a drop, although it was a sparkling one, in the great blue motion of the sunlit sea' (OFK 677).

8

The Education of Princes

It could be said of White, as of Chaucer's Clerk in *The Canterbury Tales*, that 'gladly wolde he lerne and gladly teche': ' "The best thing for being sad," replied Merlyn, beginning to puff and blow, "is to learn something" ' (OFK 185–6). White's eagerness to learn found many different opportunities, from his involvement with hawking in the 1930s, to his last years on Alderney when in the summer of 1956 he was learning the deaf/blind alphabet and taking up Braille. His interest in teaching was similarly life-long. When L.J. Potts got married, White devised a typically parodic upper-class syllabus for the baby that he supposed would soon materialise, depending on the nineteenth-century joke about learning 'the three 'r's' (Reading, Writing, 'Rithmetic): 'It will be taught the three I's (Inversion, Introversion, and Intellect), the three R's (Riding, Rogering and Rumination), and the three G's (Grace, Government and Gentility)' (LF 17). When later on a son was born to Potts and his wife, he proposed a course of instruction rather simpler to implement:

> You will have to lend me your son a good bit, as soon as he is ten years old . . . I shall teach him to fish first of all, and then, as soon as he gets into his 'teens, he shall shoot with a four-ten (a small shot-gun). Are you jealous that somebody other than yourself should already be plotting about him? (LF 67–8)

Needless to say this programme was never carried out, but still at Alderney, he took pleasure in teaching his guest, 'a little lioness in her late fifties, a maiden lady who had gone deaf/blind when she was about 12', to swim (LF 245–6).

Just after finishing *The Sword in the Stone*, White wrote to David Garnett, 'The novel . . . I have just finished . . . is satirical and about education' (W/G L 17). Throughout all four books of *The Once and Future King*, upbringing and to a lesser extent education are important topics, since they are seen to shape the development of the major characters. White's reaction against the régime at Cheltenham College which had made his early adolescence miserable, combined with the insights he gained while head of English at Stowe to produce the enlightened and progressive curriculum devised by Merlyn for the Wart. His interest in Freud and his experience as a schoolmaster made him well aware of how crucial the early years were, and in a very modernistic way he saw the chief function of education as being to teach the boy to think for himself, rather than to cram him with facts. The educational programme must at the same time develop sympathy and understanding by stimulating and enlarging the imagination. In his own professional career at Stowe White had attempted to achieve these aims through the teaching of literature and the encouragement of imaginative writing. For the Wart, the metamorphoses into other living creatures so as to gain different perspectives on human life take the place of the study of literature.

White is probably the only writer, medieval or modern, who has had any but the most superficial interest in creating 'enfances' for Arthur. Rosemary Morris, in *The Character of King Arthur in Medieval Literature*,[1] commenting on the fifteen years of Arthur's childhood before he can come to the throne, suggests that Geoffrey of Monmouth deliberately chose not to represent Arthur as a wonder-child in the tradition of Alexander and Hercules. He ignored Arthur's childhood because he wished to chronicle the important accounts of the events of his life, rather than to write a romance. While medieval writers often invented the childhood or at least the adolescence of already known heroes, including Jesus, Arthur's childhood remained untouched. Malory is almost alone even in presenting Arthur at the age of fifteen, drawing the sword from the stone, showing him as the noble, sensitive and affectionate boy whom White was to present in his own appropriately modern way. In *Le Morte Darthur*, as in Malory's source, a thirteenth-century French writer of prose romance, the boy Arthur is thus first seen just before his accession to the throne, and from that point on his childhood is at an end. Whatever his upbringing may have been, it has admirably prepared him for his rôle as king. It is the birth-tale, rather than the childhood years, that is of greatest significance: the reader is left to assume that the young Arthur will have had the appropriate education for a youth of high birth.

What such an education might have been in the Middle Ages is suggested by the story of Tristram, whose upbringing is described in some detail in the early accounts deriving from the twelfth-century *Tristan* of Thomas of Britain. Great stress is laid on the exceptional intellectual qualities of this young paragon. His education has enabled him to speak several languages, to perform skilfully on the harp, and has also made him master of the seven arts. He has learnt to excel at games such as chess, as well as at hunting, throwing the lance and wrestling. Gottfried in his twelfth-century German version of the story relates that Tristram was cared for with the most tender solicitude for the first seven years of his life by his foster mother, after which he was sent abroad with a tutor to learn foreign

1　Morris, Rosemary: *The Character of King Arthur in Medieval Literature*, Cambridge, D.S. Brewer, 1982.

languages and to begin to study books. The process of education, however, is far from being a happy one for him, for, as Gottfried paradoxically remarks, 'With his first experience of freedom his whole freedom was cut short'. The enforced study of books under stern discipline takes the place of his carefree early childhood, yet he applies himself to it with such diligence that he has soon mastered more books than any child before or since. He also devotes many hours to the playing of stringed instruments, until he has become adept. He spends his whole time in learning. His recreations are fencing, wrestling, running, jumping and throwing the javelin, and he excels at tracking and hunting, as well as at all manner of courtly pastimes. His rigorous course of study ends in his fourteenth year, when he is fetched home, with instructions to take note of the lands and people on the way, so that their characteristics will be well known to him. His noble attainments are very soon demonstrated when he encounters some merchants on the ship, plays chess and converses with them in several languages, and later when he shows some huntsmen how to break a deer correctly.* (For White, however, Tristram grows up to be merely 'a lout, a sort of copy-cat', who was 'foul to his wife, . . . always bullying poor old Palomides for being a nigger, and . . . [he] treated King Mark most shamefully' (OFK 599)).

Tristram emerges from his 'enfances' an exceptionally accomplished young man, after the miseries of his rigorous upbringing. The Wart is fortunate in that his medieval education is directed by the wisdom of Merlyn so that he is not subjected to the pressures inflicted upon Tristram. Nor is he disadvantaged by too sheltered an upbringing like that other prominent figure in Arthurian romance, Perceval. Kept at home by his mother who has her own good reasons for treating him in this way, Perceval is so ignorant that he cannot even recognise a knight when he sees one. His only skill seems to be throwing javelins, by means of which he is able to kill beasts for food. He does not know what a lance and shield are for, for his mother has taken care that he shall be completely ignorant of everything to do with knighthood. His story takes up the fairytale motif of the child who is shielded and sheltered by the parents from what is foreseen as being likely to be to his or her undoing, but who cannot ultimately be prevented from encountering the forbidden.

White's choice of Malory's *Le Morte Darthur* as source-material rather than Geoffrey of Monmouth's *Historia Regum Britanniae* gave the Wart more interesting origins. While Geoffrey gives no account of Arthur's boyhood, he does suggest that he was brought up in the house of his natural father. Malory, following the French prose author in having the infant removed by Merlin immediately after his birth, to be brought up by Sir Ector, gives Arthur's story much greater imaginative power, invoking as it does the common childhood fantasy that one's parents are not one's real parents. Malory thus makes the story more mysterious and at the same time more dramatic, with Arthur's acclamation as king following the sword-in-the-

* Malory also gives an approving account of Tristram's accomplishments (Vin 232).

stone episode. White diverges from Malory not only in inventing 'enfances' for Arthur, but also in deferring the revelation of the circumstances surrounding Arthur's birth until much later in the story. Twentieth-century novelistic techniques enable him to move backwards and forwards freely within his chosen time-scheme as his mode of telling the story requires.

White's reading of history does not seem to have interested him in the actual programmes for the education of a prince that he might have consulted, had he wished to give an accurate impression of medieval theory and practice. His main aim, in terms of history, seems to have been to impart interesting information about some of the practical activities of everyday life in the Middle Ages which particularly appealed to him, with young readers in mind. His eagerness to suggest a medieval background was not in the least concerned to give a complete picture of medieval education: instead he was content merely to suggest some of its more recondite and to him attractive aspects by occasional allusions.

The writings of such authorities as Aristotle, Thomas Aquinas, and Giles of Rome in his *De Regimine Principum*, or the later Hoccleve and Renaissance Erasmus, suggest that their chief aim in educating the heir to the throne was to inculcate virtue, justice and statecraft. Merlyn in *The Sword in the Stone*, of course, devises his own idiosyncratic programme for this purpose. But although White mentions Erasmus, he was clearly not interested in his treatise on *The Education of a Christian Prince*, nor in Hoccleve's *Regiment of Princes*. The emphasis in these works as with the earlier treatises was similarly on morals and wisdom, rather than on more specific subject-matter, though such abstract studies would have been supplemented, as in the case of Tristram, with courtly accomplishments such as harping and dancing, as well as with riding and with feats of arms.

Though in the Middle Ages education included the reading of Virgil and Ovid and the practice of rhetoric, such studies as were thought most likely to make a prince virtuous were paramount, though they were supplemented by those considered of practical use for the future ruler who needed to know something of the arts of government. Considerable attention was naturally paid to religious observance and elementary instruction: the day usually began with mass (as it does in Bertilak's castle of Haut Desert in *Sir Gawain and the Green Knight*) since the castle would have had its chapel and resident chaplain. Those who had the responsibility for the upbringing of the heir to the throne were anxious to foster piety, so as to ensure that a proper respect for God's laws should form the foundation of the virtues that they hoped to inculcate, for his own benefit and later that of his subjects. White, however, makes little reference to the religious activity that would have been customary in ordinary life in the castle. Before the Robin Hood episode, Merlyn tells the Wart to have breakfast and then go to Mass; and later, though only in the first English edition of *The Sword in the Stone*, there is a somewhat disrespectful reference to the chaplain of the castle. (He is the Reverent (sic) Sidebottom, whose tedious after-dinner reading aloud of the *Gesta Romanorum* sends the Wart into a deep sleep and his dream about the giant Galapas (SS 273 ff).).

The Wart's education does, nevertheless, fit into the usual medieval pattern for the young heir to the throne in some rather minor ways. Like Tristram, such a boy would be taken from his nurse at about the age of seven and committed to the care of an experienced and well-respected knight, referred to as *magister* or *preceptor*. The *magister* exercised only general supervision over the manners and discipline of the boy, rather than actually instructing him, a task delegated to a clerk. The Wart's education takes place in the schoolroom at the beginning of the story:

> On Mondays, Wednesdays and Fridays it was Court Hand and Summulae Logicales, while the rest of the week it was the Organon, Repetition and Astrology. The governess was always getting muddled with her astrolabe, and when she got especially muddled she would take it out of the Wart by rapping his knuckles.   (OFK 4)

White begins with a fine flourish: the programme sounds both genuinely medieval and at the same time stultifying, for he wants to make the point that such studies are inappropriate and useless, taking no account of the pupils' individual needs. Subjects are taught, but not the boys. Authentic though the programme may sound, it is nothing of the kind. Court Hand, for example, is the style of handwriting in use in English law-courts and elsewhere from the sixteenth century to the reign of George II. The *Summulae Logicales* of the thirteenth-century Petrus Hispanus would have been a most unlikely text for boys to study, as would the *Organon*, the title of Aristotle's logical treatises. The governess, still a familiar figure in upper-class English education in the first half of the twentieth century, is another comic anachronism introduced to update the scene for the young reader. When Kay is continuing his First Rate Eddication later on in the schoolroom, doing dictation with Merlyn, he might – in the actual Middle Ages – have been engaged in *dictamen*, the branch of grammar which taught how to compose letters, charters, deeds, court rolls and the like, though this would have been unusual for someone destined to become a knight. At the same time, the Wart and Kay are spared the fundamentals of medieval education, it seems, which would have begun with the Psalms as the elementary reading text, together with a collection of maxims such as Cato's *Distichs*. Instead of the *Summulae Logicales* (described even by Merlyn as 'filthy') the boys would have been more likely to have been studying such works as the *Liber Parabolarum* and *Parvum Doctrinale* attributed to the twelfth-century Alain de Lisle. Simple didactic verse would have formed the basis of their syllabus, with an enormous amount of rote-learning.[2] But the 'famous medieval mnemonic' pronounced in

2 Carruthers, Mary J.: *The Book of Memory: a Study of Memory in Medieval Culture*, Cambridge, Cambridge University Press, 1990.

measured tones by Merlyn ('Barbara Celarunt Darii Ferioque Prioris'[3] –
OFK 117–18) though perhaps well worthy of being written down and so
committed to memory by Kay, was famous as being used by university
students as an aid to learning the various types of syllogism, that is, logical
propositions, rather than in elementary education.[4]

The acquisition of skill in the arts of war and the use of weapons does
play an important part in the Wart's education, in accordance with medieval custom, despite Merlyn's disapproval. 'Tilting and horsemanship had
two afternoons a week, because they were the most important branches of a
gentleman's education in those days' (OFK 52). White gives a detailed
explanation of some of the finer points of the art of jousting or tilting, while
commenting that:

> it would take too long to go into all the interesting details of proper
> tilting which the boys had to learn, for in those days you had to be a
> master of your craft from the bottom upward.   (OFK 53–4)

His apparently serious interest in the correct techniques is immediately
undercut by the ridiculous encounter which subsequently ensues between
Pellinore and Grummore. Other gentlemanly accomplishments, knowledge
of which the medieval prince or noble youth might be expected to acquire
are, however, suggested by references to hawking and archery, as well as to
the boarhunt. White ingeniously suggests what was supposed to be common knowledge about the correct way of dealing with the boar:

> Now, as everybody knows, a quarry is a reward of entrails, etc., which
> is given to the hounds on the hide of the dead beast (sur le quir), and,
> as everybody knows, a slain boar is not skinned. It is disembowelled
> without the hide being taken off, and since there can be no hide, there
> can be no quarry. We all know that the hounds are rewarded with a
> fouail . . .   (OFK 151).

But although the Wart is an onlooker, he is not involved, as the young
Tristram is with the breaking of the deer in Gottfried.

As a page, White informs us, the Wart is also taught the practical and
domestic skills expected of a young gentleman, such as are indicated in
fourteenth- and fifteenth-century handbooks of 'courtesy' such as the *Stans
Puer ad Mensam*.[5] He knows how to lay tables, to bring in dishes from the
kitchen, to serve Sir Ector and his guests, and to offer them water for

---

3 See Crump, C.G. and Jacob, E.F. eds: *The Legacy of the Middle Ages*, Oxford, Clarendon
   Press, 1926, p. 279.
4 See Carruthers, *op. cit.*, p. 80.
5 See Furnivall, F.J.: *The Babees Book*, London 1868. Contains *The Boke of Nurture by J.R. The
   Boke of Kervynge by Wynkyn de Worde. The Boke of Nurture by Hugh Rhodes.*

washing, but unlike Chaucer's Squire, he seems not to have learnt to carve. These accomplishments are merely listed: we are given no account of how the Wart acquires them, and White does not include the cruder details relating to the appropriate behaviour for a page (such as not wiping your nose on the tablecloth), which in the medieval treatises throw interesting light on contemporary manners.

In musical skills the Wart is apparently completely lacking, nor is he seen playing such courtly games as chess and backgammon, often mentioned in medieval literature. White's mode of idealising life in Sir Ector's castle is not to represent it in romantic terms, as in *Sir Gawain and the Green Knight* and in the French romances, but to depict it in terms of a folksy realism. The Christmas celebrations in the castle, for example, are a parody of the traditional English harvest supper on a farm, such as took place regularly in the English countryside until World War II, rather than a description of courtly revelry in the Middle Ages, and perhaps thereby closer to actuality in some respects. But the scene is set in 'the old Merry England of Gramarye', and the whole village has come to dinner in hall, with no distinction between high and low. White loads the idyllic picture with anachronistic detail to create a festive atmosphere: carols in the modern sense (rather than the medieval 'carole' or dance-song) are sung, and young men and maidens dance morris dances, not recorded until the late sixteenth century. Courtly accomplishments are not required of the Wart in this fantasy world, in which modern democratic ideals are grafted on to a vaguely medieval scene. As with the writers of medieval romance, historical accuracy was not of first importance to White, but vividness was.

ii.

The Wart, it seems, is particularly fortunate in having in effect no parents – only a 'tutor of genius' – so that he is without the emotional problems of the 'Orkneys', the children of Morgause and Lot, Gawaine and his brothers. Merlyn devises for the Wart an educational programme radically different from that experienced by White, whose own schooldays at his 'rather cruel public school', as he later described it, provided a sort of anti-model for the education of his young hero. Stowe School, founded in 1923, on the other hand, was sufficiently progressive to show what a liberal education could be, and the influence of its headmaster, J.F. Roxburgh, and of the school as a whole was to have immense significance for him. It not only allowed him to see that it was possible to break away from time-honoured educational patterns in many different ways, but it must also have enabled him to some extent to continue with his colleagues something approaching the intellectual life of his Cambridge years. At first he seems to have been rather hostile to J.F. Roxburgh, despite the tolerant and supportive way in which Roxburgh had dealt with the furore occasioned by the publication of his novel, *They Winter Abroad*. White's previous unhappy experiences both as pupil and as teacher may have prejudiced him against headmasters in general but eventually, towards the end of his life, he was able to pay tribute to him in terms that suggest how charismatic a figure Roxburgh was. He had disliked him, he said, because he had loved and admired him, and 'wanted to be his blue-eyed boy as everybody else did'.

Roxburgh gave White as head of English a free hand, young and inexperienced as he was, in setting up an English 'side' (a sixth form course) at Stowe. Before he took up the appointment, White's letter to Potts shows the serious thought that he was giving to the way in which English should be taught to boys between the ages of about twelve and eighteen. His conscience, he says, was telling him 'to do something for literature: even, perhaps, to 'put it across', to popularise'. His ideas as to how this was to be done were very liberal, while at the same time he declared that his 'policy was to be jesuitical'.

> I believe that real enjoyment of reading must develop itself naturally
> from the bloodiest tripe upwards.   (LF 31)

He made out a list of books to 'give boys a background of literary appreciation', and when he took up the appointment, introduced the ideas of I.A. Richards and Cambridge literary criticism into the Upper School. He made a 'devastating impact', according to Noel Annan, who comments on the extraordinarily innovative and advanced nature of White's teaching. It was:

> at once serious and iconoclastic, and his clever pupils began to argue
> about "the meaning of meaning" and to construe Eliot or Auden as if
> they were classical specialists spotting a hendiadys or hysteron-
> proton.[6]

He wanted boys to make their own response to poetry (as I.A. Richards's epoch-making *Practical Criticism*[7] required), encouraging them to read the then comparatively unfamiliar Metaphysical poets and G.M. Hopkins, while the reading of D.H. Lawrence was also, according to Annan, obliga-

---

6   See Annan, Noel Gilroy: *Roxburgh of Stowe: the Life of J.F. Roxburgh and His Influence in the Public Schools*, London, Longmans 1965, p. 99.

7   Richards, I(vor) A(rmstrong): *Practical Criticism: a Study of Literary Judgment*, 1929, a work which revolutionized the teaching and study of English literature. Richards initiated the close study of poetry, first in lectures where he distributed unsigned and undated short poems and invited comment, in order to get away from vapid clichés learnt from superficial histories of literature. The book and Richards's method were very influential and contributed to the New Criticism in the U.S.A. in the 1930s.

tory. Although he was more *avant garde* in his literary taste and theories than his headmaster, White was nevertheless allowed to act in accordance with his own convictions. Of his teaching Annan comments, however, that 'Intellectual vitality was apt to take priority over intellectual discipline', a remark which might also be applied to *The Once and Future King*.

Under Roxburgh's headship, White was thus able to break away from traditional methods of teaching and to devise his own courses of study, based on the idea of encouraging the pupil to think for himself. Although the various teaching programmes at Stowe were not completely different from those of other public schools at the time, they were much more innovative. In the unusually liberal atmosphere that prevailed, freedom was considered an essential element in education: J.F. Roxburgh believed that boys must have leisure to follow their own interests and should to a certain extent be able to choose their activities for themselves, rather than having every moment of every day organised for them. His theories and practice were in many ways in advance of his time, and they undoubtedly coincided with White's own inclinations as a schoolmaster. In the Upper School, each boy had his own personal tutor, almost as if he were an undergraduate, who supervised his studies and gave him regular individual teaching – exactly the situation in which the Wart is placed after the coming of Merlyn. To exercise respect for the individual was considered the first duty of the teacher, an idea very different from the traditional public school ethos, and J.F. Roxburgh when speaking to boys always addressed them as if they were adults and treated them as reasonable beings. It was the school's deliberate policy to promote a close association between master and pupils for the sharing of knowledge, interests and enthusiasms. This unconventional, special relationship between teacher and taught clearly both influenced White's attitude to his pupils, and largely accounts for the confidential tone which dominates the narration in *The Sword in the Stone*. White did not need to write specifically either for adults or for juvenile readers, since the mode of address that he was accustomed to use in his professional life was presumably the same for both.

It seems likely that the personal influence of his headmaster during White's years at Stowe helped to shape the Wart's education in various other ways. In 1930, Roxburgh's book on education, *Eleutheros* (meaning 'a free man') appeared. He shocked the headmasters of other public schools by advocating in it a degree of individual freedom for his boys which went far beyond contemporary norms. The influence of this, as of many other of his ideas, can be seen in the education of the Wart and Kay, who are allowed to 'run like wild colts' by Merlyn (OFK 186). *Eleutheros* was based on Aristotle's dictum, that 'there is a form of education which should be given to our sons not because it is useful and not because it is necessary, but because it befits a free man and because it is noble'. This was the sort of education obviously required by the boy who was to be king of England, and that is actually provided by Merlyn, within the 'leisure to grow up' that

Roxburgh advocated. 'Do you think that you have learned anything?' Merlyn asks the Wart towards the end of the book. 'I have learned and been happy' is his reply (OFK 186). His education has been a joyous and successful experience because Merlyn has followed J.F. Roxburgh's precept that it is the boy who must be taught, rather than the subject, and implemented his conviction that the 'centre of every boy's education is (or ought to be) the work he does on a subject that appeals to him'. So the Wart, who has found animal life extremely interesting, has learned by being 'changed into countless different animals' (OFK 180) in the course of his educational career. Roxburgh, who had even set up a zoo at Stowe in the early days, because he believed that some boys needed a pet as an outlet for their natural affections, would no doubt have approved.

The régime at Stowe seems also to have influenced the form of the Wart's education in so far as it gave encouragement to spontaneous outdoor activities instead of the traditional team games, which White detested. J.F. Roxburgh was hostile to 'the tyranny of athleticism', and so the compulsory games that were an indispensable feature of the daily life of more conventional public schools gave place at Stowe to other forms of exercise. He introduced tennis, golf and fencing for boys who were no good at football and cricket, and allowed them to roam about the very extensive school grounds on foot, or explore the area on bicycles. They were also allowed to go fishing, shooting and hawking with White, now beginning to feel, as he wrote to Potts in April 1933, 'My real vocation is to be in the open air all day' (LF 52).

White's interest both in psychology and in politics, so apparent in *The Once and Future King*, must also have been stimulated by the years at Stowe. J.F. Roxburgh encouraged discussion of both subjects among the older boys at a time when the theories of Freud and the topic of pacifism were making particular impact. Intelligent and well-educated boys in the 1930s were aware of movements in both fields, especially in more progressive schools where they were not held strictly to the traditional curriculum. In the intellectual climate of Roxburgh's Stowe, White was able to produce a pacifist play.[8] His many references to Freud, direct or otherwise in *The Once and Future King*, probably owe something to the fact that psychology was often the subject of sixth-form discussion, and could be assumed to be not unfamiliar to his readers. J.F. Roxburgh's personal interest in psychology was apparently useful in helping him to deal with day-to-day problems, but his reading of Freud seems also to have encouraged him to regard parents with deep distrust, as potentially dangerous and likely to stunt their child's development. This view was clearly shared by White: his vision of Arthur's childhood, liberated from parental pressure, enables him

---

8   *Miracle at Verdun*, in which the dead soldiers on both sides in the First World War rose from their graves to protest at the crimes committed by politicians, both during the War and in the succeeding years.

to grow up undamaged and unwarped. Arthur's adult character can therefore be seen as a projection of what might be achieved in terms of emotional
stability as a result of an upbringing free from baneful parental influences.
It is significant that White finds no place for the episode in Malory in which
there is an affectionate first meeting between Arthur, now king, and his
mother, Igraine.

iii.

As has already been suggested, White was writing at a time when there
was widespread interest in the topic of childhood. Mid-nineteenth-century
writers had long before begun to draw attention to the suffering of children
who were harshly brought up, and had been succeeded by a later generation who represented childhood as a period of happiness, to be looked
back upon with nostalgia. The growing awareness of the importance of the
early years and of the understanding of child-psychology was reflected in
contemporary poetry and fiction, as for example in Henry James's sophisticated and subtle treatment of the child's puzzled reaction to the behaviour
of parents in *What Maisie Knew* (1898), as well as of the mysterious interaction of adult and child in *The Turn of the Screw* (1898). More mystical,
whimsical and sentimental works such as Maeterlinck's play *The Bluebird*,
very popular in the first decade of the twentieth century, and J.M. Barrie's
Peter Pan (1906), as well as Kenneth Grahame's already mentioned *Golden
Age* and *Dream Days*, ostensibly written for children, appealed more
strongly to adult nostalgia. Henry Williamson in his autobiographical
'story of the post-war years to 1924', although not published until 1945,
declares that 'A child should be allowed to grow itself naturally'. He goes
on to describe how he is given a free hand as a tutor, 'so we spent most of
our time out of doors, observing the natural world. We read some of Con-
rad together, and Jefferies' *Bevis*.' The child's mother, content with this
program, comments: ' "Well, run wild while you can." '[9]
    At the same time, recognition of the need for educational reform led to
the attempt by such pioneers as Montessori and Rudolf Steiner (and such
famous progressive schools as Abbotsholme, Bedales, Dartington Hall, St
Christopher's, Letchworth and Summerfield) to break away from obsolete
patterns and to introduce a wider curriculum and more liberal regimes,
presupposing a readiness on the part of parents to countenance change.
Merlyn's determination that the Wart should find things out and learn to

---

9   See Williamson, Henry: *The Sun in the Sands*, London, Faber, 1945. The author's autobio-
    graphical account of 'the post-war years to 1924', written in 1934 but not published for a
    decade after.

think for himself, would have been congenial to many adult readers. The 'discovery learning' by means of which the Wart is educated was of course very *avant garde* and innovative in the 1930s, though it has since become a cliché of modern education. Such a method must depend upon enlightened guidance on the part of the teacher, who has to ensure that the implications of the discovery are fully understood, conceptualised and remembered. The Wart is fortunate in having a very exceptional tutor.

The Wart, it is obvious, is by no means bookish; indeed White makes it clear that he is really rather stupid. His integrity, his patience, his fairness and his essentially loving nature are the main virtues that he later brings to the tasks of kingship. He can puzzle things out, or try to, but he is easily out-manoeuvred by the unscrupulous. Despite his intellectual shortcomings, he is as it were White's favourite pupil. Brilliantly successful as a teacher of English though White seems to have been at Stowe, there was a sense in which he disliked clever boys and the intellectual snobbery that they were liable to cultivate. Though he could be scholarly, painstaking scholarship was not his forte: his interests were too wide-ranging, and he seems to have warmed more readily to eager enthusiasm than to quick perception. He obviously enjoyed overcoming learning difficulties, as with the deaf/blind. His own emotional problems led him to value most highly those to whom he could communicate his pleasure in learning new skills and with whom he could thus establish a rapport. In this he differed markedly from the much more self-sufficient Roxburgh, for whom, though he took so warm an interest in the individual, and passionately desired to share his appreciation of art and literature, the love of art and literature remained paramount.

While he was at Stowe White, according to Noel Annan, was 'in the midst of living out a fantasy to resurrect Renaissance man who should be equally skilled in paunching a hare in the morning, stretching a canvas in the afternoon, landing an aircraft in the evening and writing poetry at night'.[10] At Stowe Ridings his interest seems to have moved backwards in time to the simpler and, as it may have appeared to him, the more childlike world of medieval man, enabling him to elaborate a system of education which would combine his vision of a happy carefree upbringing with some medieval features. The Wart and Kay are allowed to spend a great deal of time out of doors, doing just what they like. The metamorphoses into the various members of the animal kingdom, denied to Kay, allow the Wart to identify with them and so to reach his own conclusions. But even without these experiences, his education is drawn extensively from his contact with the natural world in other ways. In the depths of the greenwood, he learns from Maid Marian how to creep through the wood soundlessly, and from Robin, that you cannot 'give people as presents', so that he has to re-think

---

[10] Annan, Noel Gilroy: *Roxburgh of Stowe*, p. 100.

and re-formulate his original kind intention (OFK 113). He is instructed about the habits of birds by Merlyn and Archimedes, who discourse at length on the subject of rooks and pigeons and their modes of communication. His developing understanding of and sympathy with wild creatures is contrasted with the more predatory attitude of Kay, who breaks in upon the conversation with apologies for being late for his geography lesson, saying ' "I was trying to get a few small birds with my crossbow. Look, I have killed a thrush" ' (OFK 161).

The most significant educational experiences that the Wart undergoes are the metamorphoses. Unlike Bevis in *Wood Magic*, he is not able to speak to the animals directly as a boy, but instead depends on Merlyn to make him one of them. These magical changes greatly enhance the imaginative power of the fantasy. As in medieval art and literature, in folktale and in ballad, the animal world impinges upon that of human beings. There is also a sense in which the Wart's metamorphoses represent the descent to the underworld of classical and other mythology. In such stories, the hero must descend to the realms which ordinary living mortals cannot enter, in order to bring back knowledge of crucial importance for his future life or that of his society. Often the experience is frightening or dangerous, requiring him to make contact with the powers that inhabit the strange realm. Not only does the Wart in the form of a fish descend to the lower level of the castle moat, but he enters into a lower form of life – as he also does with his later experiences. But, paradoxically, some of the metamorphoses introduce him to what is represented as, in ethical terms, a higher form of life than that of man. From each of the creatures whom he encounters he learns different things. His change into a hawk is to enable him to talk to birds of prey because 'That is the way to learn, by listening to the experts' (OFK 71). The hawks in their spartan military mess are ready to accept him as one of themselves after certain ceremonies which take the form of an initiation. These culminate in the ordeal which he successfully undergoes, in which he has to confront the deranged and murderous Cully. From all this he learns at first hand not only about the nature of hawks, but about himself. He has to learn to overcome his fear in the face of physical danger, and to hold on. Although this episode must have originated in White's practical interest in the training of hawks at the time when he was writing *The Sword in the Stone*, his insight into their nature and his ability to represent it in human terms helps to give a mythic power to the Wart's encounter with them.

In the first, English, edition while the Wart is recovering from his broken collar-bone after the Robin Wood episode, his education takes the form of nature-walks with Merlyn. It is after his tutor has caught and shown him a grass-snake that he is changed into one himself, further instructed about the nature of snakes by T.natrix and then given a lesson in pre-history. This in turn is followed by a 'Legend' or fable about the python, narrated very much in the voice of the schoolmaster extending the general knowledge of his pupils by means of lively story-telling, in which information seems to be interpolated for its own sake. The Wart presently falls asleep and dreams that Aesculapius is teaching him 'the ancient wisdom' (SS 209), though from this experience he learns no special lesson. When he is subsequently transformed into an owl (SS 256) he is taken to visit Athene who grants him a vision of the life of trees, into which are incorporated some odds and ends of general knowledge, which include several references to trees in art and craft. Virgil's drinking bowl, the Wart is informed, was made out of beech-wood; Grinling Gibbons always used lime for his carving; Salvator Rosa loved to paint chestnuts, while Corot preferred willows (SS 267). Next, he is shown how first the solar system and then the human race evolved, until finally:

> there came a man. He split up the one pebble which remained of all that mountain with blows; then made an arrow-head of it, and slew his brother.   (SS 272)

In the later editions White cut both the dream of Aesculapius and this episode, thus removing the classical elements which he must have felt were out of keeping with the otherwise medieval atmosphere.

The addition to the 1958 edition of the visit to the ants and to the wild geese increased the seriousness of *The Sword in the Stone* and allowed it to carry a more clear-cut message than in its first form it had been able to do. From the ants, the Wart experiences the comprehensive restriction of free-dom implicit in the totalitarian régime, and then has to reflect on its impli-cations at the end of the book when the badger asks him, ' "Which did you like best, . . . the ants or the wild geese?" ' (OFK 197). The educational value of the visit is in practical terms rather limited for the Wart, since there is no likelihood of his establishing such a régime in his own kingdom. The lesson is for the reader rather than for the boy; and it goes against the commonly accepted view of ants, expressed for example in the biblical 'Go to the ant, thou sluggard. Consider her ways and be wise' and in the well-known fable of the ant and the grasshopper. The episode of the ants is too closely modelled on contemporary Nazism: while true enough as a fable it is too specific and not sufficiently assimilated to the general tone and message of the book. Yet it makes a point, if a negative point, which is always worth making, about the regulation of society, and one which the threat of Nazism, and later of Communism, made particularly important for people of White's generation.

The visit to the wild geese has other lessons for the Wart. He explains to Lyo-lyok, the young female with whom he becomes friendly, that he has been sent to join the company 'to learn his education', a process now carried out initially by question and answer. ' "Are we at war?" ' he asks (OFK 171), a question incomprehensible to the goose, who finds the topic offensive, and reprimands him with the question: ' ". . . what creatures could be so low as to go about in bands, to murder other of its own blood?" ' It is a surprisingly facile point, and over-simple, but the presentation of the goose-society is implicitly a little subtler. Amongst the geese, he sees a tolerant, good-humoured society, in which the members function as individuals, despite their communal way of life, but they are selfish. They are not at the mercy of despots or oppressed by harsh laws, and they assert no rights to any particular territory but, though White stresses their comradeship, the basic law is nevertheless every one for himself: 'Any goose who found anything nice to eat considered it his own and would peck any other one who tried to thieve it' (OFK 173). The Wart learns both positive and negative things from the geese. The lesson they offer is inconclusive, reflecting White's own recognition of the complexity of society, the inadequacy of models.

The Wart's visit to the badger's sett, included in all editions of *The Sword in the Stone*, completes his education. It occurs at a time when he is having to come to terms with his seemingly inferior position to Kay who is about to be knighted. White omits from his story the knighting of Arthur, included by Malory. Since he disapproved of the militaristic aspects of chivalry and usually treated knights facetiously, he presumably felt he could not have included the episode in an appropriately serious tone. Indeed in the 1958 edition, it is at the point when the Wart has been speaking of the glamour of chivalry and the courage and endurance and comradeship which are seen in time of war, that the badger asks his unanswered question. White's understanding of the tensions caused by sibling rivalry makes poignant the Wart's suppressed jealousy and grief that he has no proper parents and so only an inferior social position. His last metamorphosis allows him to acquire greater self-knowledge as well as understanding of human nature. As in Malory, he goes from childhood to adulthood virtually without adolescence.

The badger, caricatured as a Cambridge don with pacifist leanings, who is writing a treatise for his (much delayed) doctoral dissertation, to point out why Man has become the master of the animals, is at the same time both ridiculous and wise. He is an 'old gentleman', who after offering the Wart a glass of punch, reads him from the depths of his leather armchair the parable of the embryos. The use of such animal fantasy raises problems which remain unresolved. The Wart on first being turned into a badger, in his misery at being slighted by Kay, has determined to behave like a wild beast, but when he encounters the humble hedgehog his better (human) nature within his animal form restrains him from devouring the poor creature, as the 'old gentleman', for all his pacifist notions, would have done. White does not quite resolve this 'lesson' from the animals. His sense of reality does not quite fit in with his ideals, and his ideals are over-simple. Yet his sympathy for other than human forms of life conveys a larger generosity than more complex or more penetrating fables might do. The episodes are original and entertaining with a simple wisdom that enlarges the book's scope.

With this episode, the Wart's formal education comes to an end, though Merlyn remains for some time as his adviser, endeavouring to inculcate his ideals and ideas as the young king prepares for the battle of Bedegraine. The education that Arthur has received has been at the same time liberal and limited; limited to some lessons about human and animal behaviour. Merlyn has tried to teach him to think, and has eventually succeeded to a considerable extent. He has not imparted many facts, except a few about the animal kingdom, and those selected to form part of the course owe their inclusion to the author's current interests. The course of instruction has contained a strong moral element, but it is the morality of the nineteen-thirties pacifist, rather than of the educators of the Middle Ages. The military training that later enables Arthur to be successful as a knight and leader in war is constantly mocked by Merlyn: White was never able to share Malory's fascination with and admiration for chivalry.

Altogether the 'education of Arthur' rather well illustrates the strengths and weaknesses of the extreme liberal version of an English public school education in the nineteen-thirties. It is strong in an (ungrounded) sense of decency, kindness and curiosity, weak in intellectual discipline and information, curiously sexless. As it turns out, not altogether intentionally, it was a good education for those whose duty it was to lead men in battle, a good education for a king, if not for the specialist administrators who must save him. It was not a good education for a modern advanced industrial society; but it reminds us of the world we have lost, even if it was only a fantasy world.

White never lost his interest in education, nor his distrust of the inclination towards the scientific and practical which tends to exclude the study of the humanities in modern education. In the end paper of his copy of Bulfinch's *Mythology* he wrote:

> A still more important human problem than that of warfare, though perhaps a less pressing one, is that of Wisdom versus Ingenuity. It seems unlikely to be solved except by education, and this education will have to be in the humanities, the ethics, the arts, the philosophies, the histories, the beauties and the living biological sciences of life – not in what has hitherto been considered valuable, namely the "practical" sciences. Man is quite practical enough already far too bloody practical – and we shall have to sit on this side of him for the time being, until his wisdom has caught up with his ingenuity.

In his journal for 24 February 1942 he recorded the educational programme that he would institute if he were 'the Dictator of the world':

> If I were the Dictator of the world, I would only try to improve the human mind. I would aim at a really educated proletariat.
> From birth till ten years of age my subjects should run wild.
> From 10–22, they would be sent to school and university.
> From 22–42, they would work four hours a day for the state . . .

From 42, the individual would be regarded as adult and would cease to work for the state. He would now for the first time be allowed to be baptised, confirmed, legally married . . .

In addition, those aged between 22 and 42 'would each have to read good books for 2 hours a day'. It is an educational system ideal for producing Peter Pans.

iv.

White creates a most interesting contrast to the education of Arthur, thus widening the views of education conveyed in *The Once and Future King*, by showing the 'young princelings of Lothian' growing up in a very different way. White invents for Gawain, Agravaine, Gaheris and Gareth 'enfances' just as he had done for Arthur, but the influences brought to bear upon them are less enlightened. In the early drafts of his second volume he had indirectly expressed his bitter resentment against Constance White through his portrayal of Morgause as – amongst other things – an utterly heartless mother to her sons. Even in *The Queen of Air and Darkness* toned down and diminished though she is, she remains a crucial influence on her sons' development. The childhood of the four boys, therefore, involves psychological pressures from which the Wart is almost entirely free. Their lives are blighted by their continual need to win their mother's love and approval: 'They adored her dumbly and uncritically, because her character was stronger than theirs' (OFK 217). They are bewildered by her frequent and arbitrary changes of attitude to them. Agravaine, it is suggested, already has an unnatural relationship with his mother. Their unhappy striving for her attention also means that they grow up undisciplined and unsatisfied in a stultifying state of isolation.

They might have been a solar system of their own, with nothing else in space, as they went round and round among the dunes and coarse grass of the estuary. Probably the planets have few ideas in their heads, either.   (OFK 247)

White perceptively suggests the varying characters that might arise from this harsh and oppressive environment. Nowhere is his unsentimental knowledge of boys' characters better illustrated. In accordance with Malory's representation of the adult Gawaine, White shows him as a boy whose sturdy uprightness of character develops into a noble steadfastness that never leaves him, while for Agravaine he devises a thoroughly unpleasant nature, and convincingly lays the foundations in boyhood of a growing perversion that is to account for his later actions. While Gaheris invariably 'did and felt what the others did' Gareth, like Gawaine, shows how a good nature may survive even in such a dehumanising setting. White shows how, without the benefit of Merlyn's instruction and restraining hand, their situation and natural instincts make them sadistic, so that they think nothing of tormenting the donkeys: 'On the rim of the world they knew too much about cruelty to be surprised by it.' They have, moreover, been brought up by Morgause 'with an imperfect sense of right and wrong. It was as if they could never know when they were being good or when they were being bad' (OFK 217). The moral training central to medieval education is thus indirectly suggested, but for these boys it is completely neglected. Even though each is shown as a distinct individual, they are all very largely what their mother has made them, 'through indifference and through laziness or even through some kind of possessive cruelty'. It is about her that the murderous quarrel breaks out in the store-room, presaging the later quarrel when Mordred and Agravaine are about to accuse Lancelot and Guenever to Arthur (OFK 557). Fighting comes naturally to them.

As with the education of Arthur, the upbringing of the 'Orkneys' is made accountable for their later development. Though they talk together in Gaelic, they have been taught 'the Old Language of chivalry' because they will need it when they are grown-up. In the remote, more primitive world, so vividly evoked, in which their childhood is passed, the story is the dominant cultural medium. They rehearse again and again the tale that their mother has taught them concerning their family history and the wrongs done to their clan by the 'bloody King of England', with the insistence of young children on exact form. They thus build up and strengthen the sense of family grievance which will later seek revenge through Mordred. (White learnt much from Ireland in these matters.) The oral and traditional nature of their education – such as it is – is further suggested by the use of proverbs, once again taught them by their mother, in Agravaine's quotation:

> "Four things . . . that a Lothian cannot trust – a cow's horn, a horse's
> hoof, a dog's snarl, and an Englishman's laugh."   (OFK 220)

The brutalising nature of their childhood experience is further suggested by White's narrative method: while the storytelling is proceeding, Morgause is boiling the cat in the room below. Her children are listening to her 'secret movements', though they are ignorant of what she is actually doing. The focus shifts from one scene to the other and back again, ending with the children's affirmation of their intention to avenge their family wrongs, because they love their mother. They are not entirely dependent on Morgause for their education, however, since they also have the benefit of St Toirdealbhach's tuition, such as it is. He is described as a relapsed saint, who had fallen into the Pelagian heresy of Celestius, and who believed that the soul was capable of its own salvation. This belief allows him to indulge freely in the 'mountain dew', 'water-of-life' or 'usquebaugh' (whiskey) of which there are nineteen empty bottles in Mother Morlan's dark little cabin. Here he is to be found sitting in front of the turf fire when the boys come for a story. He is the 'source of mental nourishment to them . . . who gave them what culture they were ever to get' (OFK 662). He has taught them to read and write, rather more effectively than one would expect, in view of the letter that Gawaine writes to Lancelot at the end of his life:

> Gawaine had hardly been the sort of person you thought of as a writer. Indeed it would have seemed more natural if he had been illiterate, like most of the others. Yet here . . . was the lovely old Gaelic miniscule, as neat and round and small as when he had learned it from some ancient saint in dim Dunlothian. He had written so unfrequently since, that the hand had retained its beauty. It was an old-maid's hand, or an old-fashioned boy's, sitting with his feet hooked round the legs of a stool and his tongue out, writing carefully . . .   (OFK 662)

The mental nourishment for which the boys go to St Toirdealbhach, however, is conveyed by stories, and White shows the old holy scoundrel plainly enjoying them. The boys ask for stories about murders, about magic, and particularly about fighting, and this is shown to be the saint's special subject. They are thus presented as being brought up in the old Gaelic tradition, untouched by Gallic sophistication, and the fantasies and attitudes nourished by the folklore and hero tales with which they have grown up effectually shape their later behaviour. In the earlier versions of this book, it was Sir Palomides the Saracen knight who had been their tutor, but in changing the role of Palomides and sacrificing the comedy of the schoolroom scenes, White tightened the logic of the whole story. The cancelled prep-school Latin lesson was more amusing than St Toirdealbhach's tale of King Conor Mac Nessa which replaced it, but less appropriate. In rewriting the second book to satisfy the criticisms that the first version had aroused, White abandoned his teaching experience as source and made use instead of the Irish tradition in which he was immersed at Doolistown.

He also made the bestiary which he later translated as *The Book of Beasts* part of the educational experience of Gawain and his brothers. In response to their demands, St Toirdealbhach brings out his *Liber de Natura Quorundam Animalium* ('Book on the Nature of Certain Animals'), and is made to 'turn the vellum quickly . . . skipping the enchanting Griffins, Bonnacons, Cocodrills, Manticores, Chaladrii' etc. until they come to the Unicorn. We are not told whether the boys are able to read the Latin for themselves, or whether the saint has to translate it for them. White did not know that in the Middle Ages, the bestiary was thought of as a beginner's book, an entertaining way of retaining moral precepts, which was also used for complex mnemonic purposes. Whatever may have been St Toirdealbhach's knowledge of the bestiary, it is clear that Gawain and his brothers are not being forced to study it with a view to making it the basis of a memory-system for future use. When they finally reach the required page in the book, moreover, their knowledge on the subject of the unicorn is revealed as being of its sexual connotations, rather than of the moral lessons that it was supposed to teach. They are led to the senseless murder of the unicorn, a moving fable of man's wanton destruction of innocence, beauty and love, yet perfectly in accord with boyish nature. It has something in it of that other great book written by a schoolmaster, William Golding's *Lord of the Flies*.

Gareth, the youngest of the four brothers, is ten when they are first introduced to the reader at the beginning of *The Queen of Air and Darkness*, so that, when Mordred is begotten at the end of that book, there is a gap of ten years or more between him and his half-brothers. He is therefore represented as having been brought up virtually as an only child. He is presented as an extreme example of the damaging effects of maternal possessiveness: alone with Morgause throughout his childhood, he has not only had instilled into him an obsessive sense of grievance against his father, but has become a sadist. When he enters the story he, unlike his half-brothers, has not married, the implication being that his relationship with his mother has stood in the way. His proposal to marry Guenever at the end of the book becomes, in the light of this, the more perverted.

Mordred's bodily weakness and slight deformity have also increased his grudge against Arthur, but have not excused him the weapons-training undergone by his half-brothers. Unlike them he has no taste for fighting: he seems to have escaped St Toirdealbhach's inflammatory influence. When he eventually comes to Camelot it is as a sophisticated young courtier, despite the rough, uncourtly environment in which like his half-brothers he has grown up.

v.

Before describing the upbringing of Lancelot, in Chapter III of *The Ill-Made Knight* White says:

> There was a feature about the great families which centred round the doom of Arthur. All three had a resident genius of the family, half-way between a tutor and a confidant, who affected the character of the children in each. At Sir Ector's there had been Merlyn, who was the main influence in Arthur's life. In lonely and distant Lothian there had been St Toirdealbhach, whose warlike philosophy must have had something to do with the clannishness of Gawaine and his brothers.

The importance of the teacher's personality is thus emphasised before White goes on to present yet another aspect of education in the growing up of Lancelot. His 'enfances' immediately follow the arrival at Arthur's court of Morgause and her sons and the begetting of Mordred, and once again,

White invents an upbringing since there is in Malory no hint of what the childhood of Lancelot might have been like. Again, psychological factors play as important a part in his development as in that of Gawaine and his brothers, although his circumstances are very different. Lancelot is introduced as a small page of the King's household, who excels at round games, at the wedding which ends *The Queen of Air and Darkness*. Back home in the castle of Benwick at the beginning of the next book, he is still described as a small boy, although he is aged fifteen. White hints at his own adolescent problems through his introduction of his character: 'The boy thought there was something wrong with him'; but he cautions the reader against intrusive curiosity with, 'We do not have to dabble in a place which he preferred to keep secret' (OFK 327). White's identification with Lancelot thus prompts him to glance at the origin of his own psychological and sexual problems, but in dissociation from the devouring mother-figure of Morgause. Lancelot's mother is as innocuous as she could well be, a great lady doing her embroidery and entertaining guests in a conventional manner. Nevertheless, we are told, something 'must have gone wrong in the depths of his spirit to make a face like that' (OFK 329), for White, contrary to the medieval tradition, makes Lancelot quite extraordinarily ugly in face. His desire for understanding, to know what he is, indicated by his study of his reflection in his helmet, further suggests the extent to which White had his own problems in mind. The sense of his own ugliness, apparently instilled in him in childhood by his mother's comments – though those who knew him as an undergraduate described him as extremely handsome – also suggests that Lancelot is to some extent a self-portrait. 'Shame and self-loathing' had been planted in Lancelot while he was tiny, yet White gives no explanation as to how this had happened: his brother Sir Ector has it seems no emotional problems. White's constant awareness of psychological factors is further suggested at this point by his reference to dreams, taken as seriously by medieval people, he says, as psychiatrists take them today, though here the dream only looks forward to Lancelot's later inability to achieve the Grail quest.

Lancelot's is an obsessive character, and the description of his education and upbringing is concerned solely with his training in the martial arts which are later to bring him lasting fame. He is a hero-worshipper: he falls in love with Arthur as a young boy, and from this point to the end of the story it is Arthur whom he really loves. (Later on, the impression is given that he has been entrapped by Guenever.) White reverts several times to Lancelot's problems: there is the 'impediment of his nature' (OFK 383), as well as the 'unhappy and inextricable tangles' which cause the boy to be emotionally 'disabled by something which we cannot explain'. From the beginning, he is the Ill-Made Knight, his ugliness also symbolically representing White's sense of his own inner 'ugliness'. In the armoury where he spends the long days training with Uncle Dap (and such exercises seem to constitute the whole of his education) there are sticks for beating him when he is stupid, as he strives 'to perfect himself for Arthur' (OFK 334). These sticks, White says, lie 'on the desk', creating an image more suggestive of the house-master's study than of the armoury in a medieval castle. Sometimes (OFK 337), Uncle Dap 'was tantalized into beating' Lancelot, perhaps indicating that Dap is himself sadistic. This mention of corporal punishment scarcely seems enough to account for the sadism that afflicts Lancelot in later life, however, making him shudder 'at the cruelty in himself' (OFK 375) when he has to deal with a knight who has cut off a lady's head before his eyes. Malory gives no suggestion of this trait in his hero.

The immense amount of detail with which White describes Lancelot's weapons-training, which takes him from the age of fifteen to eighteen, is functional in creating atmosphere and providing for the reader a clear account of the technicalities of such training. It is yet another example of the author's delight in such information and his desire to share it, while at the same time it illuminates Lancelot's character. It also draws attention to the immense importance of the teacher, in this case Uncle Dap, as the 'resident genius of the family' from whom could be learned 'everything the boy wanted' (OFK 337). Of the other aspects of Lancelot's education and home-life nothing is said, however, though it is obvious that he is neither unintelligent nor ignorant. Even as a small page, he understands at once when Arthur tells him about the Order of Chivalry that he wants to establish, so as to fight against Might.

> "We call it Fort Mayne in France," he had explained. "The man with the strongest arm in a clan gets made the head of it, and does what he pleases. That is why we call it Fort Mayne. You want to put an end to the Strong Arm, by having a band of knights who believe in justice rather than strength. Yes, I would like to be one of those very much. ..."   (OFK 328)

The knight who emerges from this narrow and stringent upbringing, this 'obscure and mystic life' (OFK 334), is very unlike Malory's confident, charismatic and seemingly well-balanced hero. The prowess which he acquires by this rigorous training, to which he gives himself so single-mindedly, is devalued by White's constant reference to the martial arts as mere games. Lancelot is top of the battling averages like the cricketers Bradman or Woolley. It is an art, like cricket, that he practises, but White though he admired skill despised games.

There is nothing in Lancelot's upbringing to suggest the growth of his spiritual nature. His desire to do a miracle, his strong feelings about chastity, and his commitment to the Grail quest and the way of perfection after it are idiosyncrasies which White does not attempt to account for, except as products of his unexplained self-loathing. Though he had to make Lancelot a deeply religious man, he did so without himself having much feeling for religion.

Although White describes the upbringing of the 'Orkneys' and Lancelot in some detail, Arthur alone is made to comment in later life on his early education. ' "Don't ever let anybody teach you to think, Lance: it is the curse of the world" ' (OFK 455), he remarks when things begin to go wrong after the Grail quest. No power of reasoning can solve problems of such complexity as he must face: Merlyn's *avant garde* programme has only made Arthur too sympathetic, too gentle to deal with the situation with which he is about to be confronted. White's scheme for the education of a prince was at the same time both liberal and limited. Though it included a strong moral element, it was the morality of the '30s pacifist that informed it. In the interests of historical realism, it included military training, but always undercut by Merlyn's disdainful mockery. Shaped above all by the author's current interests, it consisted mainly in lessons about animal behaviour and thus, by deduction, that of human beings.

9

White's Historical Imagination

'To tell a story you must first of all construct a world' says Umberto Eco[1] – and the characters must act in accordance with its laws. White's 'Old England of the twelfth century, or whenever it was' (OFK 205) is an historical never-never land, 'A glorious dream of the Middle Ages as they never were but as they should have been', in the words of a *New York Times* reviewer of *The Once and Future King*.

White's dependence on Malory as his source largely controlled his use of historical material. The fact that he was not attempting to write an historical novel about King Arthur released him from any obligation to try to create an authentic setting, and allowed him to devise a unique amalgam of historical fact and fantasy, enlivened with humour while moving progressively towards more serious concerns. The relationship of his work to Malory's is the key to the fantasy world of *The Once and Future King*, since the setting of *Le Morte Darthur*, though imaginatively powerful, is so lacking in visual and historical realism that it was easy for White to devise his own background, and to justify the enormous time-span covered by *The Once and Future King*. His carefully chosen historical detail is of the kind that a good teacher selects to 'make the subject come alive' for the beginner, and is vividly presented in White's own voice, as narrator. While he was creating pictures of some aspects of English medieval life, often from different periods, he was not afraid to exploit the opportunities for humour and comedy that they offered, nor did his doing so arise out of contempt for the past. Inconsistencies and anachronisms, he claimed, were justified by Malory's own practice. Historical burlesque, moreover, was very popular in the late nineteenth and early twentieth centuries, when English history was systematically learned by every little child, so that such books as Arthur Moreland's *The Humors of History*[2] and Gilbert Abbot A'Beckett's *Comic History of England*,[3] a copy of which White possessed and actually

---

1 Eco, Umberto, *op. cit.*, p. 24.

2 Moreland, Arthur: *The Humors of History*, 80 Drawings by Arthur Moreland, Reprinted from the *Morning Leader*, London, The Star Newspaper Co., 1903 (2 vols).

3 A'Beckett, Gilbert Abbott: *The Comic History of England*, with engravings by John Leech, new ed. 1907. Originally published in 1847.

referred to in *The Book of Merlyn*, were widely enjoyed. Mark Twain's *A Yankee at the Court of King Arthur* (1889) similarly offered an earlier example of the comic possibilities to be found in a backward glance at the Middle Ages, while the popularity of Sellar and Yeatman's *1066 and All That*, published in 1930, would have suggested that the taste for facetious history was still very much current when White was writing.

White's years at Stowe and Stowe Ridings gave him a strong sense of the historic nature of the English countryside. In *England Have My Bones*, he sees every place he sets foot in as packed with history, and although he remarks that Buckinghamshire is undistinguished, he obviously had a strong sense of how much more interesting it had been in the past. He speaks of the 'prodigious forest . . . as full of highwaymen and outlaws as any woodland of Robin Hood's' (EHMB 86). It is easy to see how the diminished forest of White's day could still become the Forest Sauvage of the Wart's boyhood. In the time of the crusades, he says, the Buckingham-shire forests had been full of boar, and he quotes the story of a farmer who, when bringing a stretch of this woodland under cultivation, cleared and dug up a mound overgrown with brambles and bracken, inside which he found a conch shell, a crusader's sword, and the bones of an enormous boar. Whether such stories were fact or fiction, they helped to supply a sense of continuity with the past and inspiration for *The Sword in the Stone*, furthered it seems by the presence of some of the old county families, some of whom had occupied the same house for five hundred years. A 'feeling of time telescoped and eternity' is produced by such unbroken tradition: 'I daresay you would find a pair of crusader's boots under your bed . . . and probably there are a couple of battle axes or rapiers mixed up with the umbrellas in the hall' (EHMB 170). The unbroken rural tradition of the harvest supper, described by A.G. Street in *Farmer's Glory* (1932), a book which White admired, and which tallies in many details with harvest suppers that he too had attended[4] undoubtedly inspired Sir Ector's Christmas feast.

White seems to have set out to represent, in *The Sword in the Stone*, a more or less idealised medieval world, centred upon Sir Ector's castle and the Forest Sauvage, and only later when he was working closer to *Le Morte Darthur*, to have begun to think out and formulate a mode of representing historical development to fit his story. In Chapter I a timeless scene is presented as Sir Ector directs the hay-making in which every able-bodied man and woman on the estate is participating. 'The best mowers mowed away in a line where the grass was still uncut, their scythes roaring in the strong sunlight'. From the hayfield the Wart and Kay move to the Mews which are 'neatly kept, with sawdust on the floor to absorb the mutes, and the castings taken up every day' (OFK 9). White loves to dwell on the detail

4 See *England Have My Bones*, p. 321ff.

of how traditional arts and crafts and rural tasks are carried out, abandoning comedy and caricature for realism and seriousness. The castle itself is more like a town or a village than any one man's home, and the villagers go to church in its chapel, wearing their best clothes: 'Everybody went to church in those days, and liked it.'

White, unlike most historical novelists, likes to exploit his position as a modern narrator, and he varies the situation in time. We are so to speak 'present' at Sir Ector's harvest supper and on many other occasions when the fictional happenings are fully realised. In Chapter V, a very different though even more detailed picture of Castle Sauvage is presented: it is still standing, but we are now in the author's present, and the castle is ruined. White guides the modern tourist around what remains of it, pointing out its features and their original purpose. During this conducted tour the reader is urged, 'if a sensible person', to spend days or possibly weeks there, recreating for himself the life of the castle in its heyday. One of White's greatest talents is this nimble shifting between the past times of legend, of popular imagination, of known historical fact and twentieth-century actuality. It reinforces the sense of continuity and historicity without breaking the narrative spell and lends a timeless quality to the story.

The visual images of life in Old England are familiar ones, often apparently drawn from illuminated manuscripts such as the Luttrell Psalter (to which White refers as a source in Chapter III of *The Candle in the Wind* (OFK 565)) with its marginal illustrations depicting scenes of everyday activities. On Sir Ector's domains:

> In the autumn everybody was preparing for the winter. . . . The pigs were driven into the purlieus of the forest, where boys beat the trees to supply them with acorns. . . . From the granary there proceeded an invariable thumping of flails; in the strip fields the slow and enormously heavy wooden ploughs sailed up and down for the rye and the wheat. . .   (OFK 130)

The images suggest the traditional Labours of the Months represented in medieval manuscripts such as the Duc de Berry's *Très Riches Heures*, or in the sculpture of the period, where a different country activity for each month of the year is depicted. In *The Sword in the Stone*, indeed, White makes the reader aware of the passing of the year and the cyclical pattern of medieval life by beginning his story in summer, moving on through the seasons of autumn and winter to spring, and then to summer and haymaking once again.

White sees nothing wrong in the feudal system itself, although he later makes it clear that not all landowners were as humane and altruistic as Sir Ector appears to be. His villeins knew that they:

> were more valuable to him than his cattle even . . . He walked and worked among his villagers, thought of their welfare, and could tell the good workman from the bad. . .

In other parts of Gramarye, of course, there did exist wicked and des-
potic masters – feudal gangsters whom it was to be King Arthur's
destiny to chasten – but the evil was in the bad people who abused it,
not in the feudal system.   (OFK 131)

White's journey back in time differs markedly from Mark Twain's in *A
Yankee at the Court of King Arthur*, where the superstition, brutality and
harshness of the medieval world are frequently suggested, even though by
means of comedy. White's nostalgic picture is nevertheless entirely appropriate to the fantasy pastoral setting that he is creating for the Wart's
'enfances'. He presents a world reminiscent of the 'edited' recollections of
childhood of many adults, in which:

in the summer it was beautifully hot for no less than four months . . .
and in the winter . . . the snow lay evenly, three feet thick, but never
turned to slush.   (OFK 137)

The nature of the historical detail grafted on to the story of Arthur
changed as White progressed with the work. In *The Sword in the Stone* it is
enormously varied, sometimes authentic but frequently chosen to create an
idyllic picture in conformity with the popular notion of the Middle Ages, or
else an absurd one in the manner of the once-popular comic histories. His
account of the Mews in Sir Ector's castle in Chapter I, for example, has the
stamp of authenticity since all the details must have been gathered from
White's books on hawking, but on the other hand, in the old Merry England of Gramarye fact often gives way to outright fantasy with touches of
humour that save it from being no more than weak nostalgia:

the rosy barons ate with their fingers, and had peacocks served before
them with all their tail feathers streaming, or boar's heads with the
tusks stuck in again . . . when the forests rang with knights walloping
each other on the helm, and unicorns in the wintry moonlight stamped
with their silver feet and snorted their noble breaths of blue upon the
frozen air.   (OFK 137)

As an example of the fully comic mode, the memorable fight between
King Pellinore and Sir Grummore Grummursum in Chapter VII is typical,
and may be compared with the entirely serious treatment of the same topic
in Chapter IV of *The Ill-Made Knight*, in which Arthur and Lancelot encounter each other without recognition and Lancelot unhorses the young
King (OFK 343).

The 'historical' background of *The Once and Future King* succeeds because
of the wealth of concrete detail which makes it immensely vivid. It has two
other distinctive features: firstly there is a prevailing tendency to the grotesque, and secondly it often takes the form of lists of medieval objects or
other matters. Even the Queen's bath comes in for this dual treatment in
The Ill-Made Knight: it is 'like a large beer barrel' and she is sitting in it
'naked, except for a pearl necklace', while:

> All over the floor between the puddles, there was a confusion of linen
> towels for drying herself, and of jewellery boxes, brocades, garments,
> garters, shifts . . . There were some condemned headdresses lying in
> disgrace – strange shapes of starch like candle extinguishers, and me-
> ringues, and the double horns of cows.   (OFK 496)

Similarly, as Arthur invents 'Law as Power' and Lancelot and Guenever
approach their Indian Summer, the kingdom settles down to a period of
peace, while:

> Housewives of a provident turn of mind filled their cupboards with
> treacle as a medicine for bad air, and with home-made plasters called
> Flos Unkuentorum for the rheumatics and muskballs to smell. . . . In
> the new law courts – for Fort Mayne was over – the lawyers were as
> busy as bees, issuing writs for attainder, chancery, chevisance, dis-
> seisin, distraint, distress, embracery, exigent, fieri facias, maintenance,
> replevin, right of way, oyer and terminer, scot and lot, Quorum bono-
> rum, Sic et non, Pro et contra, Jus primae noctis, and Questio quid
> juris?   (OFK 540)

White's attempt to achieve the ideal of Renaissance man, conceived as
being capable of a great range of accomplishments, while he was a master
at Stowe, combined with his antiquarian and practical interests, helped to
provide much of the background detail for his book. It was probably also
the restlessness produced by his deep unhappiness that drove him to the
exploration of such practical activities as the training of hawks, and the
need to learn something as the 'best thing for being sad'. Although it has
been suggested that he was less successful at some of the sports and skills
that he attempted than he liked to maintain, there seems no doubt that his
experiment with hawks represented a genuine revival of medieval prac-
tices, involving quite considerable research and a very great deal of per-
severance. The theme of hawking is recurrent throughout *The Once and
Future King* from the first chapter through to the symbolic hawk-imagery
that so effectively conveys an atmosphere of menace in *The Candle in the
Wind*. It is so ingeniously woven into the narrative that the large amount of
technical detail that White manages to include is never intrusive. In *The
Sword in the Stone,* he transmutes his knowledge of an almost forgotten
aspect of medieval life into the Wart's initiation as a hawk in the mews,
beginning this episode with a hawk's-eye view of a woolly bear caterpillar
fifteen yards away out of doors. He then blends this with an anthropomorphic view of the hawks as army officers, and reports their modern dialogue
in an amusing set of literary parodies. In *The Ill-Made Knight*, it is the
hawking episode – again presented to some extent in technical terms –
which causes Lancelot to fall in love with Guenever, whom he has previously regarded only as 'that woman', as he realises that his exasperation
with her ineptitude has caused him to hurt 'a real person'.

The Boxing-Day boarhunt demonstrates still more clearly White's use of authentic medieval material, even though he is not here able to make use of his own practical firsthand experience. For this chapter he drew on *Le Art de Venerie* by William Twiti, royal huntsman under Edward II, incorporating its author into his book as Master William Twyti, 'who turned out to be a shrivelled, harassed-looking man, with an expression of melancholy on his face' (OFK 142). White embeds the technicalities involved – the calls, the 'undoing' of the boar and so forth – into a vivid description of the whole episode, blending in several strands of comedy and the poignant account of the death of the hound Beaumont, the name of Twiti's hound in real life.

White seizes the opportunity of enlightening the reader about medieval customs whenever he can. When the Wart wants to know 'what happens when you are made a knight', his natural curiosity as a sibling rival about the 'rite de passage' which Kay is about to experience allows White to describe in detail what the ritual actually involved. Such information is never divulged in Malory, whose contemporary readers would probably not have needed to be told. To the Wart's complaint that Kay won't tell him what happens because it is too sacred, Merlyn replies with a description of the process in his best throw-away, anachronistic manner, which nevertheless gives an accurate, if up-dated impression of the process.

> "... What does happen?"
> "Only a lot of fuss. You will have to undress him and put him into a bath hung with rich hangings, and then two experienced knights will turn up ... and they will both sit on the edge of the bath and give him a long lecture about the ideals of chivalry such as they are. ... Then you dress him up as a hermit and take him off to the chapel, and there he stays awake all night, watching his armour and saying prayers. People say it is lonely and terrible for him in this vigil, but it is not at all lonely really, because the vicar and the man who sees to the candles and an armed guard, and probably you as well, as his esquire, will have to sit up with him at the same time. In the morning you lead him off to bed to have a good sleep – as soon as he has confessed and heard mass and offered a candle with a piece of money stuck into it as near the lighted end as possible – and then, when you are all rested, you dress him up again in his very best clothes for dinner. ..."   (OFK 183)

By basing the narrative of events loosely on Malory, and omitting a great deal, White was able to allow himself very considerable freedom in the handling of time. The 'Old England' in which the story begins seems at first to be identified with Norman times of perhaps the early twelfth century, but when Sir Ector with Kay and the Wart set out for London for the tournament, they apparently move from the twelfth century to the later Middle Ages. White, suggesting that if the reader happens not to have lived in 'Old England', he will find it difficult to imagine the wonders of the journey (OFK 204), takes him directly to the tilting ground itself, strangely represented as 'a huge green pit in the earth', ten feet below surface level, which has been carefully kept free of snow by being temporarily covered with straw. Wooden grandstands and pavilions for the famous people surround it, adorned with pennons and pennoncels, and White completes his colourful picture by suggesting how the armour will flash in the sunshine when the combatants arrive. It seems as if time has moved on from the twelfth century with which the chapter began, to an unspecified date at which plate-armour was in common use, since mail would be unlikely to flash in the sun. Plate armour began to come into general use in the fourteenth century. White also seems to suggest that the tournament is to take the form of jousts (since Kay apparently envisages himself engaging in single combat), although the form of the tournament before the fourteenth century was almost exclusively the mêlée (mentioned in fact in Chapter VII of *The Ill-Made Knight*) in which large numbers of knights engaged simultaneously.

White, as we know, considered anachronisms entirely justifiable, on the grounds that Malory is 'simply riddled' with them, and also since they could provide an amusing and effective means of communicating ideas about the past. Most but not all of his anachronisms are obviously intentional, some of them perhaps to be accounted for by his vagueness about the actual point in time of which he is writing. Sometimes they are signalled, sometimes not: King Pellinore's helmet is secured by means of nuts, bolts and screws, not known until the seventeenth century and so surely a deliberate anachronism, but there is nothing to prevent the reader from thinking that helmets really were fastened on in this way in the Middle Ages. Elsewhere, some time after Arthur has become king, he together with Merlyn and Kay are munching the half-ripe heads of corn in the harvest field, 'tasting the furry milkiness of the wheat, and the husky, less generous flesh of the oats. The pearly taste of barley would have been strange to them, for it had not yet come to Gramarye' (OFK 237). This is simply wrong. 'Barley' is an Old English word and the cereal was known to the Anglo-Saxons. But the pseudo-historical detail reinforces the impression of accuracy and historical detail. It is quite an ingenious stroke of imagination and who among his expected readers was going to check it?

White's manipulation of time, variously discussed elsewhere, is always ingenious and masterly, frequently through the brilliant device of Merlyn's different perspective which allows White a dramatic excuse to give historical surveys of varying accuracy where he feels the narrative needs them. Arthur and Kay are placed outside time when Merlyn explains the attitudes of various monarchs:

> Look at the Norman myths about legendary figures like the Angevin kings. From William the Conqueror to Henry the Third, they indulged in warfare seasonally. The season came round, and off they went to the meet in splendid armour which reduced the risk of injury to a foxhunter's minimum. Look at the decisive battle of Brenneville in which

a field of nine hundred knights took part, and only three were killed.
Look at Henry the Second borrowing money from Stephen, to pay his
own troops in fighting Stephen.   (OFK 240)

Here White is making political and moral points through simplified
history, and walks a tightrope between fiction and instruction. The informative passages naturally become less frequent as *The Once and Future King*
progresses, since the scene has already been set. *The Queen of Air and Darkness*, however, opens with the vivid description of the draughty, smokey,
damp and thoroughly uncomfortable tower room in which Gawaine and
his brothers sleep, covering themselves as best they can with straw and
plaids. White may well have had in mind as a model the castle at Trim, to
which Doolistown was very close, of which the huge and extensive ruins
can still be seen. This passage is one of genuine historical imagination,
vividly realised, though it needed little academic knowledge. The plain of
Bedegraine provides the opportunity for another extended set-piece:

> there were joculators, gleemen, tumblers, harpers, troubadours, jesters,
> minstrels, tregetours, beardancers, egg-dancers, ladder-dancers,
> ballette-dancers, mountebanks, fire-eaters, and balancers. In a way it
> was like Derby Day.   (OFK 271)

Into the list of authentic medieval entertainers, White anachronistically
inserts mountebanks, a term not used in England until the late sixteenth
century, but again, as the reference to Derby Day shows, he makes a reasonable deduction about medieval life and enlivens it for the modern reader.
Similarly in *The Ill-made Knight* and *The Candle in the Wind*, he introduces
some detailed passages of description such as the Armoury in the castle of
Benwick, in which Lancelot grows up. Here he visualises for the reader the
contents of this large room, explaining the function of the various weapons
and pieces of armour, with a very great deal of incidental information, well
spiced with touches of anachronism 'to give you the feel'. A feeling for the
past is accompanied by a strong sense of the present: the two combine to
create a vivid impression. His extensive reading must have been carefully
digested and then redeployed in such a way as not only to create a lively
picture but also to make it possible for the reader both to envisage the scene
and to understand something of the method of training the medieval
knight. Later, when Lancelot makes his escape from Elaine and rides back
to Camelot we see Uncle Dap:

> standing with Lancelot's old charger . . . and all his accustomed armour
> neatly stowed on the saddle, as if for a kit inspection. Everything was
> correctly folded and strapped in the proper military place. The haber-
> geon was rolled in a tight bundle. The helm, pauldrons, and vambraces
> were polished, literally by weeks of polishing . . .   (OFK 440)

These passages make apparent White's special interest in armour and heraldry: his copy of Charles Boutell's *Heraldry, Historical and Popular*[5] had been presented to him by Sir Sydney Cockerell, and he made good use of his knowledge of the subject at a number of points, particularly in *The Ill-Made Knight*. His interest in the technicalities of armour is also suggested by his annotations of his copy of F.P. Barnard's *Medieval England*.[6] He labelled each item of armour on a diagram of the brass of John Gray Esq., 1390 in this book. His notes also suggest his constant habit of seeing the medieval in terms of the twentieth century: tournaments are described as the 'medieval race meeting'. A comment beside a diagram of a bascinet reads 'The blind and hoggish expression of a man in a gas-mask'. In *The Sword in the Stone* we are told that 'Tilting was a great art and needed practice', and White devotes almost two pages to explaining how it was done, before declaring that 'It would take too long to go into all the interesting details of proper tilting that the boys had to learn', leaving the reader with the distinct impression that tilting is a very worthwhile activity.

While White was keenly interested in technique, in exactly how it was all done, on another level he strongly disapproved of the whole business of tilting, jousting and tournaments as he frequently makes plain. As a serious activity, it was ludicrous. As leading to 'Games-Mania' it was reprehensible, while worse still, it encouraged aggression and the waging of war for its own sake. When the Wart's longing to see some real knights fighting is gratified by Merlyn, as King Pellinore and Sir Grummore encounter each other in a 'terrible battle', White presents the combat as neither romantic nor exciting but as simply ridiculous. Although he delights in giving the details of the construction of the tilting helm, and of the weight of metal carried by each knight, as well as of the problems of conducting the sword-fight which follows the tilting, when he quotes Malory: 'They hurtled together as it had been two boars', he undercuts the splendour and excitement implicit in Malory's allusions to such combats by making the whole episode both absurd and childish. Just occasionally he forgets his disapproval of chivalric encounters and allows himself to be intrigued by the task of bringing to life for the reader the technicalities involved in them, as he does with great vividness in the account of Lancelot's fight with Sir Turquine:

> then they retreated in the usual way, fewtered their spears, and charged together like thunder. Lancelot, at the last moment, noticed that he was wrong about Turquine's seat. In the last flash he realized that Turquine was the finest tilter he had met, that he was coming with a hurl as great as his own, and that his aim was sure.
>
> The knights ducked and drew themselves together; the spears struck at the same moment; the horses checked in mid-career, reared up and fell over backward; the spears burst and went sailing high in the air,

---

5   Boutell, Charles: *Heraldry, Historical and Popular*, London 1864.
6   Barnard, F.P.: *Medieval England*, Oxford 1902.

turning over and over gracefully like the results of high explosive; and the lady on the palfrey looked away. When she looked again, both horses were down with their backs broken, and the knights lay still.

Two hours later, Lancelot and Turquine were still fighting with their swords.   (OFK 367–8)

White can never have seen such a combat, and there are no descriptions of such encounters in Malory or indeed anywhere in medieval literature, but he imagines the contest in an entirely convincing way, except perhaps for the detail of the broken-backed horses. Since despite his fascination with the technical aspects, he detested the very idea of chivalry, White usually insists on deglamourising, ridiculing and devaluing it, as the self-indulgent and reprehensible activity of barbarians, thugs and fools. He refuses to attribute any civilising power or intrinsic worth to it, or even to recognise its value in the commonly used modern sense of generosity and courtesy in social situations. ' "What is all this chivalry, anyway?" ' asks Merlyn: ' "It simply means being rich enough to have a castle and a suit of armour, and then, when you have them, you make the Saxon people do what you like." ' (Here he adopts the Normans versus Saxons themes first popularised in Scott's *Ivanhoe*.) Chivalry is equated with oppression: a view which conflicts with Chaucer's idealised portrait of the knight in *The Canterbury Tales*,[7] as well as with Langland's image of the knight as protector and of Christ as knight in *Piers Plowman*,[8] a concept found elsewhere in the fourteenth century, as for example in the poet William Herebert's similar image of Christ in the medieval lyric, 'What is he, this lordling, that cometh from the fight?'[9] Above all, White here runs counter to Malory's frequently recurring concept of the High Order of Knighthood, and its exalted chivalric ideal. But for White, chivalry is to be understood as implying that Might is Right. Malory's influence only comes through indirectly when Arthur as a young king is to institute a 'sort of order of chivalry' whose members will strike only on behalf of what is good (OFK 254).

ii.

In deciding to take Malory's *Morte Darthur* as the basis of his narrative, White was well aware of the complexity and difficulty of the undertaking in terms of devising an appropriate background. In an entry in his journal on 24th June, 1940, he commented on Malory's treatment of the past:

7 See the General Prologue to *The Canterbury Tales*, lines 43–78.
8 See *The Vision of Piers Plowman*, a Complete Edition of the 'B-Text, ed. A.V.C. Schmidt, London, Dent 1978, Passus XVIII, lines 10–28.
9 See ed. Davies, R.T.: *Medieval English Lyrics*, London, Faber, 1963, pp. 94–5.

Malory wrote at the end of the 15th century a description of very shadowy events supposed to have taken place in the 5th (6th?) century. Himself an antiquarian, he pictured them against the hazy background of the 12th century: he had in his mind's eye a picture of antiquity three hundred years ago, much as if a writer of the present day (in 1940) were to describe the Norman conquest against the sleepy background of the Stuart countryside.

After correctly remarking that Malory could have had no 'picture of 5th-century Britain', he continues:

> So far as the Morte d'Arthur is concerned, therefore, we have a man in 1470 describing events attributed to 479 (?) as if they had taken place in the 12th century.

In the same journal entry, he makes explicit the problem that this poses for him:

> Now, when I come upon the scene, I am faced by a composite figure indeed. I have, in the 20th century, to make the best of a 19th century version of the 15th century looking at the 5th century as if it were the 12th!

By '19th century version' he presumably means the Strachey edition of Malory that he was using. It is hardly surprising that he admits to trying to make 'a sort of fanciful fairyland out of the whole of the M.A.' (in a note written on the end-paper of his copy of Lytton's *The Last of the Barons*), though this intention co-existed with what was almost its opposite. In revising *The Sword in the Stone*, he comments in one of his notebooks:

> In Bk I emphasise the Norman Conquest state of affairs either in early description of Forest or in remarks about serf-agriculture.
> In Bk 4 insert a Wars of the Roses date.

The actual action of *The Once and Future King* takes place roughly between the beginning of the thirteenth century (the Wart becomes King in 1216) and the end of the fifteenth century, at the point at which Malory probably completed *Le Morte Darthur*, although White looks back to the beginning of the Norman period. King Pellinore comments on the announcement of the death of Uther: 'Uther the Conqueror, 1066 to 1216', so that Uther's reign is thus made to cover a hundred and fifty years and the reigns of no less than seven monarchs, from William I to King John, and Arthur's many more. No wonder that when actual monarchs are mentioned, White refers to them as coming from 'mythological families such as Plantagenets, Capets and so forth', and speaks of them as 'legendary kings like John', 'fictional kings', and 'an oaf like the imaginary Richard Coeur de Lion' (OFK 560–3). This cavalier attitude to historical fact greatly benefits White's book. It enables him to move easily between fact and fiction without puzzling the reader, since there is no consistent attempt at historical realism. We knowingly enter a fairyland, but a fairyland with many points of connection with past and present.

White seems to have had very little interest in political history: his fascination was with the past, with people's lives, with how they did things. Understanding the complexities and technicalities involved in such activities as hawking and jousting required considerable research, and took him closer to those who had originally performed those actions and the times in which they had lived. The political history of the Middle Ages was only marginally relevant to his narrative. Although like Sir Walter Scott he had a strong sense of the romance of the Middle Ages, his approach to his subject – as has been suggested – did not allow him to follow Scott's method. In *The Sword in the Stone* he looks back beyond the Conquest to the 'immortal feud of Gael and Gall', as Merlyn explains to Arthur and Kay how the Gaels – or Celts – or Old Ones – had been harried out of England by the Normans. White, like Scott in *Ivanhoe*, represents the enmity between Saxon and Norman as persisting long after the Conquest, but although he must have been familiar with Scott's novel, even though like Scott he includes the figure of Robin Hood (or Wood, who, he adds, was a Saxon partisan (OFK 233)), the differences between the two writers are in most respects more apparent than the similarities. White does not seem to have thought very highly of his great predecessor, complaining in *The Book of Merlyn* that his characters 'talk like imitation warming pans'.

As he proceeded with *The Once and Future King*, he was becoming increasingly anxious to discover implications for his own time from past history, and to draw lessons from it. Merlyn, lecturing Arthur before the battle of Bedegraine, sees the Norman Conquest as 'a process of welding small units into bigger ones', and comments that the revolt of the 'Gaelic Confederation' (later crushed in the course of the battle) 'is a process of disintegration'. He goes on to express the view that it is the destiny of Man to unite, not to divide. Norman attitudes not unnaturally still persist after the death of Uther, as Arthur recognises in the scene when he institutes his 'sort of order of chivalry', in the Round Table, although they are for the most part seen as rather reprehensible, as Arthur's reference to ' "our Norman idea about the upper classes having a monopoly of power, without reference to justice" ' implies (OFK 254).

Like many nineteenth- and some twentieth-century historians, White seems to favour a theory of progress, as he draws attention to the process of unification under the Normans, and reflects on the achievements of the Middle Ages. Arthur's strenuous efforts to civilise his realm by various means correspond (very roughly) to the developments that took place between the Conquest and the life-time of Malory. White – in his moments of seriousness – sees history as a series of transformations and changes, taking the form of a long struggle out of barbarism towards order, justice and tolerance, a slow process of gradual achievement which is ever in danger of being reversed by the return of chaos. Arthur's reign is shown again and again as illustrating this progress towards civilisation, as he tames the aggressive instincts of his followers and eventually imposes order and institutes the rule of law. White, able to look back – as Malory was not – with some historical knowledge makes clear the advances that he felt had been made:

> When the old King came to his throne it had been an England of armoured barons, and of famine, and of war. It had been the country of trial by ordeal with red-hot irons . . . In the baron's castle, in the early days, you would have found the poor men being disembowelled . . . You have only to turn to the literature of the period . . . to see how the land lay. . . . And all the while, before Arthur came, the common people . . . had cried aloud that Christ and his saints were sleeping. (OFL 559)

(This last reference is an echo of the *Peterborough Chronicle* concerning the period of anarchy in Stephen's reign in the early twelfth century.) 'Such had been the surprisingly modern civilisation which Arthur had inherited', White continues ironically. But now Lancelot and Guenever are looking out over 'the fabled Merry England of the Middle Ages' which has become the 'Age of Individuals'. White turns from the barbarism that he has been contemplating to consider seriously, if briefly, the achievements of the Middle Ages: the splendours of its architecture, its stained glass, the work of goldsmiths and carvers in ivory, the book-production, the whole 'ferment of creative art which existed in our famous ages of darkness' (OFK 563). With enormous zest he continues to elaborate his vision in one of his best set pieces, supplying his own evaluation of what the medieval scene might have offered with the alchemist 'who was, most sensibly, trying to turn lead into gold'. With seeming approval he describes the palmer whose bogus relics, 'if he were a well-travelled one':

> might have included a feather from the Angel Gabriel, some of the coals on which St Lawrence was grilled, a finger of the Holy Ghost "whole and sound as ever it was", "a vial of the sweat of St Michael whereas he fought with the devil", a little of "the bush in which the Lord spake to Moses", a vest of St Peter's, or some of the Blessed Virgin's milk preserved at Walsingham.   (OFK 566)

Even more remarkably, it seems:

> The Countess of Anjou always used to vanish out of the window at the secreta of the mass. Madame Trote de Salerno used her ears as a handkerchief and let her eyebrows hang down behind her shoulders, like silver chains.   (OFK 563)

What is so amazing is the success with which White controls his heterogeneous mixture of fact and fantasy. He does it partly by taking neither too far, and by his controlling, imaginative but not unduly solemn concern. The careless ease with which he packs in a vast amount of recondite and learned material is only equalled by the enthusiasm with which he elaborates it with imagination and invention. Even at the end of his story, when Lancelot returns the Queen to King Arthur in the presence of the Bishop of Rochester, White constructs a 'pageant of reconciliation' which piles one concrete detail upon another until, 'heavy with majesty', Arthur enters. Much of the illustrative detail which so successfully enlivens all four volumes of *The Once and Future King* White seems to have drawn from the comparatively small number of historical studies which were actually in his possession. Yet as a voracious reader to whom books were available from many different sources, at least before he went to Doolistown, his mind must early have been extraordinarily well-stocked with historical information. It is often far from easy to identify his sources in *The Once and Future King*, though the origin of a number of passages can be found in some of the books from his library which were found in his house in Alderney after his death.

Of these, Strutt's *Sports and Pastimes of the People of England*, first published in 1801, supplied a good deal of information on the size and use of longbows and on archery in general, as well as on the use of the quintain. Here also White probably found the small detail about the mutilation of dogs 'so that they could not hunt in the woodlands of the lord', as well as many more such facts. The pages devoted to the subject of medieval roads in J.J. Jusserand's famous book, *English Wayfaring Life in the Middle Ages*, which first appeared (in French) in 1884 probably came to mind when White was describing the journey of Sir Ector's party to London towards the end of *The Sword in the Stone*. The method of both writers is not dissimilar: Jusserand, too, brings imagination to his task:

> While battling each one against the weather which hampered his journey, prelates, barons, or knights, must have been obliged to stop their animals in some isolated inn, and as they listened to the sound of the sleet on the wooden panels which closed the window, feet at the fire in the smoky room . . . they thought on the royal displeasure which soon, no doubt, would show itself in the "painted chamber" at Westminster. (86)

The 'painted chamber' is to become the tapestried Justice Room at the end of White's story, from which Lancelot 'in the felon's way' is to leave for Dover, taking sanctuary as he goes. White quotes Jusserand's footnote to p.161, 'He was to be "un-girt, un-shod, bare-headed, in his bare shirt, as if he were to be hanged on the gallows" ' on p. 638 of *The Once and Future King*. Very many more examples could be given of his indebtedness to this source, in particular for some of the more bizarre details in Chapter III of *The Candle in the Wind*.

In drawing on these works, White made use of the facts – or fictions – with which they supplied him with great ingenuity. In Crump and Jacob's

Legacy of the Middle Ages, for example, he found information about hand-writing in the Middle Ages[10] which suggested the description of the letter written by the dying Gawaine in 'the lovely old Gaelic minuscule' (OFK 662). In the same book, Eileen Power in her chapter on 'The Position of Women' quotes 'the refrain of a French *ballade* of the fourteenth century, 'En ciel un dieu, en terre une deesse" (405) which White also quotes, inge-niously fitting the line into his adaptation of Malory's comments on 'love in kynge Arthurs dayes' (OFK 559; Vin 649), as he presents one of the last glimpses of Lancelot and Guenever together in peace. His notes in the end-papers of Crump and Jacob comment on the 'humanistic miniscule' (sic), and he marked many passages in the Introduction and in the chapters on 'Decorative and Industrial Arts', 'The Position of Women' and 'Custom-ary Law', as well as on 'Handwriting'. From Crump and Jacob he probably also took the medieval mnemonic 'Barbara Celarent Darii Ferioque Prioris' pronounced by Merlyn in Chapter XII of *The Sword in the Stone* which White includes again when it is 'sung antiphonally' by Arthur and Kay in Chapter III of *The Queen of Air and Darkness*. In his text he did not hesitate to inform the reader of the actual source of his information where it suited him to do so: in the long historical sketch at the beginning of Chapter XXV, in *The Ill-Made Knight*, he refers to Duruy's *History of France*[11] (more fully discussed later in this chapter), an early nineteenth-century study that he possessed and used extensively. He does not, however, mention other writers to whom he was indebted at this point, such as J.R. Reinhard from whose *Medieval Pageant*[12] he took the story of the Countess of Henneberge who gave birth to 365 children at one time. (*Medieval Pageant* is a compila-tion of stories, freely retold in very much the spirit of White, the author's purpose being to share with the Gentle Reader his own interest and pleasure in the tales. In his preface Reinhard explains that he has 'taken such liberties as seemed to me necessary to convey to the Gentle Reader of the twentieth century the same impression or idea as that received by the Gentle Auditor of the eleventh, twelfth or thirteenth.')

Elsewhere, Chaucer as well as the historians was pressed in to enliven the scene, as White alludes to the *Miller's* and *Reeve's Tales*:

> In this direction, if you happened to be broad-minded, you might have been amused to see the saucy Alison who cried "Tee-Hee!" after she had been given the unusual kiss which Chaucer tells about. In that one, you might notice an exasperated Miller and his family, trying to straighten out the hurrah's nest which happened last night through the displacement of a cradle, as the Reeve tells in his Tale.   (OFK 568)

[10] See Crump, C.G. and Jacob, E.F., *op. cit.*, p..197, Lowe, E.A.: *Handwriting*.

[11] Duruy, Victor: *Histoire de France, op. cit.*

[12] Reinhard, J.R.: *Medieval Pageant*, London, Dent 1939.

Though White would have liked to have been a professional historian and a scholar, he relied mainly upon secondary sources for much of the historical information he used in *The Once and Future King*. Such a method was perfectly adequate for his purposes; there would have been little point in searching out more recondite material. He was, when necessary, well able to work from original texts, for example on the subject of the training of hawks, for which he used medieval and early Renaissance manuals. He could easily read late Middle English prose, accessible in modern editions: the description of the boarhunt in Chapter VII of *The Sword in the Stone*, as has already been mentioned, draws heavily upon *Le Art de Venerie*,[13] and he probably also made use of *The Master of Game*.[14] He certainly knew *The Book of St Albans*,[15] since he refers to 'the Abbess Juliana Berners', its author, as a source of information on the subject of hawks appropriate to the various ranks (OFK 347). He also read Latin without difficulty (he had, after all, been engaged to teach it in the prep-school at Reigate) as his translation of Friar Clynn's[16] 'message' in *The Book of Merlyn* shows: ' "Seeing these many ills," he had written in Latin, "and as it were the whole world thrust into malignancy . . ." ' (BM 127).

White's fascination with the past for its own sake is unmistakable, but he was an antiquarian rather than an historian. The skill with which he contrived to load his narrative with miscellaneous historical information – and indeed with pseudo-historical information – without ever boring the reader is remarkable. His historical set-pieces are among the most successful features of his book.

In deliberately basing *The Once and Future King* on *Le Morte Darthur*, he neither wished to be consistent in setting his narrative in the fifteenth century, nor wanted to adopt Malory's mentality and ethos, because of his antipathy to the very idea of chivalry and, for the most part, the ideals of the Round Table. Undoubtedly his purpose changed as he wrote his 'quadruplets': from wishing simply to devise a light-hearted fantasy which would combine some of the features of *The Midnight Folk* with a picture of Merry England, so as to delight young readers, he became more and more anxious to communicate to adults a message for his own time, as the

---

13 Twiti/Twyti/Twici Guillaume: *Le Art de Venerie* (The Art of Hunting), 1327.
14 *The Master of Game* by Edward, second Duke of York, written 1406–13.
15 *The Book of St Albans*, the last work issued by the press that was set up at St Albans about 1479, containing treatises on hawking and heraldry, and one on hunting by Dame Julians Barnes.
16 Friar Clynn: White describes him as 'a historian . . . who had died in 1348. This friar, employed as the annalist of his abbey to keep the historical records, had seen the Black Death coming to fetch him . . . Carefully leaving some pieces of blank parchment with the book in which he was to write no longer, he had concluded with the following message . . . "Seeing these many ills," he had written in Latin, ". . . I am now leaving some paper . . . in case by any chance a man may remain alive in the future . . . to carry on the labour once begun by me." '

horrors of World War II impinged more acutely on his consciousness, but his historical background remained fantastic.

His interest, as has already been suggested, was selective, his desire to 'give you the feel' of medieval times confined to the aspects that particularly appealed to him. Religion, which impinged upon life at so many points in the Middle Ages, he almost entirely neglected. Chaucer's *Canterbury Tales*, by including among the Pilgrims a high proportion professionally concerned with religion, suggest how important the Church was in the everyday life of the fourteenth century. White must have been aware of this fact: he includes the Rev. Sidebottom among the inhabitants of the Castle Sauvage, and St Toirdealbhach as the mentor of Gawaine and his brothers, it is true, but they are comic and idiosyncratic figures. He is not interested in the spiritual dimensions of his story, as have been, for example, a number of more recent Arthurian writers who have devoted attention to the pagan rituals which might have been conducted in the reign of a Romano-British Arthur. He also preferred to handle as indirectly as possible the theme of the quest of the Holy Grail, to which many of his predecessors in the nineteenth century had been strongly attracted, as a topic otherwise too pious for the modern reader to accept without embarrassment.

White's historical imagination encouraged him to empathise with certain medieval figures, notably Henry II. In the end-papers of Vol. II of his copy of Thierry's *Norman Conquest of England*[17] he wrote an extensive note on Henry II, 'by far the most interesting of the English kings', in which he indicates his sympathy with Henry's attraction to Becket. With Thomas Becket the King:

> seems to have had one of the most important relations of his life. Sodomy was a Norman vice, and Becket beautiful as well as strong, but there need have been no physical relationship. Indeed, it is most unlikely. But he did have a most intense emotional relationship with Becket, and I have no doubt that he submitted sincerely to the rods . . . Consider this fat, grey-eyed, bloodshot, strangely attractive sportsman kneeling to be whipped before the tomb of that beautiful person whom he had personally known to be a saint long before he was canonised, whom he had persecuted all his life ("hell knows no fury like a woman scorned") and whom he had driven to revolt because he loved him and could not for that reason permit him to live his own life. Henry is a very real person.

The interest in White's notes lies in the terms in which he speaks of Henry II, suggestive of a number of perceived similarities with himself. He indicates the King's loneliness, his friends alienated, and says that 'Like most unhappy men, he was a great hunter', a 'fat . . . attractive sportsman'. His understanding of the possibility of 'a most intense emotional relationship' of a homosexual nature, but without a physical relationship surely springs from

---

[17] Thierry, Augustin: *op. cit.*

his own proclivities, as does his comment on the inherent sadism of the King's refusal to allow Becket to live his own life 'because he loved him'. It calls to mind White's revelation to David Garnett, that his sadism made sexual relationships impossible for him because of his urge to hurt those whom he loved. It also helps to illuminate the nature of his passion for the boy Zed when White was living on Alderney towards the end of his life, in that he accepts that an intense emotional relationship of a homosexual nature can exist without necessarily being accompanied by physical relations.

Although White always seems to have kept his sadistic inpulses under control, he was undoubtedly interested in descriptions of torture and other forms of physical cruelty. In his copy of Victor Duruy's *History of France* which gives a number of particularly explicit accounts of medieval cruelties, he was sufficiently interested to mark all such passages. When illustrating the progress from barbarism to civilisation in the course of Arthur's reign he subsequently drew on some of them for *The Once and Future King*. Duruy's book probably supplied the passage in Chapter VII of *The Ill-Made Knight* in which he describes 'the state of England, which forced King Arthur to work for his theory of justice', for example. He refers directly to Duruy in Chapter XXV of the same book, as the source of the horrible examples of the 'burst of lawlessness and brutality' which had followed the discovery that the world had not ended, as feared and expected, in the year one thousand (OFK 444). Similarly, in Chapter III of *The Candle in the Wind*, White again described the state of the country when Arthur came to the throne, contrasting it with the achievements of his reign, in terms of the torments inflicted on the populace by the barons (OFK 559–61). It seems indisputable that Duruy influenced White's attitude to the conquering Normans by describing their cruelties at length, in the passages on which White drew specifically, and throughout his book.

White's interest in the personality of Henry II found further expression in his journal for 24 June 1941. Here, he suggests that Malory 'thought of Arthur as a contemporary of Henry II. His chivalry is the Norman chivalry of that King'; and he goes on to suggest a number of similarities between the two kings:

> His Arthur stands, to my mind, in a sort of poeticised aura of the twelfth century: that extraordinary century of Individualism, in which the second Henry, like Arthur, had a wife who was not above reproach (?), a bosom friend (Becket) with whom, as Arthur with Lancelot, he had an intense emotional bond, an empire beyond the channel, and sons like Mordred to betray him. But I have not, for this reason, confined my own version of A. to the 12th century.

Although White chose not to confine the historical background to his narrative to the twelfth or any other century, he had little tolerance for the nineteenth-century enthusiasts who, feeling under no more obligation than he to work within strict historical limits, allowed themselves considerable artistic licence. His journal for 24 June 1941 continued with a spirited criticism presumably directed principally against Burne-Jones:

> The great Victorian revival of Arthur took hold of the already complicated time-sequence (1475 looking at 479 (?) as if it were 12th century) and transformed it into a fantastic century which existed nowhere except in the minds of Tennyson and Rossetti and Burne-Jones. Malory's knights, whose main armament was the chain mail, were now tricked out in a fantastic version of plate, in which the pauldrons were iron ivy-leaves and God knows what. They were transported to the ruins of Victorian lunatic asylums, where, with brambles circling round their ivy-plated knees, they looked upwards swooningly into a misty nimbus surrounding the vicar's communion chalice.

One of White's major aims in dealing with historical material in *The Once and Future King* was to draw parallels between past and present, as in his own way Malory had done, not simply to give his readers 'the feel' of earlier centuries, but to allow himself to comment more freely on the tragic consequences of man's belligerent nature. His horror at the carnage of World War II inevitably affected his view of the past, making him indifferent to the ideals of chivalry and only able to see, for the most part, its evil aspects. There is no doubt that his attitude was influenced by the pacifism of the nineteen-thirties. His views were shared by many, particularly in the universities, before the outbreak of war; and his production of the pacifist play, *Miracle at Verdun*, while he was at Stowe indicates the extent to which such attitudes were current, even widely accepted. Contemplation of the past, however, only made White feel the more dismayed that the course of the centuries had brought no progress in civilisation in terms of peace. Indeed, the lapse into barbarism represented by the War was perhaps the more terrible to him because of the advances that had been made in some aspects of civilisation, so that the descent was necessarily the more profound. Such signs of progress as had been taken for granted by western society must therefore be deceptive, as fragile and short-lived as the ideals for which Arthur had striven in *Le Morte Darthur*. Nevertheless he does not leave his account without hope for the future, based on what he believed was his justification in telling Arthur's story in the first place. There must be a new Round Table 'without boundaries between the nations who would sit to feast there.' Hope for the future lies in culture alone, as White asserts at the end of his story. It is this concern, this commitment to communicating the ideals, not of a chivalric dream-world, but of modern western society at its best, that gives White's Aristotelian tragedy its power and its lasting greatness. Mark Twain's *Yankee* fizzles out in spleen and hopelessness; most more recent Arthurian fictions are mere entertainments, though often delightful. *The Once and Future King*, both modern and old-fashioned at the same time, is still read and remains a flickering candle shedding light as its author hoped it would.

10

White and Malory

On April 28th, 1939, before the idea of ending *The Once and Future King* with *The Book of Merlyn* had occurred to White, he wrote in his journal of his intention of writing 'a little Introduction' to his 'quadruplets about Arthur':

> It will have to be on these lines: "These books are only a marginal embroidery upon the immortal work of Sir Thomas Malory."

In this proposed introduction, which seems never to have been published, he intended to explain what he had been trying to do, how his work related to *Le Morte Darthur*, and to 'confess the alterations which I have made in his earlier work'. Above all, it was to be a tribute to Malory who, he says in this journal-entry, is 'generally read, if read at all nowadays, as if he were a sort of rambling old buffer with a charming vocabulary'; and to rectify contemporary attitudes to 'one of our greatest national poets'. White suggests that Malory is neglected because he is considered quaint, and because it is commonly supposed that his characters lack individuality in an age which attaches great importance to realistic characterisation. His desire to lead the modern reader back to *Le Morte Darthur*, to provide a preface to Malory, is formulated here as he refers to 'the master, to whom anybody who has been amused by my scribbling should turn for the true fount now.' If the 'universal ignorance of the general reader' of Malory's very existence is now at all diminished, it is surely true that enjoyment of *The Once and Future King* has enabled many who would otherwise have ignored *Le Morte Darthur* to read it for themselves. White's genius is particularly apparent in his power to select from Malory's huge work what can even now readily capture the imagination, and to transform it so that it can still be appreciated today. *The Sword in the Stone* can dissolve the prejudices of those who believe that the medieval is dull, remote and irrelevant, as it creates interest in the Arthurian characters and draws the reader into the story, even if it does not present a veracious picture of medieval life.

In his projected Introduction White also sets out to explain his reasons for the alterations he had made in his handling of his source-material. He could regard his work as no more than 'marginal embroidery' because he believed that he had preserved Malory's 'great characters, his sequence of events, and all the motives which he clearly laid down 450 years ago', even if he had 'omitted perhaps too much of glorious undergrowth' for the sake of the main plot. The changes that he himself has introduced he dismisses as trifling: 'I have made Morgause the youngest of the Cornwall sisters. . . . I have made Agravaine kill his mother. . . . I have omitted a wife of Sir Ector's. . . . I have let Sir Launcelot kill Agravaine first. . . . I have falsified the fact that King Uther Pendragon died when Arthur was two years of age.' He then goes on to justify the fusion of the two Elaines: 'as Lancelot already had a mother called Elaine, I felt it was profuse to give him two mistresses of the same name.'

For White it was a 'fact altogether neglected' that Malory's characters are real characters, not "knights-in-armour", for whom he seems to have had an enduring distaste. But while Malory presents his characters simply and directly through event and speech, White as narrator speculates in an entirely modern way about their motivation and their emotions. He defines Gawaine as passionate, Lancelot as muddled, Guenever as domineering, and Arthur as kind. In attributing to each major character a leading trait he may seem to oversimplify, but in fact the definition of their leading characteristics allows him also to individualise them and to reveal for the reader the 'real people' within the types that he found them to be, as he himself rediscovered *Le Morte Darthur*. So, where Malory had drawn his characters with 'the strength of a few lightning strokes', White confesses to discussing their motives, which are interesting to us now in the twentieth century, although they were not important for the medieval reader.

On the subject of his introduction of anachronisms White also felt it necessary to justify his mode of handling his source. 'Alas, I cannot forbear from pointing out, Mallory himself is simply packed with anachronisms', he comments. He sees Malory as fixing for the modern reader the imaginary Arthurian world, 'a world in which there were giants, dragons, miracles and other phenomena uncommon under Edward' (Edward IV, in whose reign in the 1460s Malory was writing). Into this fantasy world of his creation, Malory introduces the 'armour and chivalry and domestic arrangements of his own day – or of one a little before it'. White goes on to remark that Arthur 'if he existed at all' must have lived in the fifth century, and vividly pictures him 'plodding about in cross-gartered small clothes, stuffed with straw, plotting an occasional ambush upon Saxons equally insignificant. This was not the man that Mallory was thinking about.' He adds the comment that Shakespeare, like Malory, had similarly updated the accoutrements of his characters, dressing his 'Scottish barbarian' [Macbeth] in Elizabethan armour.

It is because he saw Malory as a romantic who created his own setting for the story of Arthur that White feels justified in taking the process of updating the story one stage further. He was, in fact, only doing what many medieval authors as well as Malory had done before him, as they retold an already extant story in their own way, often at the same time changing parts of it and giving it a new meaning. So White elaborates on Malory's characters while simplifying the main story itself in order to bring out its essential features, ignoring what is irrelevant to his own purpose and interests. He devises a setting for the action derived from his idealised vision of medieval England: where Malory shuns surface realism and visualises almost nothing of the circumstances of his story, White supplies a wealth of historical or pseudo-historical detail as background for his characters. To the possible objection that he has produced a character (Merlyn) who talks anachronistically about psychoanalysis and plastic surgery, he asserts that he has allowed himself any anachronism that he wanted when it was connected with a wizard or witch. Since Merlyn had second-sight, which must come from knowledge of the future, references to the twentieth century must be legitimate. As to the 'g'-dropping knights of *The Sword in the Stone*, the resulting evocation of a comparatively modern fox-hunting society can be justified as 'a genuine comment on the ideals of chivalry'. Thus, even though White claimed to despise *A Yankee at the Court of King Arthur* (although he was a member of the Mark Twain Society), there are similarities between the work of the two authors, since Twain's book also bridged the gap between past and present at many points.

White discusses the problem of dialogue in his notes for an Introduction. He has decided to modernise so as to avoid 'placing a gulf of unreality between the old world and our own', and in so doing, he suggests that it had 'seemed more sensible to recognise the unity of the human soul in all ages, to throw a light of reality upon the old days'. He could hardly have done otherwise without making the dialogue intolerably precious. So, throughout *The Once and Future King*, Malory's laconic, dramatic yet ceremonious speech gives way to the flatter tones of twentieth-century realistic dialogue. Everywhere White takes pleasure in expanding his source to explicate the thoughts and emotions of his characters. Guenever, for example, is for him 'what they used to call a "real" person' (OFK 497) who 'behaved like herself' and who (thanks to White's timely reading of the Russian novelists) is able to some extent at least to reveal the complexities and contradictions that go to make up her personality through idiosyncratic speech.

There is an interesting exception to White's use of modernistic and, it must be admitted, sometimes banal (when not deliberately comic) dialogue. It illustrates both White's sensitivity to the noble exalted strain in Malory, and his remarkable balancing act upon Malory's work, both flippant and serious. The exception occurs when White realises the need to elevate the tone and deal seriously with certain ideals and events. He is usually skilful in modulating from the modernising level of his ordinary style to these more elevated passages. Their use illustrates the delicate ambiguity of his handling of Malory, the tight-rope he walks between modernistic triviality and pseudo-historical pomposity – the dangers of each being very clear to him.

White therefore invokes at times what he calls the High Language of Chivalry (in fact, Malory's ordinary style), justifying it by saying 'for in those days there were two kinds of speech like High and Low Dutch or Norman French and Saxon English' (OFK 356). The High Language is usually direct quotation from Malory. White thus suggests that such apparently stylised discourse was a chivalric convention, suitable for special occasions, rather than the language of everyday converse. In general, the device works well, though there are points at which his attempt to insert the language of ceremony or of liturgical solemnity into the modern does not entirely succeed. Nor is he able to make use of the subtle 'modulations from the polite and dignified plural to the insulting singular'[1] of the second personal pronoun that enables Malory to convey to his fifteenth-century readers a whole range of changes of tone. Where Malory can indicate some of the complexities of the relationship and status of his speakers by their use of 'you' and 'thou' in addressing each other, modern speech cannot represent such nuances in this way.

White's analysis of Malory's method sees him as an 'historical novelist in three layers', thereby suggesting that he worked in a more systematic and sophisticated manner than is at all likely, both because of Malory's literary temperament and the state of knowledge available to him. The first layer is represented, he says, by Malory's allusion to fifth-century Britain and his correct enumeration of its kings. Malory's 'romantic twelfth-century picture of the flower of chivalry' constitutes the second layer, substantiated by White's reading of de Joinville and the bestiaries of that century. He sees the third layer as being contemporary with Malory himself, indicated by his very brief references to fifteenth-century costume and custom. White goes on to express his awareness of the complexity and magnitude of Malory's task in speaking of his sources:

> The roots of the Arthurian legend are buried among confused narrative ballads and prose romances in half the European languages, including French, German and Welsh. These tedious roots, which are uniformly contradictory about almost all the relative facts, were synthesised by the amiable and immortal Sir Thomas Mallory into a consistent whole.

The success attributed rather inaccurately to Malory in thus re-ordering his source-material into a narrative which has beginning, middle and end suggests to White that he must have been a man, not only of the most penetrating intellect, but also of 'profound education . . . in classical criticism', since *Le Morte Darthur* 'satisfies every rule of Aristotle's definition of

---

[1] See Brewer, D.S., ed.: *Malory: The Morte Darthur, Parts Seven and Eight*, York Medieval Texts, London, Arnold, 1968, p. 16ff.

tragedy.' White was much mistaken both about the state of the sources available to Malory, and about his classical education, but his criticism has the essence of the matter. Malory did indeed remarkably recreate the Arthurian legend in *Le Morte Darthur*, as witnessed by its continuing life, though in ways different, as modern scholarship now shows, from the ways attributed to him.

Although White would have liked to be a scholar himself, his projected Introduction nevertheless contains a spirited criticism as by an equal of Arthurian scholars, as well as of some of Malory's sources. Naming no names, he goes on to give a very shrewd, justified and at the time rather original evaluation of those misguided academics who neglected Malory in favour of his sources as:

> pedantic jackdaws, who have asserted that Mallory's work is decadent, in comparison with the vernal blooms of their illiterate troubadours: an assertion and an attitude which could only be parallelled if Shakespearian scholars unanimously decided to neglect Macbeth in favour of North's Lives.

The reference to 'illiterate troubadours' is wildly mistaken but the essence of the comment is true. Arthurian scholars were prone to posit 'lost sources' always greatly superior to those works we have, and Malory in particular suffered from such denigration. This unhappy state of affairs, White explains, has led him to devote a quarter of a million words to what he now modestly describes as 'at best . . . a footnote to the older writer.' He seems to have had little or no interest himself in the earlier Arthurian literature out of which Malory had fashioned *Le Morte Darthur*, nor in the discovery of the Winchester MS of Malory's *Works* in 1934. Though he possessed several copies of Malory,[2] he seems to have worked from the Globe edition edited by Sir Edward Strachey, which he heavily annotated, and which is now preserved in the Harry Ransom Centre in the University of Texas at Austin. The Globe edition prints Caxton's version of 1485, which until the Winchester College MS was discovered was the only version known, and which is still the basis of the Everyman and Penguin editions.

In his work of making the story of Arthur available to English readers of the fifteenth century, from the collection of French prose and English verse sources at his disposal, Malory's aim seems essentially to have been to 'reduce' the complex mass of stories to an historical sequence, a narrative history of England centred on Arthur. As such, it was a difficult task: he had to deal with texts of immense length, consisting of interwoven stories, described by Vinaver as 'an elaborate fabric woven out of a number of

---

[2] White owned the Globe edition, edited by Sir Edward Strachey, London, Macmillan 1899; the Dent Everyman edition of Caxton (1935); *Arthur Pendragon*, New York, George Putnam's Sons, 1943; and Vinaver's first edition of the Winchester MS, *The Works of Sir Thomas Malory*, Oxford 1947.

themes which alternated with one another like the threads of a tapestry.' (Vin, Introduction, p. vii). Malory had often to unravel the threads, in order to follow consistently the progress of a dominant character, cutting out the intervening episodes and incidents which involved other knights. As the work proceeded, the process of selection began to indicate a shape and purpose forming in Malory's mind: to depict the establishment of a noble institution, an ideal society, and the cause of its destruction. It seems that his choice of material began necessarily to be subordinated to this overriding intention, and in the process, he often not only excised what was not to his purpose, but shaped the narrative and added his own words to the account. For him, the unfolding drama of Arthur's rise and fall was a history, a chronicle of events of which some were perhaps to be doubted at times, but which in the main gave a trustworthy account, progressing from the mystery of Arthur's birth and his recognition as rightful king, through the successful building up of the kingdom, to his tragic death at the hands of his own son, and the shattering of all that he had achieved. Part of this story consisted of the exploits of various knights, including the huge section on Tristram and associated knights and their adventures, but during which Launcelot comes to be seen as the outstanding knight of the Round Table. Malory recounts this series in a laconic style, with virtually no interest in visual detail or inner personality, but there is no doubt of the underlying moral concern for chivalry, for England, and the leading characters in the drama.

From beginning to end Malory's tone is consistently serious. His Merlin is a serious figure, whose magic is not in itself amusing. Although in *The Book of Sir Tristram*, Dinadan is to some extent a butt for the laughter of the court, as well as a joker himself, there is little comedy for the modern reader in the sequences in which he figures. Palomydes is treated seriously, while for White he is a figure of fun partly because he is a foreigner, and partly because of his desperate love for Isoud (particularly in *The Witch in the Wood*, in passages mostly omitted from *The Queen of Air and Darkness*). In such a work as *Le Morte Darthur* there could be little place for humour, though Malory does not reject it entirely. When, for example, sir Launcelot is smitten in the 'thycke of the buttok' by the huntress as he sleeps beside a forest spring, he 'whorled up woodly' and exclaimed, ' "Lady, or damesell, what somever ye be, in an evyll tyme bare ye thys bowe. The devyll made you a shoter!" ' (Vin 643), which is surely meant to elicit at least a wry smile on the part of the reader. By contrast, from beginning to end of *The Once and Future King* White sets out to amuse as well as to move the reader: he loses no opportunity for humour. He frequently selects elements from *Le Morte Darthur* which he knows are not meant to be funny, but which he can make superbly comic, as when Queen Morgan le Fay, accompanied by three other queens, kidnaps the sleeping Lancelot and carries him off to Castle Chariot, insisting next morning that he shall choose one of them as his mistress, which he refuses to do. Similarly, when Guenever is kidnapped by

Meliagrance, White creates a splendidly ludicrous scene as the 'cockney knight' tries to get his castle in a fit state for the Queen's reception. White's method of treating his material, though in many respects different, is again not totally unlike Mark Twain's in that the aim of both writers is often to find absurdity in the medieval.

Malory begins very unusually and directly with the birth of his hero. White's way into his story was different. In *Le Morte Darthur*, Arthur's origins are unknown to almost everyone, and are mysterious and exceptional in themselves. He grows up in complete obscurity, but destiny awaits him at the appointed time. Mysterious circumstances surround the birth of many other mythical heroes as Lord Raglan[3] pointed out many years ago: the obscurity makes the moment of recognition more impressive. When Arthur draws the sword from the stone he is eventually, but reluctantly, accepted as rightful king by the barons and people. Since the story of magical intrigue on the part of Merlin, as a result of which Arthur was begotten, proved intractable for White and too adult for his intended readership in *The Sword in the Stone*, he preferred to shift his story out of the traditional, away from the chronicle genre, and into the genre of 'poetry' and the twentieth-century version of the medieval 'enfances' of the hero that earlier writers had denied Arthur. In thus supplying Arthur with an apocryphal childhood, White could in his own way follow the convention dear to the writers of Arthurian stories and hagiography in the Middle Ages, by inventing suitable events in the early life of his subject. White's recourse to invention was such that he took very little from Malory's Book I (*The Tale of King Arthur*) before Chapter XXIII of *The Sword in the Stone* in which he mentions the Wart's parentage and fostering.

White's skill in handling the story appears in his power to select what was germane to his purpose from a mass of material, and to expand it. From Merlin's reproach in *Le Morte Darthur* after the battle of Bedegrayne (Vin 24), 'Thou hast never done. Hast thou nat done inow?', for example, White developed the whole topic of Merlyn's attempt to curb Arthur's enthusiasm for conquest, at the deepest level of seriousness of which he was capable. On the other hand, he could characterise his nigromancer as a comic figure from the hint that Malory gives, when Merlin is so disguised that Arthur does not know him, 'all befurred in blacke shepis skynnes, and a grete payre of bootis' with 'wylde gyese in hys honde' (Vin 25). White postpones to the end of Book II, where the nettle must inevitably be grasped, the arrival of 'kyng Lottis wyf of Orkeney' and the seduction of Arthur, although this occurs much earlier in *Le Morte Darthur*, while he finds a place early in *The Sword in the Stone* for King Pellinor and the Questing Beast, which come later in Malory, since they fit in with his vein

---

3 Raglan, Lord: *The Hero: a Study in Tradition, Myth and Drama*, London 1936. See also *Jocasta's Crime: an Anthropological Study* (1933).

of comic fantasy. The poetry of his first book and the comedy of the second preclude tragic themes, however, so that King Pellinor remains a figure of fun instead of the more serious figure that he is in Malory, where he fails to save the life of his own daughter. The motif of unwittingly slaying 'the beste frende that ye have and the man that ye moste love in the worlde' (Vin 39–40), recurrent throughout *Le Morte Darthur*, which first appears at the beginning of Malory's narrative in the tale of Balin and Balan, is also omitted. This theme is too tragic and perhaps too primitive for White. On the other hand, White also leaves out the episode of Arthur's happy reunion with his mother Igraine, of which Malory gives a brief account (Vin 31), except by way of direct quotation in the 'preface' to *The Witch in the Wood*. In taking what he wanted from *Le Morte Darthur* and rejecting what was for him irrelevant, White was doing very much what Malory had originally done with his own sources, completely ignoring the relatively brief *Tale of Sir Gareth* and the enormous *Book of Sir Tristram de Lyones*, for example, in order to focus directly on the story of Arthur. His omission of much material that was not to his purpose allowed him to do what really interested him, to invent the 'enfances' not only of Arthur but also of Gawaine and his brothers, and to a lesser extent Lancelot. By condensing and compressing and cutting out the jousts, the tournaments and the knightly adventures and encounters which had appealed so strongly to Malory, but which often bemuse and bore the modern reader, he was able to concentrate on a modernised version of the human relationships at the heart of the tragic story. At the same time he was able to devise for it a tight, coherent structure.

He also rejected much of the magical, the mythical and the mystical that had found a place in *Le Morte Darthur* unless, with a few exceptions, it could be turned to comic purposes. While Lancelot is allowed to perform his miracle with the healing of Sir Urre, for example, Gawaine in his great battle with Lancelot is denied the magical gift of supernatural strength which increases until noon and then declines, attributed to him by Malory, following his source. This gift, and Launcelot's discovery of it as he fights sir Gawayne, leads in *Le Morte Darthur* to the further and more significant revelation of Launcelot's exceptional might, as well as of his nobility and generosity. He keeps his adversary in play until his strength becomes normal rather than supernatural, and then when he has him at his mercy, refuses to strike. Terrible though the strife and enmity are, sir Launcelot's physical and moral grandeur in this battle creates a deep impression on the reader, focusing attention on the greatness and noble qualities of the individuals involved rather than on the baffling problems of man's belligerent nature. White prefers to deepen the sense of tragedy by making his characters entirely human, as when his Gawaine writes his last letter. Subsequently, White again avoids the mythical and symbolic when he omits Arthur's dreams before the Last Battle, first of Fortune's wheel, and then of sir Gawayne's warning to him. In *Le Morte Darthur*, the dreams with their clear significance enhance paradoxically both the sense of destiny taking its ineluctable course, and the possibility of avoiding it. They charge the story with greater tension, as the second dream seems to offer the hope that Arthur will heed it and escape the downfall symbolically indicated by his first, terrible dream. Such revelations also enhance the stature of Arthur as the most significant agent, still shown as a powerful and active warrior-king. He is never to become, in Malory, the weary and baffled old man of *The Candle in the Wind*, and still more *The Book of Merlyn*. Indeed Malory tells us that, at the end, Arthur 'did full nobely, and fainted never', until only Mordred is left standing against him on the battlefield, and on Mordred he was 'passing glad to be avenged'. Malory's Arthur has no guilt-ridden sympathy and forbearance for his son: entreated to let Mordred go by Lucan and Bedivere, the sole survivors on his side, he is determined to finish him off, cost what it may.

White, in composing his 'footnote' was carrying much further what Malory had done earlier with the so-called 'tedious roots' of the Arthurian legend, which he had found among what White himself confusingly calls 'confused narrative ballads and prose romances'. Both authors (like most other Arthurian writers) give a new interpretation to old stories. Terence McCarthy[4] points out that it could be argued that the *Morte Darthur*:

> constitutes a movement away from romance, or that it presents that genre in a new light. Malory's *matière* is the *matière* of romance, but the *sen*, the 'feeling', is perhaps not.

While romance takes us close to its heroes and allows us to see into their hearts, Malory, suggests McCarthy, takes us further away, 'replacing intimacy by respect'. If Malory writes as an historian, treating his characters with deference and maintaining a respectful distance from them, White by adopting the novelistic guise of the (almost) omniscient narrator reverses Malory's method. For him, the individuality of his characters is all-important. It is this strong desire for total understanding of them that drives him to invent or to speculate about their childhood experience in order to achieve the right degree of psychological realism. Malory on the other hand has no desire to analyse feeling: it is 'given', a factor of greater or lesser significance in the tale that he has to unfold. He sees no need to investigate motives or to search out the secrets of upbringing, content to allow mystery to surround the origins of his characters, and the mystical to account for some of the happenings. Deeply concerned though he is with how the tragedy of the downfall of the Round Table came about, he is less interested in the personal and private factors involved than in the public ones.

---

4 McCarthy, Terence: *Le Morte Darthur and Romance*, in *Studies in Medieval English Romances*, ed. and publ. D.S. Brewer, Cambridge 1988, p. 148.

Malory's knights are first and foremost members of the social group to which they belong, and very little differentiated as individals.

Malory's soldierly preference for affairs of state,[5] rather than for the affairs of the heart which supply the subject-matter of romance thus leads him away from consideration of the individual to the world of public affairs (though hardly in a modern political sense). It is the institution of the Round Table, rather than the personalities of its members that concerns him. His purpose was to chronicle the establishment of the honourable company, and to record the events that led both to the destruction of the noblest society ever to have been created and to the death of Arthur. Even here the practicalities of government, or of ordinary everyday life, find no place. For White, on the other hand, the downfall of the Round Table, leading inevitably to the death of Arthur, since he saw it as an Aristotelian tragedy, was necessarily a personal tragedy directly resulting from Arthur's past actions and told with much material and emotional realism. White's admiration for Malory and passionate commitment to the task of retelling his story still did not force him to share Malory's ethos or system of values. In *Le Morte Darthur*, the first duty of the knight is to seek to acquire honour (which is not quite the same thing as goodness) by the performance of brave deeds and by associating with others who have already achieved a noble reputation. At all costs the knight must avoid shame, the opposite of honour, and the consequence of dishonourable actions such as cowardly behaviour, and must uphold his reputation. A woman's honour depends on her chastity, or if married, on her faithfulness to her husband. In the case of both men and women honour is also good reputation. Malicious talk, slander, 'evil noise', also destroy honour and cannot be allowed. We see that in *Le Morte Darthur* even after Launcelot and Guenever have been trapped together and accused by Mordred, Launcelot is endeavouring to protect the queen from slander by insisting on her innocence and by maintaining that she 'ys a trew lady untyll her lorde' (Vin 680). He in turn is urged by sir Bors:

> 'insomuch as she ys in payne for youre sake that ye knyghtly rescow her; for and ye ded ony other wyse all the worlde wolde speke you shame to the worldis ende. Insomuch as ye were takyn with her, whether ye ded ryght othir wronge, hit ys now youre parte to holde wyth the quene, that she be nat slayne and put to a myschevous deth. For and she so dye, the shame shall be evermore youres.'
> 'Now Jesu deffende me from shame,' seyde sir Launcelot. . . .'
>
> (Vin 680)

Loyalty is part of honour, of 'good name'. For Malory's knight his good

name, regardless of whether the facts support his reputation or not, is thus
of the greatest importance, while for White, on the other hand, innocence
and guilt take the place of honour and shame. The honour/shame system,
resting upon reputation, is the means by which control over behaviour is
exercised, and anti-social behaviour outlawed. White's ethical system, by
contrast, is based upon a higher level of personal development, dependent
not upon the judgment of the peer-group but upon the internalisation of
values, so that it is the integrity of the individual that controls or is supposed to control conduct. But, 'It seems, in tragedy, that innocence is not
enough' (OFK 323). It is Arthur's 'innocent' guilt which brings about disaster, and the guilt of Lancelot and Guenever which allows Mordred to attack
them, and through them to attack Arthur.

What White saw as of central significance in the story of Arthur was
therefore not the concept of honour, itself bound up with the paramount
duty of loyalty. Sir Bors' reply to sir Launcelot after Mordred's attack in *Le
Morte Darthur*, when it becomes plain that war is now inevitable, suggests
the inescapable sense of obligation which loyalty demanded:

> 'Sir,' seyde sir Bors, 'all ys wellcom that God sendyth us, and as we
> have takyn much weale with you and much worshyp, we woll take the
> woo with you as we have takyn the weale.'   (Vin 679)

He speaks not only for himself but for his friends and kinsmen. Gareth, the
brother of Gawayne, is equally devoted to Launcelot who had knighted
him as a young man. He is described as loving 'sir Launcelot of all men
erthly'. In his brother sir Gawayne's words:

> 'I dare say my brothir loved hym bettir than me and all hys brethirn
> and the kynge bothe. Also I dare say, an sir Launcelot had desyred my
> brothir sir Gareth with hym, he wolde have ben with hym ayenste the
> kynge and us all.'   (Vin 686)

Le Morte Darthur glorifies such loyalty, as it also celebrates knightly
achievement and deeds of prowess conducted in strict accordance with a
recognised code, based on an ethos or ideal which remains valid for Malory
throughout his book. Arthur's knights strive to win honour for themselves,
to enhance the reputation of the Round Table, and to guard their good
name. The tournament and the joust as well as the spontaneous encounter
of single knights or small parties offer opportunities for augmenting the
glory both of the individual and the society. Malory has nothing but admiration and approval for Launcelot's and Tristram's ability to sweep their
opponents from their saddles in the tournaments at Surluse, Lonezep and
elsewhere. The noble deeds of his heroes must nevertheless be in conformity with the oath which Arthur had made them swear at his first Pentecost
feast, and which they annually renewed:

never to do outerage nothir mourthir, and allwayes to fle treson, and to
gyff mercy unto hym that askith mercy, uppon payne of forfiture [of
their] worship and lordship of kynge Arthure for evirmore; and allwayes to do ladyes, damesels, and jantilwomen and wydowes [so-
cour:] strengthe hem in hir ryghtes, and never to enforce them, uppon
payne of dethe. Also, that no man take no batayles in a wrongefull
quarell for no love ne for no worldis goodis.   (Vin 75–6)

For White, there is a certain ambiguity about this oath which sums up the
ethos of the Round Table in *Le Morte Darthur*. When, in *The Queen of Air and
Darkness*, Arthur first formulates his idea of 'a sort of order of chivalry', he
says that he will make the oath of the order that Might is only to be used for
Right, binding the knights:

to strike only on behalf of what is good, to defend virgins against Sir
Bruce and to restore what has been done wrong in the past and to help
the oppressed and so forth.   (OFK 254–5)

For Malory's knights, jousting is an essential activity. When they encounter worthy opponents, they are as merciful as they are strong. White
sees jousting as encouraging the reprehensible predominance of Might over
Right, and refuses to allow his historical imagination to acknowledge its
essential predominance in the romance lives of knights errant. Lancelot is
diminished by being described as 'top of the battling averages', and his
achievement is without real significance, merely the medieval equivalent of
the despised and detested 'Games-Mania' of twentieth-century public
schools.

For Malory, the knight's prowess also involves a number of different
virtues, since chivalry is the means by which justice is established and
maintained, and aggression held in check. It allows women to be protected
and championed. As it exalts comradeship and loyalty, so it condemns
treachery. In *Le Morte Darthur*, Launcelot's conflicting loyalties open the
way for the treachery of Mordred and Agravaine. The Round Table has
been built up into a noble institution, the glory of England, only to be
destroyed as a result of Launcelot's divided allegiance and undue reliance
on his own strength.

White, unable to accept Malory's view of the Round Table and the value
of the chivalry which it represents, focusses on the individuality and
achievement of Arthur, his personal ideals, uncertainties and shortcomings,
and represents his tragic downfall as a more personal disaster. The destruction of the Round Table seen from a different perspective is therefore less
tragic. The cause of the downfall stems, for White, more directly from
Arthur's disastrous early and, as it were, unwitting liaison with Morgause,
and the birth and attempted murder of Mordred, than from the actions of
Lancelot. As White's books progress, and Arthur is gradually persuaded by

Merlyn to regard jousting and other knightly activities as morally unacceptable, White's aim becomes increasingly to present an antidote to war,
an emphasis not to be seen in Malory. Malory regards war as disastrous
indeed, as bringing about the inevitable if temporary destruction of the
chivalric ideal society, but naturally we do not find in him the pacifist
attitudes so typical of the 1930s.

While Caxton could assert in his Preface to *Le Morte Darthur* that he had
printed the 'noble history of King Arthur' 'to the entente that noble men
may see and lerne the noble actes of chyvalrye', White's view of such acts
thus remained very different; though he might have been able to agree with
Caxton as to the inspirational nature of the stories from which his readers
might 'take the good and honest actes in their remembraunce', and follow
the same.

Although for Malory the institution of the Round Table represented in
the terms of historical romance, the supreme public ideal, White seems to
have seen it only as a stage in the development of human civilisation, and
in the process of being as it were outgrown. Already, by Chapter IX of *The
Ill-Made Knight*, it has ceased to function properly:

> "This Round Table," said the older man slowly, "was a good thing
> when we thought of it. It was necessary to invent a way for the fighting
> men to express themselves without doing harm. I can't see how we
> could have done it otherwise than by starting a fashion, like children.
> To get them in, we had to have a gang, as kids have in schools. Then the
> gang had to swear a darksome oath that they would only fight for our
> ideas. You could call it for civilization. What I meant by civilization
> when I invented it, was simply that people ought not to take advantage
> of weakness – not violate maidens, and rob widows, and kill a man
> when he was down. People ought to be civil. But it has turned into
> sportsmanship. . . . My scheme is going wrong. . . . I wish I had never
> invented honour, or sportsmanship, or civilization."   (OFK 380–1)

Since he associated the ideals of the Round Table with the idea of 'sports-
manship', which according to Merlyn is 'the curse of the world', White
could only regard them with disfavour. While, for Malory's Arthur, 'true
honour coincides with virtue and law, and all together constitute the supreme value of fellowship',[6] White could not accept and approve the concept of honour on which Malory's society is founded, any more than he
could admire chivalry. For White's Arthur, the Round Table is founded
upon an ideal that is merely temporary and temporal, to be superseded in
the course of time, first by the Grail quest which he hopes will prove to be a
means of turning its energies into a spiritual channel and thus of making

6   Ed. Brewer, D.S.: *Malory: The Morte Darthur, op. cit.*, p. 30.

Might work for God (OFK 457). Eventually, after the quest has ended, the rôle of the Table is taken over by Arthur's new system of Justice and the rule of Law. Ultimately White rejects Malory's ideals as represented by the Round Table for the simple, and for White modern – though now old-fashioned – virtue of decency, mocked by Mordred in *The Candle in the Wind* as 'the Done Thing' (OFK 548), while Malory's concept of a loyalty which links all the members of the society has become a personal affection between the King and some of his knights, and thus apparently much more limited in its extent.

Since for White it is Arthur's unwitting sin of incest that ultimately brings about the tragedy, Lancelot's conflict of loyalties is inevitably less important in *The Once and Future King* than in *Le Morte Darthur*. This helps to accommodate White's somewhat different attitude to the love between Lancelot and the Queen. Although Malory is interested neither in analysing romantic sentiment nor in describing physical love-making, he regards love as intrinsically good: Launcelot's love for Guenever is itself represented as virtuous. Malory takes love for granted and rarely troubles to inform the reader of exactly what Launcelot and Guenever were doing when they were alone together, since he sees 'kissing and clipping' as a 'kyndly thing', very natural. Similarly, in telling the story of Tristram and Isoud earlier in *Le Morte Darthur*, he shows little interest in their passionate love-affair but instead concentrates on Tristram's prowess in arms, and his rivalry with Launcelot. Malory is nevertheless able to suggest Elaine of Ascolat's passion for Launcelot with delicate perception, and Launcelot's devotion to the Queen with understanding. That there was such love between his characters is a fact of the utmost significance for Malory's story, but it is its implications with which he is primarily concerned. He does not represent the love of Launcelot and Guenever for each other as 'romantic' but rather as tormenting and dangerous, even while it is at the same time 'vertuouse'. In drawing the reader's attention to the nature of love in former times he emphasises its strength, purity and greater faithfulness, in comparison with love in his own day:

> But nowadayes men can nat love sevennyght but they muste have all their desyres. . . . And ryght so faryth the love nowadayes, sone hote sone colde. Thys ys no stabylyte. But the olde love was nat so. For men and women coude love togydirs seven yerys, and no lycoures lustis was betwyxte them, and than was love trouthe and faythefulnes. And so in lyke wyse was used such love in kynge Arthurs dayes.
>
> (Vin 649)

He ends his whole story by showing the redeeming power of faithful love: after almost a lifetime of adultery, Launcelot and Guenever are saved. Guenever is to be accepted as – in Launcelot's words – the 'Moste nobelest Crysten quene' (Vin 676), and furthermore, we are told, 'whyle she lyved she was a trew lover, and therefor she had a good ende' (Vin 649). When

Launcelot dies, the Bishop sees in a vision 'the angellys heve up syr Launcelot unto heven, and the yates of heven opened ayenst hym' (Vin 724). Such love as theirs, when its carnal aspect was renounced and repented, could only be good, and part – as it were – of the divine love itself. Yet its power, because it cannot be controlled or suppressed, is such that it nevertheless brings about the ever-widening rift in the Round Table, leading to its final destruction, as the Queen herself confesses after the death of King Arthur:

> 'Thorow thys same man and me hath all thys warre be wrought, and the deth of the moste nobelest knyghtes of the worlde; for thorow oure love that we have loved togydir ys my moste noble lorde slayne.'
>
> (Vin 720)

White, by contrast with Malory, sees the love of Lancelot and Guenever as unfortunate rather than intrinsically virtuous. His main interest is in trying to understand and to explain the motivation and the relationships of the three participants in the love-triangle. He makes the affair seem the more remarkable by depicting Lancelot against all tradition as exceptionally ugly as well as by exploring Guenever's states of mind and representing her at her worst as a jealous virago. Although he even shows her in her bath, endeavouring to enhance her charms so as to entice Lancelot back to her after the Grail quest, we never see her in bed with Lancelot. When the ageing lovers are together before the attack by Mordred and his party, the scene is made effective by the very vivid account of Lancelot's defence, rather than by the noble and moving eloquence of the farewell speeches attributed to them by Malory. The relationship that White depicts between them suggests a conflict at the very heart of Lancelot's attraction to the Queen, distinct from the opposing force of his religious longings and aspirations. Nor is there any redemptive power in their love: that is to come only from Arthur's generosity and affection. His attitude is to some extent clarified by a letter he wrote to David Garnett towards the end of 1955, commenting on Garnett's book, *Aspects of Love* which he had recently received. He much disliked it because:

> you will think it quite dotty – but I can't help it – . . . I believe human beings ought to be monogamous . . . – that if they consciously take a solemn vow in public they should stick to it – or not take it.
>
> (W/G L 274)[7]

White's attitude to extra-marital relationships and his concept of honour

---

7 Later in the same letter White expresses his delight that Princess Margaret had decided *not* to marry Group Captain Townshend, because: 'Mr Townshend had made a solemn, voluntary oath, in public, to marry Mrs Townshend till death did them part. If the princess had afterwards married him, she would have been an accessory to the fact of a public lie.'

were inevitably different from Malory's, but his convictions were as firmly held.

At the end of *The Once and Future King*, unlike the end of *Le Morte Darthur*, the characters have distinctly aged, as the pattern of destiny works itself out. Arthur is weary and beginning to despair, while Lancelot is presented with a touch of pathos as a white-haired old warrior. Though his spiritual potential is shown, as in Malory, by his healing of Urre, White does not allow him to become quite the charismatic figure that he is at the end of *Le Morte Darthur*. He is not shown as attracting the devotion of Sir Lavaine, the young brother of Elaine of Ascolat, for example. Subsumed into Elaine the mother of Galahad, Elaine of Ascolat has been allowed to become middle-aged and subsequently to die in Chapter XL of *The Ill-Made Knight*. Time and the process of ageing have left Lancelot a figure of legendary grandeur and undiminished prowess, but not one for whom young girls pathetically pine away out of love. Although for Malory he is always the centre of interest, this is not so for White in *The Candle in the Wind*. It is Arthur who remains dominant, all the more if *The Book of Merlyn* is regarded as the true end of *The Once and Future King*.

For Malory the traditional aspects of his story were of particular importance, having a resonance that White did not attempt to achieve. Arthur is always the great king of England even when not active in a central role. He is the pivot around which the others revolve. Launcelot is Malory's favourite knight who achieves grandeur. Gawayne too, especially towards the end has his greatness and some complexity of character. Guenever is above all the Queen, the icon of beauty and womanly appeal. Launcelot is divided in loyalty between King and Queen. Gawayne, at first loyal to Launcelot, cannot forgive him the accidental slaying of Gareth. These great figures are not closely personified, nor seen in a domestic context. They are large simple figures in a tragic pattern even more general than they.

Launcelot is of course the key figure who instigates, by his love for the Queen, the complex series of actions. He dominates the narrative after his return from the Grail quest until the insurrection of Mordred. Launcelot becomes increasingly charismatic and seemingly quite untouched by time, until at the very end sir Ector pronounces his splendid eulogy over his brother's dead body. Malory has made no attempt to analyse Launcelot's internal conflict which is to lead to disaster. He makes no claim to knowledge of what is going on in Launcelot's mind other than what is made manifest by his spoken words. He does not even tell us what is going on when Launcelot and the Queen are alone together on the night of Mordred's armed attack.

White, by contrast, can tell us exactly what they were doing – and it is entirely innocent – but his invention takes him far beyond Malory in the exploration of the motives of Mordred and Agravaine as they plot to catch Lancelot and Guenever together and to denounce them. While Malory never suggests that Mordred's illegitimacy, or Arthur's attempt to get rid of him in infancy, provided him with motives for trying to trap Launcelot and the Queen alone together, or for proposing to marry the Queen, White makes it clear that Mordred is aware of his origins and in consequence embittered. He elaborates Malory's narrative by constructing scenes between Gawaine and his brothers, and between them and Arthur and Guenever, making Mordred's bitter enmity the mainspring of the action and the centre of interest for much of the fourth book. At this stage of his story, Malory communicates a greater sense of tragic loss and waste, at a more universal level, and when Mordred attacks, he allows Launcelot and Guenever to rise to heights of grandeur, expressed in formal and ceremonious language, that White's more psychological approach cannot compass. But White's penetrating analysis of the reasons for and the growth of Mordred's anger and of his sadism, dramatically represented in scene after scene, add a new dimension to the story of Arthur. The sense of the incursion of the private and personal into public affairs is now intensified, as Mordred comes into the foreground of the action.

Malory's attitude to war, writing as he was at a time of civil strife when the combatants were apt to change sides and were even more closely drawn into fighting their own kind than in the World Wars of the twentieth century, was necessarily very different from White's. His concern is with the fickleness and lack of discernment of his contemporaries, whom he implicitly condemns in denouncing the changeable Englishmen of Arthur's time who side with Mordred when it seems to their advantage, unable to distinguish between the noble and the base. In an address to his readers he says:

> Lo ye all Englysshemen, se ye nat what a myschyff here was? For he that was the moste kynge and nobelyst knyght of the worlde, and moste loved the felyshyp of noble knyghtes, and by hym they all were upholdyn, and yet myght nat thes Englyshemen holde them contente with hym. Lo thus was the olde custom and usayges of thys londe, and men say that we of thys londe have nat yet loste that custom. Alas! thys ys a greate defaughte of us Englysshemen, for there may no thynge us please no terme.
>
> And so fared the peple at that tyme: they were better pleased with sir Mordred than they were with the noble kynge Arthur, and muche people drew unto sir Mordred and seyde they wolde abyde wyth hym for bettir and for wars. And so sir Mordred drew with a greate oste to Dovir, for there he harde sey that kyng Arthur wolde aryve, and so he thought to beate hys owne fadir fro hys owne londys. And the moste party of all Inglonde hylde wyth sir Mordred, for the people were so new-fangill.   (Vin 709)

Subsequently, the people returned to Arthur's side, declaring that Mordred 'warred upon kynge Arthur wyth wronge', when it seemed to their advantage to do so. Malory, therefore, had a message for his own time just as White did, but it was a different one.

For Malory it is important that the circumstances of Arthur's death should be as exceptional as his birth. The pattern must be worked out in its entirety: Excalibur returned, and Arthur carried off by the weeping queens. As *Le Morte Darthur* moves towards its tragic conclusion, Malory achieves a sense of an ending by the mounting force of the events that make disaster inevitable for all the participants, rather than by emphasising the passing of time, bringing with it change and decay. Completion is essential: Malory could not have left Arthur at the end with his story unfinished, even though in a sense he could not finally complete it, since he could not himself confirm either that Arthur was dead or that he would come again. For Malory another important strand still remained after the death of Arthur: he had still to relate the bitter repentance of Guenever and Launcelot and how their deaths came about, and to make clear the splendour and the tragedy of it all. He shows Guenever as the 'moste nobelest Crysten quene' that Launcelot had called her, as she takes responsibility for the disastrous train of events in her address to the ladies in the nunnery to which she has fled.

Launcelot's comment, when he finally reaches the hermitage, suggests at the most fundamental level the cause of the tragedy: 'Alas! Who may truste thys world?' Malory's continuing concern with Launcelot's part in the story is made apparent in his confession when Guenever is buried. He declares 'how by my defaute and myn orgule and my pryde' Arthur and Guenever were both 'layed ful lowe, that were pereles that ever was lyvyng of Cristen people'. Malory does not puzzle over why men should want to war against each other and kill their own kind, or how an antidote can be found, or even how it can happen that deep and faithful love on the part of so noble a knight as Launcelot can destroy the kingdom and all he loves with it. He presents these facts of life and death with a sober acceptance. For Malory it is Launcelot's love, rather than the terrible trick of fate that had caused Arthur to beget Mordred, that is to blame for the tragedy. But he does not allocate blame nor speculate how tragedy may be avoided. Like White, he offers hope for the future, when after Arthur's death, syr Costantyn is chosen king of England and rules 'worshypfully'.

In finishing off his narrative in *The Candle in the Wind* before the Last Battle and the death of Arthur, White omits not only the return of Excalibur to the Lady of the Lake, but also the deaths of Guenever and of Lancelot: he merely tells us that 'it was Lancelot's fate and Guenever's to take the tonsure and the veil.' Malory, by following his account of the Last Battle with Arthur's departure in the 'lytll barge wyth many fayre ladyes in hit' (Vin 716), and the subsequent deaths of Guenever and Launcelot, achieves a much greater sense of finality – of the end of all that Arthur had accomplished after a lifetime's effort, of the noble order of chivalry, of Arthur himself, of the lovers, of sir Gawayne and his entire family. It is comprehensively tragic, and yet, as Christian tragedy, not totally without hope. Arthur may come again; Guenever and Launcelot are redeemed by love and faith; the viper Mordred is destroyed; the evil has been stamped out. Arthur's return to the animals in *The Book of Merlyn*, by contrast, takes the story back to the level of fantasy with which it started, while in *The Candle in the Wind* in the final, 1958 edition, White ended his epic with a positive sense of life continuing, by leaving the Last Battle as yet unfought, as 'the Majesty of England drew himself up to meet the future with a peaceful heart.'

Bibliography

Part I

Publication of *The Once and Future King*

The Sword in the Stone: London 1938
    New York 1939
    In *The Once and Future King*, 1958.
The Witch in the Wood: New York 1939
    London 1940.
As *The Queen of Air and Darkness*, in *The Once and Future King*, London 1958.
The Ill-Made Knight: New York 1940
    London 1941
    In *The Once and Future King*, 1958.
The Candle in the Wind, in *The Once and Future King*, London and New York, 1958.
The Book of Merlyn, University of Texas Press, 1977.

Part II

Townsend Warner, Sylvia: *T.H. White: A Biography*. London, Cape with Chatto and Windus, 1967.

Gallix, François ed.: *T.H. White: Letters to a Friend, The Correspondence between T.H. White and L.J. Potts*. Gloucester, Alan Sutton, 1984.

———— *T.H. White: an Annotated Bibliography*. New York and London, Garland Publishing Inc., 1986.

Garnett, David, ed.: *The White/Garnett Letters*. London, Cape, 1968.

———— *The Familiar Faces*. London, Chatto and Windus, 1962.

Maxwell, William ed.: *Letters: Sylvia Townsend Warner*. London, Chatto and Windus, 1982.

Sprague, Kurth: *A Joy Proposed: Poems by T.H. White*. London, Bertram Rota, 1980.

A'Beckett, Gilbert Abbott: *The Comic History of England*. New ed. London, 1907.

Annan, Noel G.: *Our Age: Portrait of a Generation*. London, Weidenfeld and Nicolson, 1990.

———— *Roxburgh of Stowe: the Life of J.F. Roxburgh and His Influence in the Public Schools*. London, Longmans, 1965.

Brewer, D.S. ed.: *Malory: The Morte Darthur, Parts Seven and Eight*. York Medieval Texts. London, Arnold, 1968.

Brewer, D.S. ed.: *Studies in Medieval English Romances*. Cambridge, D.S. Brewer, 1988. See McCarthy, Terence: *Le Morte Darthur and Romance*.

Campbell, Joseph: *The Hero with a Thousand Faces*. Princeton, 1968.

Carruthers, Mary J.: *The Book of Memory: a Study of Memory in Medieval Culture*. Cambridge, University Press, 1990.

Coveney, Peter: *The Image of Childhood*. Penguin, Harmondsworth, 1967.

Crane, John J.: *T.H. White*. New York, Twayne Publishers Inc., 1974.

Eco, Umberto: *Postscript to The Name of the Rose*. Translated by William Weaver. San Diego, New York and London, Helen and Kurt Wolff, 1983.

Enck, J.J.: *The Comic in Theory and Practice*. New York, Appleton-Century-Crofts, 1960.

Foley, Barbara: *Telling the Truth: the Theory and Practice of Documentary Fiction*. Ithaca, Cornell University Press, 1986.

Freud, S.: *Totem and Taboo. Resemblances between the Psychic Lives of Savages and Neurotics*. Authorised English Translation. London, Routledge, 1919.

Freud, S., ed. Rickman, J.: *Civilisation, War and Death: Selections from 3 Works by S. Freud*. London, Hogarth Press, 1939.

Furnivall, F.J.: *The Babees Book*. London, 1868.

Hume, Kathryn: *Fantasy and Mimesis*. New York and London, Methuen, 1984.

Jung, E. and von Franz, M.L.: *The Grail Legend*. Translated by A. Dykes. London, Hodder and Stoughton, 1971.

Kellman, Martin: *T.H. White and the Matter of Britain. A Literary Overview*. Studies in the Historical Novel, Vol. 2. Lewiston/Queenston, the Edwin Mellen Press, 1988.

Manlove, C.N.: *The Impulse of Fantastic Literature*. London, Macmillan, 1983.

Marsh, Jan: *Back to the Land*. London, Quartet Books, 1982.

Moreland, Arthur: *The Humours of History*. 2 vols. London, 1903.

Morris, Rosemary: *The Character of King Arthur in Medieval Literature*. Cambridge, D.S. Brewer, 1982.

Potts, L.J.: *Comedy*. London, Hutchinson's University Library, 1948.

────── *Aristoteles: On the Art of Fiction. An English translation of Aristotle's Poetics with an introductory essay and explanatory notes*. Cambridge, University Press, 1953.

Raglan, Lord: *The Hero: a Study in Tradition, Myth and Drama*. London, Methuen, 1936.

Richards, Ivor Armstrong: *Practical Criticism: A Study of Literary Judgment*. London, Kegan Paul, 1929.

Savater, Fernando: *Childhood Regained: the Art of the Storyteller*. Tranlated by Frances M. Lopez-Morillas. New York; Guildford: Columbia University Press, 1982.

Swinfen, Ann: *In Defence of Fantasy: A Study of the Genre in English and American Literature since 1945*. London, Routledge, 1984.

Thompson, Ray: 'Modern Fantasy and Medieval Romance' in Schlobin, R.C., ed.: *The Aesthetics of Fantasy Literature and Art*, pp. 211–25. Indiana, University of Notre Dame Press/Harvester, 1982.

Twain, Mark: *A Yankee at the Court of King Arthur*. London, 1899.

Vinaver, Eugéne: *The Works of Sir Thomas Malory*. Oxford, The Clarendon Press, 1947. Second edition, London, Oxford University Press, 1971.

Weston, Jessie L.: *From Ritual to Romance*. Cambridge, University Press, 1920.

Whitaker, Muriel: *Arthur's Kingdom of Adventure: the World of Malory's Morte Darthur*. Cambridge, D.S. Brewer, 1984.
Williamson, Henry: *The Sun in the Sands*. London, Faber, 1945.

Part III

Books in White's library at his death, which may have influenced his writing of *The Once and Future King* and *The Book of Merlyn*.

A'Beckett, Gilbert Abbott: *The Comic History of England*. London, 1907.
Aldrovandi, Ulisse: *De animalibus insectis libri septem*. 1638.
Barnard, Francis P.: *Medieval England*. Oxford, 1924.
Boutell, Charles: *Heraldry, Historical and Popular*. London, 1864. (Given by Sir Sydney Cockerell)
Breasted, James H.: *Ancient Times, a History of the Early World*. Boston, c.1916.
Browne, Sir Thomas: *Pseudodoxia Epidemica*. London, 1646.
Bulfinch, Thomas: *Mythology: the Age of Fable. The Age of Chivalry*. London, John Lane, the Bodley Head, n.d.
Cole, G.D.H.: *The Intelligent Man's Guide through World Chaos*. London, 1932.
Cross, Tom Peete, and Slover, Clark Harris, eds.: *Ancient Irish Tales*. London, Harrap, 1936.
Crump, G.C. and Jacob, ed.: *Legacy of the Middle Ages*. Oxford, 1938.
Curtis, Edward: *History of Medieval Ireland from 1086–1513*. 1938.
D'Alton, Edward Alfred: *History of Ireland*. 1911.
Duruy, Victor: *History of France*. Everyman. London, Dent, 1928.
Forel, Auguste: *The Social World of the Ants Compared with that of Man*. Translated by C.K. Ogden. 1928.
Freeman, Edward Augustus: *History of the Norman Conquest of England: Its Causes and Its Results*. Oxford, 1877.
Freud, S.: *Introductory Lectures on Psychoanalysis*. 1923.
Goad, Harold Elsdale: *The Making of the Corporate State: a Study of Fascist Development*. 1932.
Hartley, Dorothy: *Life and Work of the People of England: a Pictorial Record from Contemporary Sources*. London, 1925–31. (6 vols., from the library of Stowe School)
Huxley, Julian: *Ants*. London, 1935.
Huxley, Julian and Suschitzky, W.: *The Kingdom of the Beasts*. London, Thames and Hudson, 1956.
Imram Brain: *The Voyage of Bran*. 2 vols. 1895–7.
Jefferies, Richard: *Wild Life in a Southern County*. London, 1934.
Jusserand, J.J.: *English Wayfaring Life in the Middle Ages*. London, Benn, 1939.
Lytton, Lord: *The Last of the Barons*. London, Dent, 1933.
Macalister, R.A.S.: *Ireland in Pre-Celtic Times*. Dublin, Talbot, n.d.
———— The Story of the Crop-eared Dog; the Story of Eagle-boy; two Irish Arthurian Romances. London, 1908. Inscribed "T.H. White. This addition to Mallory from David Garnett".

Malory, Sir Thomas: *Le Mort D'Arthur*. Everyman. London, Dent, 1935.

—— *Le Morte Darthur*. Edited and with an introduction by Sir Edward Strachey, Bt. New York and London, Macmillan, 1899.

Mandeville: *The Travels of Sir John Mandeville . . . with 3 narratives . . . from Hakluyt's "Navigations, voyages and discoveries"*.

—— (The voyage of Johannes de Piano Carpini.

—— The journal of Friar William de Rubruquis.

—— The journal of Friar Odoric.) London, 1923.

Mann, J.G.: *Armour in Essex*. British School of Archaeology, n.d.

Masefield, John: *The Midnight Folk: A Novel*. London, Heinemann, 1927.

—— *Midsummer Night and Other Tales in Verse*. London, Heinemann, 1928.

—— *The Box of Delights*. London and New York, 1935.

Reinhard, John Russell: *The Medieval Pageant*. London, Dent, 1939.

Smith, Grafton Elliot: *The Evolution of Man*. London, 1927.

Spitteler, Carl: *Laughing Truths*. London, 1927.

Street, A.G.: *Hedge-trimmings*. London, 1935.

Strutt, James: *Sports and Pastimes of the People of England*. London, Chatto and Windus, 1876.

Theobaldus Episcopus: *Physiologus, a metrical bestiary of twelve chapters*. 1492. Translated by Rendell, A.W., London, 1928.

Thierry, Augustin: *The Norman Conquest of England*. London, Dent, 1927.

Tolstoy, Leo: *Anna Karenina*. Translated by Townsend, Rochelle. Everyman. Dent.

Weston, Jessie L.: *The Legend of Sir Lancelot du Lac*. London, Nutt, 1901.

Wilde, Jane Francesca: *Ancient Cures, Charms and Usages of Ireland: Contributions to Irish Lore*. 1890.

Index

ARTHURIAN STUDIES